THE JUNIOR CLASSICS
Vol. - 1

AF147367

by

ED. WILLIAM PATTEN

The Junior Classics
Vol - 1
by ED. William Patten

Copyright © 2024

All Rights reserved.
No part of this publication may be reproduced,
stored in a retrieval system, or transmitted in any
form or by any means, electronic, mechanical,
photocopying or Otherwise, without the written
permission of the publisher.

The author/editor asserts the moral right to
be identified as the author/editor of this work.

ISBN: 978-93-57489-55-3

Published by

DOUBLE 9 BOOKS

2/13-B, Ansari Road, Daryaganj
New Delhi – 110002
info@double9books.com
www.double9books.com
Tel. 011-40042856

This book is under public domain

ABOUT THE EDITOR

Born around 1510, William Patten was a government official, author, and scholar during the reigns of King Edward VI and Queen Elizabeth I. He was the son of Richard Patten, a clothworker, and Grace, the daughter of John Baskerville. Patten's grandfather was Richard Patten of Boslow, Derbyshire, who was the brother of William Waynflete (also known as Patten), Bishop of Winchester. Patten attended Gonville Hall, Cambridge, and served as a minor chaplain and parish clerk of St Mary-at-Hill, Billingsgate, London, from 1528 and 1533, respectively. He was married twice, and his second wife was Anne, the daughter and heiress of Richard Johnson of Boston, Lincolnshire. Patten was the father of seven children, all from his second marriage, and he referred to himself as "unfortunate Patten...the sorrowing father."

CONTENTS

INTRODUCTION

The purpose of The Junior Classics is to provide, in ten volumes containing about five thousand pages, a classified collection of tales, stories, and poems, both ancient and modern, suitable for boys and girls of from six to sixteen years of age. Thoughtful parents and teachers, who realize the evils of indiscriminate reading on the part of children, will appreciate the educational value of such a collection. A child's taste in reading is formed, as a rule, in the first ten or twelve years of its life, and experience has shown that the childish mind will prefer good literature to any other, if access to it is made easy, and will develop far better on literature of proved merit than on trivial or transitory material.

The boy or girl who becomes familiar with the charming tales and poems in this collection will have gained a knowledge of literature and history that will be of high value in other school and home work. Here are the real elements of imaginative narration, poetry, and ethics, which should enter into the education of every English-speaking child.

This collection, carefully used by parents and teachers with due reference to individual tastes and needs, will make many children enjoy good literature. It will inspire them with a love of good reading, which is the best possible result of any elementary education. The child himself should be encouraged to make his own selections from this large and varied collection, the child's enjoyment being the object in view. A real and lasting interest in literature or in scholarship is only to be developed through the individual's enjoyment of his mental occupations.

The most important change which has been made in American schools and colleges within my memory is the substitution of leading for driving, of inspiration for drill, of personal interest and love of work for compulsion and fear. The schools are learning to use methods and materials which interest and attract the children themselves. The Junior Classics will put into the home the means of using this happy method.

Committing to memory beautiful pieces of literature, either prose or poetry, for recitation before a friendly audience, acting charades or plays, and reading aloud with vivacity and sympathetic emotion, are good means of instruction at home or at school This collection contains numerous admirable pieces of literature for such use. In teaching English and English literature we should place more reliance upon processes and acts which awaken emotion, stimulate interest, prove to be enjoyable for the actors, and result in giving children the power of entertaining people, of blessing others with noble pleasures which the children create and share.

From the home training during childhood there should result in the child a taste for interesting and improving reading which will direct and inspire its subsequent intellectual life. The training which results in this taste for good reading, however unsystematic or eccentric it may have been, has achieved one principal aim of education; and any school or home training which does not result in implanting this permanent taste has failed in a very important respect. Guided and animated by this impulse to acquire knowledge and exercise the imagination through good reading, the adult will continue to educate him all through life.

The story of the human race through all its slow development should be gradually conveyed to the child's mind from the time he begins to read, or to listen to his mother reading; and with description of facts and actual events should be mingled charming and uplifting products of the imagination. To try to feed the minds of children upon facts alone is undesirable and unwise. The immense product of the imagination in art and literature is a concrete fact with which every educated human being should be made somewhat familiar, that product being a very real part of every individual's actual environment.

The right selection of reading matter for children is obviously of high importance. Some of the mythologies, Old Testament stories, fairy tales, and historical romances, on which earlier generations were accustomed to feed the childish mind, contain a great deal that is barbarous, perverse, or cruel; and to this infiltration into children's minds, generation after generation, of immoral, cruel, or foolish ideas is probably to be attributed in part the slow ethical progress of the race. The commonest justification of this thoughtless practice is that children do not apprehend the evil in the bad mental pictures with which we foolishly supply them; but what should we think of a mother who gave her children dirty milk or porridge, on the theory that the children would not assimilate the dirt? Should we be less careful about mental and moral food materials? The Junior Classics have been selected with this principle in mind, without losing sight of the fact that every developing human being needs to have a vision of the rough and thorny road over which the human race has been slowly advancing during thousands of years.

Whoever has committed to memory in childhood such Bible extracts as Genesis i, the Ten Commandments, Psalm xxiii, Matthew v, 8-12, The Lord's

Prayer, and I Corinthians xiii, such English prose as Lincoln's Gettysburg speech, Bacon's "Essay on Truth," and such poems as Bryant's "Waterfowl," Addison's "Divine Ode," Milton's Sonnet on his Blindness, Wotton's "How happy is he born or taught," Emerson's "Rhodora," Holmes's "Chambered Nautilus," and Gray's Elegy, and has stamped them on his brain by frequent repetition, will have set up in his mind high standards of noble thought and feeling, true patriotism, and pure religion. He will also have laid in an invaluable store of good English.

While the majority of the tales and poems are intended for children who have begun to do their own reading, there will be found in every volume selections fit for reading aloud to younger children. Throughout the collection the authors tell the stories in their own words; so that the salt which gave them savor is preserved. There are some condensations however, such as any good teller of borrowed stories would make; but as a rule condensation has been applied only in the case of long works which otherwise could not have been included. The notes which precede the condensations supply explanations, and answer questions which experience has shown boys and girls are apt to ask about the works condensed or their authors.

The Junior Classics constitute a set of books whose contents will delight children and at the same time satisfy the legitimate ethical requirements of those who have the children's best interests at heart.

Charles W. Eliot

PREFACE

There are some things in this world we can get along without, but, the experience of many thousand years has shown us that the fairy tale is not one of them. There must have been fairy tales (or fables, or folk tales, or myths, or whatever name we choose to give them) ever since the world began. They are not exclusively French, German, Greek, Russian, Indian or Chinese, but are the common property of the whole human family and are as universal as human speech.

All the world over, fairy tales are found to be pretty much the same. The story of Cinderella is found in all countries. Japan has a Rip Van Winkle, China has a Beauty and the Beast, Egypt has a Puss in Boots, and Persia has a Jack and the Beanstalk.

Those wise people who have made a careful study of literature, and especially of what we call folk tales or fairy tales or fables or myths, tell us that they all typify in some way the constant struggle that is going on in every department of life. It may be the struggle of Summer against Winter, the bright Day against dark Night, Innocence against Cruelty, of Knowledge against Ignorance. We are not obliged to think of these delightful stories as each having a meaning. Our enjoyment of them will not be less if we overlook that side, but it may help us to understand and appreciate good books if we remember that the literature of the world is the story of man's struggle against nature; that the beginnings of literature came out of the mouths of story-tellers, and that the stories they told were fairy tales—imaginative stories based on truth.

There is one important fact to remember in connection with the old fairy tales, and that is that they were repeated aloud from memory, not read from a book or manuscript.

The printing of books from type may be said to date from the year 1470, when Caxton introduced printing into England. It is said that the first book printed in English which had the pages numbered was a book of tales, "Æsop's Fables."

As late as 1600 printed books were still so rare that only rich men could own them. There was one other way of printing a story—on sheepskin (split and made into parchment) with a pen—but that was a long and laborious art that could only be practiced by educated men who had been taught to write. The monks were about the only men who had the necessary education and time, and they cared more for making copies of the Bible and Lives of the Saints than they did of fairy tales. The common people, and even kings and queens, were therefore obliged to depend upon the professional story-teller.

Fairy tales were very popular in the Middle Ages. In the long winter months fields could not be cultivated, traveling had to be abandoned, and all were kept within doors by the cold and snow. We know what the knight's house looked like in those days. The large beamed hall or living room was the principal room. At one end of it, on a low platform, was a table for the knight, his family, and any visiting knights and ladies. At the other tables on the main floor were the armed men, like squires and retainers, who helped defend the castle from attack, and the maids of the household.

The story-teller, who was sometimes called a bard or skald or minstrel, had his place of honor in the center of the room, and when the meal was over he was called upon for a story. These story-tellers became very expert in the practice of their art, and some of them could arouse their audiences to a great pitch of excitement. In the note that precedes the story "The Treason of Ganelon," in the volume "Heroes and Heroines of Chivalry," you can see how one of these story-tellers, or minstrels, sang aloud a story to the soldiers of William the Conqueror to encourage them as he led them into battle.

The fairy tales collected by the Brothers Grimm were first published in 1812. They spent thirteen years collecting them, writing them down as they were told by the peasants in Hesse, a mountainous province of Germany lying far removed from the great main roads.

Their friends helped them, but their best friend was the wife of a cowherd, a strong, intelligent woman of fifty, who had a perfect genius for storytelling. She knew she told the stories well, and that not many had her gift. The Grimms said that though she repeated a story for them three times, the variations were so slight as to be hardly apparent.

The American Indian stories of Manabozho the Mischief-Maker and his adventures with the Wolf and the Woodpeckers and the Ducks were collected in very much the same way by Henry R. Schoolcraft (1793–1864), the explorer and traveler, who lived among the Indian tribes for thirty years.

Mrs. Steel has told us how she collected her Hindu stories, often listening over and over to poor story-tellers who would spoil a story in trying to tell it, until one day her patience would be rewarded by hearing it from the lips of the best storyteller in the village, who was generally a boy.

As all nations have their fairy tales, you will find in this collection examples of English, Irish, French, German, Scandinavian, Icelandic, Russian, Polish, Serbian, Spanish, Arabian, Hindu, Chinese, and Japanese fairy tales, as well as those recited around the lodge fires at night by American Indians for the entertainment of the red children of the West.

I hope the work may prove for many a boy and girl (of any age up to a hundred) the Golden Bridge over which they can plunge into that marvelous world of fairies, elves, goblins, kobolds, trolls, afreets, jinns, ogres, and giants that fascinates us all, lost to this world till some one wakes us up to say "Bedtime!"

Such excursions fill the mind with beautiful fancies and help to develop that most precious of our faculties, the imagination.

WILLIAM PATTEN.

MANABOZHO, THE MISCHIEF-MAKER

Adapted from H. R. Schoolcraft

There was never in the whole world a more mischievous busybody than that notorious giant Manabozho. He was everywhere, in season and out of season, running about, and putting his hand in whatever was going forward.

To carry on his game he could take almost any shape he pleased. He could be very foolish or very wise, very weak or very strong, very rich or very poor — just as happened to suit his humor best. Whatever anyone else could do, he would attempt without a moment's reflection. He was a match for any man he met, and there were few manitoes* (*good spirits or evil spirits) that could get the better of him. By turns he would be very kind or very cruel, an animal or a bird, a man or a spirit, and yet, in spite of all these gifts, Manabozho was always getting himself involved in all sorts of troubles. More than once, in the course of his adventures, was this great maker of mischief driven to his wits' ends to come off with his life.

To begin at the beginning, Manabozho, while yet a youngster, was living with his grandmother near the edge of a great prairie. It was on this prairie that he first saw animals and birds of every kind; he also there made first acquaintance with thunder and lightning. He would sit by the hour watching the clouds as they rolled by, musing on the shades of light and darkness as the day rose and fell.

For a stripling, Manabozho was uncommonly wide-awake. Every sight he beheld in the heavens was a subject of remark, every new animal or bird an object of deep interest, and every sound was like a new lesson which he was expected to learn. He often trembled at what he heard and saw.

The first sound he heard was that of the owl, at which he was greatly terrified, and, quickly descending the tree he had climbed, he ran with alarm to the lodge. "Noko! noko! grandmother!" he cried. "I have heard a monedo."

She laughed at his fears, and asked him what kind of a noise it made. He answered. "It makes a noise like this: ko-ko-ko-ho!"

His grandmother told him he was young and foolish; that what he heard was only a bird which derived its name from the peculiar noise it made.

He returned to the prairie and continued his watch. As he stood there looking at the clouds he thought to himself, "It is singular that I am so simple and my grandmother so wise; and that I have neither father nor mother. I have never heard a word about them. I must ask and find out."

He went home and sat down, silent and dejected. Finding that this did not attract the notice of his grandmother, he began a loud lamentation, which he kept increasing, louder and louder, till it shook the lodge and nearly deafened the old grandmother.

"Manabozho, what is the matter with you?" she said, "you are making a great deal of noise."

Manabozho started off again with his doleful hubbub, but succeeded in jerking out between his big sobs, "I haven't got any father nor mother, I haven't."

Knowing that he was of a wicked and revengeful nature, his grandmother dreaded to tell him the story of his parentage, as she knew he would make trouble of it.

Manabozho renewed his cries and managed to throw out for a third or fourth time, his sorrowful lament that he was a poor unfortunate who had no parents or relatives.

At last she said to him, to quiet him, "Yes, you have a father and three brothers living. Your mother is dead. She was taken for a wife by your father, the West, without the consent of her parents. Your brothers are the North, East, and South; and being older than you your father has given them great power with the winds, according to their names. You are the youngest of his children. I have nursed you from your infancy, for your mother died when you were born."

"I am glad my father is living," said Manabozho, "I shall set out in the morning to visit him."

His grandmother would have discouraged him, saying it was a long distance to the place where his father, Ningabinn, or the West, lived.

This information seemed rather to please than to discourage Manabozho, for by this time he had grown to such a size and strength that he had been compelled to leave the narrow shelter of his grandmother's lodge and live out of doors. He was so tall that, if he had been so disposed, he could have snapped off the heads of the birds roosting on the topmost branches of the highest trees, as he stood up, without being at the trouble to climb. And if he had at any time taken a fancy to one of the same trees for a walking stick, he would have had no more to do than to pluck it up with his thumb and finger and strip down the leaves and twigs with the palm of his hand.

Bidding good-by to his old grandmother, who pulled a very long face over his departure, Manabozho set out at a great pace, for he was able to stride from one side of a prairie to the other at a single step.

He found his father on a high mountain far in the west. His father espied his approach at a great distance, and bounded down the mountainside several miles to give him welcome. Apparently delighted with each other, they reached in two or three of their giant paces the lodge of the West which stood high up near the clouds.

They spent some days in talking with each other—for these two great persons did nothing on a small scale, and a whole day to deliver a single sentence, such was the immensity of their discourse, was quite an ordinary affair.

One evening Manabozho asked his father what he was most afraid of on earth.

He replied—"Nothing."

"But is there nothing you dread here—nothing that would hurt you if you took too much of it? Come, tell me."

Manabozho was very urgent, so at last his father said: "Yes, there is a black stone to be found a couple of hundred miles from here, over that way," pointing as he spoke. "It is the only thing on earth I am afraid of, for if it should happen to hit me on any part of my body it would hurt me very much." The West made this important circumstance known to Manabozho in the strictest confidence.

"Now you will not tell anyone, Manabozho, that the black stone is bad medicine for your father, will you?" he added. "You are a good son, and I know you will keep it to yourself. Now tell me, my darling boy, is there not something that you don't like?"

Manabozho answered promptly—"Nothing."

His father, who was of a steady and persevering nature, put the same question to him seventeen times, and each time Manabozho made the same answer—"Nothing."

But the West insisted—"There must be something you are afraid of."

"Well, I will tell you," said Manabozho, "what it is."

He made an effort to speak, but it seemed to be too much for him.

"Out with it," said the West, fetching Manabozho such a blow on the back as shook the mountain with its echo.

"Je-ee, je-ee—it is," said Manabozho, apparently in great pain. "Yes, yes! I cannot name it, I tremble so."

The West told him to banish his fears, and to speak up; no one would hurt him.

Manabozho began again, and he would have gone over the same make-believe of pain, had not his father, whose strength he knew was more than a match for his own, threatened to pitch him into a river about five miles off. At last he cried out:

"Father, since you will know, it is the root of the bulrush." He who could with perfect ease spin a sentence a whole day long, seemed to be exhausted by the effort of pronouncing that one word, "bulrush."

Some time after Manabozho observed: "I will get some of the black rock, merely to see how it looks."

"Well," said the father, "I will also get a little of the bulrush root, to learn how it tastes."

They were both double-dealing with each other, and in their hearts getting ready for some desperate work. They had no sooner separated for the evening than Manabozho was striding off the couple of hundred miles necessary to bring him to the place where the black rock was to be procured, while down the other side of the mountain hurried Ningabinn, the West.

At the break of day they each appeared at the great level on the mountain-top, Manabozho with twenty loads, at least, of the black stone, on one side, and on the other the West, with a whole meadow of bulrush in his arms.

Manabozho was the first to strike—hurling a great piece of the black rock, which struck the West directly between the eyes, and he returned the favor with a blow of bulrush that rung over the shoulders of Manabozho, far and wide, like the long lash of the lightning among the clouds.

First one and then the other, Manabozho poured in a tempest of black rock, while the West discharged a shower of bulrush. Blow upon blow, thwack upon thwack—they fought hand to hand until black rock and bulrush were all gone. Then they betook themselves to hurling crags at each other, cudgeling with huge oak trees, and defying each other from one mountain top to another; while at times they shot enormous boulders of granite across at each other's heads, as though they had been mere jackstones. The battle, which had commenced on the mountains, had extended far west. The West was forced to give ground. Manabozho pressing on, drove him across rivers and mountains, ridges and lakes, till at last he got him to the very brink of the world.

"Hold!" cried the West. "My son, you know my power, and although I allow I am now fairly out of breath, it is impossible to kill me. Stop where you are, and I will also portion you out with as much power as your brothers. The four quarters of the globe are already occupied, but you can go and do a great deal of good to the people of the earth, which is beset with serpents, beasts and monsters, who make great havoc of human life. Go and do good, and if you put forth half the strength you have to-day, you will acquire a name that will last forever. When you have finished your work I will have a place provided for you. You will then go and sit with your brother, Kabinocca, in the north."

Manabozho gave his father his hand upon this agreement. And parting from. him, he returned to his own grounds, where he lay for some time sore of his wounds.

WHY THE DIVER DUCK HAS SO FEW TAIL FEATHERS

Adapted from H. R. Schoolcraft

Having overcome the powerful Pearl Feather, killed his serpents and escaped all is wiles and charms, the heart of Manabozho welled within him. An unconquerable desire for further adventures seized upon him. He had won in a great fight on land, so he determined his next success should come to him from the water.

He tried his luck as a fisherman and with such success that he captured an enormous fish, a fish so rich in fat that with the oil Manabozho was able to form a small lake. Wishing to be generous, and at the same time having a cunning plan of his own, he invited all the birds and beasts of his acquaintance to come and feast upon the oil, telling them that the order in which they partook of the banquet would decide how fat each was to be for all time to come.

As fast as they arrived he told them to plunge in and help themselves.

The first to make his appearance was the bear, who took a long and steady draft; then came the deer, the opossum, and such others of the family as are noted for their comfortable covering. The moose and the buffalo were late in arriving on the scene, and the partridge, always lean in flesh, looked on till the supply was nearly gone. There was not a drop left by the time the hare and the marten appeared on the shore of the lake, and they are, in consequence, the slenderest of all creatures.

When this ceremony was over Manabozho suggested to his friends, the assembled birds and animals, that the occasion was proper for a little merrymaking; and taking up his drum he cried out:

"New songs from the South! Come, brothers, dance!"

They all fell in and commenced their rounds. Whenever Manabozho, as he stood in the circle, saw a fat fowl which he fancied pass him, he adroitly wrung its neck and slipped it under his belt, at the same time beating his drum and singing at the top of his lungs to drown the noise of the fluttering, crying out in a tone of admiration:

"That's the way, my brothers; that's the way." At last a small duck of the diver family, thinking there was something wrong, opened one eye and saw what Manabozho was doing. Giving a spring, and crying: "Ha-ha-a! Manabozho is killing us!" he made a dash for the water.

Manabozho was so angry that the creature should have played the spy that he gave chase, and just as the Diver Duck was getting into the water he gave him a kick, which is the reason that the diver's tail feathers are few, his back flattened, and his legs straightened out, so that when he is seen walking on land he makes a sorry looking figure.

The other birds, having no ambition to be thrust in Manabozho's belt, flew off, and the animals scampered into the woods.

MANAIBOZHO IS CHANGED INTO A WOLF

Adapted from H. R. Schoolcraft

One evening, as Manabozho was walking along the shore of a great lake, weary and hungry, he met a great magician in the form of an Old Wolf, with six young ones, coming toward him.

The Wolf no sooner caught sight of him than he told his whelps, who were close beside him, to keep out of the way of Manabozho, "For I know," he said, "that it is that mischievous fellow whom we see yonder."

The young wolves were in the act of running off when Manabozho cried out, "My grandchildren, where are you going? Stop and I will go with you. I wish to have a little chat with your excellent father."

Saying which, he advanced and greeted the Old Wolf, expressing himself as delighted at seeing him looking so well. "Whither do you journey?" he asked.

"We are looking for a good hunting-ground to pass the winter," the Old Wolf answered. "What brings you here?"

"I was looking for you," said Manabozho. "For I have a passion for the chase, brother. I always admired your family; are you willing to change me into a wolf?"

The Wolf gave him a favorable answer, and he was forthwith changed into a wolf.

"Well, that will do," said Manabozho. "But," he said, looking at his tail, "could you oblige me by making my tail a little longer and more bushy, just a little more bushy?"

"Certainly," said the Old Wolf; and he straightway gave Manabozho such a length and spread of tail that it was continually getting between his legs, and it was so heavy that it was as much as he could do to carry it. But, having asked for it, he was ashamed to say a word, and they all started off in company, dashing up the ravine.

After getting into the woods for some distance they ran across the tracks of moose. The young ones scampered off in pursuit, the Old Wolf and Manabozho following at their leisure.

"Well," said the Old Wolf, by way of starting the conversation, "who do you think is the fastest of the boys? Can you tell by the jumps they take?"

"Why," he replied, "that one that takes such long jumps, he is surely the fastest."

"Ha! ha! you are mistaken," said the Old Wolf. "He makes a good start, but he will be the first to tire out; this one who appears to be behind will be the one to kill the game."

By this time they had come to the spot where the boys had started in chase. One had dropped what seemed to be a small medicine-sack, which he carried for the use of the hunting party.

"Take that, Manabozho," said the Old Wolf.

"Why, what will I do with a dirty dog skin?"

The Old Wolf took it up; it was a beautiful robe.

"Oh, I will carry it now," cried Manabozho.

"Oh, no," said the Wolf, who had used his magical powers, "it is a robe of pearls. Come along!" And away he sped at a great rate of speed.

"Not so fast," called Manabozho after him; and then he added to himself as he panted after, "Oh, this tail!"

Coming to a place where the moose had lain down, they saw that the young wolves had made a fresh start after their prey. "Why," said the Old Wolf, "this moose is thin. I know by the tracks. I can always tell whether they are fat or not." A little farther on, one of the young wolves, in dashing at the moose, had broken a tooth on a tree.

"Manabozho," said the Old Wolf, "one of your grandchildren has shot at the game. Take his arrow; there it is."

"No," replied Manabozho, "what will I do with a dirty dog's tooth?"

The Old Wolf took it up, and behold it was a beautiful silver arrow.

When they at last overtook them, they found that the youngsters had killed a very fat moose. Manabozho was very hungry, but the Old Wolf just then again exerted his magical powers, and Manabozho saw nothing but the bones picked quite clean. He thought to himself, "Just as I expected; dirty, greedy fellows. If it had not been for this log at my back I should have been in time to have got a mouthful"; and he cursed the bushy tail which he carried to the bottom of his heart.

The Old Wolf finally called out to one of the young ones, "Give some meat to your grandfather."

One of them obeyed, and coming near to Manabozho he presented him the end of his own bushy tail, which was now nicely seasoned with burs gathered in the course of the hunt. Manabozho jumped up and called out: "You dog, do you think I am going to eat you?" And he walked off in anger.

"Come back brother," cried the Wolf. "You are losing your eyes. You do the child injustice. Look there!" and behold a heap of fresh meat was lying on the spot, all prepared.

Manabozho turned back, and at the sight of so much good food put on a smiling face. "Wonderful!" he said, "how fine the meat is!"

"Yes," replied the Old Wolf, "it is always so with us; we know our work and always get the best. It is not a long tail that makes the hunter."

Manabozho bit his lip.

WHY THE WOODPECKER HAS RED HEAD FEATHERS

Adapted from H. R. Schoolcraft

When his wounds had all been cured by his grandmother's skill in medicine, Manabozho, as big and sturdy as ever, was ripe for new adventures. He set his thoughts immediately upon a war excursion against the Pearl Feather, a wicked old manito, living on the other side of the great lake, who had killed his grandfather.

He began his preparations by making huge bows and arrows without number, but he had no arrow heads. At last his grandmother, Noko, told him that an old man who lived at some distance could furnish him with some, and he sent her to get them. Though she returned with her wrapper full, he told her that he had not enough and sent her again for more.

In the meanwhile he thought to himself, "I must find out the way of making these heads."

Instead of directly asking how it was done, he preferred — just like Manabozho — to deceive his grandmother, in order to learn what he wanted by a trick. "Noko," said he, "while I take my drum and rattle, and sing my war songs, do you go and try to get me some larger heads, for these you have brought me are all of the same size. Go and see whether the old man is not willing to make some a little larger."

He followed her at a distance as she went, having left his drum at the lodge, with a great bird tied at the top, whose fluttering wings should keep up the drumbeat, the same as if he were standing there beating the drum himself. He saw the old workman busy, and learned how he prepared the heads; he also beheld the old man's daughter, who was very beautiful. Manabozho discovered for the first time that he had a heart of his own, and the sigh he heaved passed through the arrow maker's lodge like a young gale of wind.

"My how it blows!" said the old man.

"It must be from the south, though," said the daughter, "it is so fragrant."

Manabozho slipped away, and in two strides he was at home, shouting forth his songs as though he had never left the lodge. He had just time to untie the bird which had been beating the drum when his grandmother came in and gave him the big arrowheads.

In the evening the grandmother said, "My son, you ought to fast before you go to war, as your brothers do, to find out whether you will be successful or not."

He said he had no objection. Having privately stored away in a shady place in the forest two or three dozen juicy bears, a moose, and twenty strings of the tenderest birds, he would retire from the lodge so far as to be entirely out of view of his grandmother and fall to and enjoy himself heartily. At nightfall, having dispatched a dozen birds and half a bear or so, he would return, tottering and forlorn, as if quite famished, so as to make his grandmother feel sorry for him.

When he had finished his term of fasting, in the course of which he slyly dispatched twenty fat bears, six dozen birds, and two fine moose, Manabozho sung his war song and embarked in his canoe, fully prepared for war.

Besides his weapons he took along a large supply of oil.

He traveled rapidly night and day, for he had only to will or speak, and the canoe went. At length he arrived in sight of the fiery serpents, and stopped to study them. He noticed that they were of enormous length and of a bright color, that they were some distance apart, and that the flames which poured forth from the mouths reached across the pass, so he said good morning and began talking with them in a very friendly way. They were not to be deceived, however.

"We know you, Manabozho," they said, "you cannot pass."

Turning his canoe as if about to go back, he suddenly cried out with a loud and terrified voice: "WHAT IS THAT BEHIND YOU?"

The serpents thrown off their guard, instantly turned their heads, and in a moment Manabozho glided silently past them.

"Well," said he, softly, after he had got by, "how about it?"

He then took up his bow and arrows, and with deliberate aim shot every one of them easily, for the serpents were fixed to one spot and could not even turn around.

Having thus escaped the sentinel serpents, Manabozho pushed on in his canoe until he came to a part of the lake called Pitch-Water, as whatever touched it was sure to stick fast.

But Manabozho was prepared with his oil and, rubbing his canoe freely with it, from end to end, he slipped through with ease—and he was the first person who had ever succeeded in passing through the Pitch-Water.

"Nothing like a little oil," said Manabozho to himself.

Having by this time come in view of land, he could see the lodge of the Shining Manito, high upon a distant hill. At the dawn of day he put his clubs and arrows in order and began his attack, yelling and shouting and beating his drum, and calling out so as to make it appear that he had many followers:

"Surround him! surround him! run up! run up!"

He stalked bravely forward, shouting aloud, "It was you that killed my grandfather," and shot off a whole forest of arrows.

The Pearl Feather appeared on the height, blazing like the sun, and paid back Manabozho with a tempest of bolts which rattled like hail.

All day long the fight was kept up, and Manabozho had fired all of his arrows but three without effect, for the Shining Manito was clothed in pure wampum. It was only by immense leaps to right and left that Manabozho could save his head from the sturdy blows which fell about him on every side, like pine.trees, from the hands of the Manito. He was badly bruised, and at his very wits' end, when a large Woodpecker flew past and lit on a tree. It was a bird he had known on the prairie, near his grandmother's lodge.

"Manabozho," called out the Woodpecker, "your enemy has a weak point; shoot at the lock of hair on the crown of his head."

The first arrow he shot only drew a few drops of blood. The Manito made one or two unsteady steps, but recovered himself. He began to parley, but Manabozho, now that he had discovered a way to reach him, was in no humor to trifle, and he let slip another arrow which brought the Shining Manito to his knees. Having the crown of his head within good range Manabozho shot his third arrow, and the Manito fell forward upon the ground, dead.

Manabozho called the Woodpecker to come and receive a reward for the timely hint he had given him, and he rubbed the blood of the Shining Manito on the Woodpecker's head, the feathers of which are red to this day.

Full of his victory, Manabozho returned home, beating his war drum furiously and shouting aloud his song of triumph. His grandmother was on the shore to welcome him with the war dance, which she performed with wonderful skill for one so far advanced in years.

MANABOZHO IS ROBBED BY THE WOLVES

Adapted from H. R. Schoolcraft

Shortly after this the Old Wolf suggested to Manabozho that he should go out and try his luck in hunting by himself. When he chose to put his mind to it he was quite expert, and this time he succeeded in killing a fine fat moose which he thought he would take aside slyly and devour alone.

He was very hungry and he sat down to eat, but as he never could go to work in a straightforward way, he immediately fell into great doubts as to the proper point at which to begin.

"Well," said he, "I do not know where to commence. At the head? No, people will laugh, and say, 'He ate him backward.'"

He went to the side. "No," said he, "they will say I ate him sideways."

He then went to the hind quarter. "No, that will not do, either; they will say I ate him forward. I will begin here, say what they will."

He took a delicate piece from the small of the back, and was just on the point of putting it to his mouth when a tree close by made a creaking noise. He seemed vexed at the sound. He raised the morsel to his mouth the second time, when the tree creaked again.

"Why," he exclaimed, "I cannot eat when I hear such a noise. "Stop, stop!" he cried to the tree. He put down the morsel of meat, exclaiming. "I CANNOT eat with such a noise," and starting away he climbed the tree and was actually pulling at the limb which had bothered him, when his forepaw was caught between the branches so that he could not free himself.

While thus held fast he saw a pack of wolves advancing through the wood in the direction of his meat. He suspected them to be the Old Wolf and his cubs, but night was coming on and he could not make them out. "Go the other way, go the other Way!" he cried out; "what do you expect to get here?"

The Wolves stopped for a while and talked among themselves, and said: "Manabozho must have something there, or he would not tell us to go another way."

"I begin to know know him," said the Old Wolf, "and all his tricks. Let us go forward and see." They came on and, finding the moose soon made away with it.

Manabozho looked wistfully on while they ate until they were fully satisfied, when off they scampered in high spirits. A heavy blast of wind opened the branches finally, and released him. The wolves had left nothing but bare bones. He made for home.

When he related his mishap, the Old Wolf, taking him by the forepaw, condoled with him deeply on his ill luck. A tear even started to his eye as he added: "My brother, this should teach us not to meddle with points of ceremony when we have good meat to eat."

MANABOZHO AND THE WOODPECKERS

Adapted from H. R. Schoolcraft

Manabozho lost the greater part of his magical power through letting his young wolf grandson fall through the thin ice and drown. No one knew where his grandmother had gone to. He married the arrow maker's daughter, and became the father of several children, but he was very poor and scarcely able to procure a living. His lodge was pitched in a distant part of the country, where he could get no game, and it was winter time. One day he said to his wife, "I will go out walking and see if I can find some lodges."

After walking some time he finally discovered a lodge at a distance. There were children playing at the door, and when they saw him approaching they ran in and told their parents Manabozho was coming.

It was the home of the large Red-Headed Woodpecker. He came to the door and asked Manabozho to enter, and the invitation was promptly accepted. After some time the Woodpecker, who was a magician, said to his wife: "Have you nothing to give Manabozho? he must be hungry."

She answered, "No."

"He ought not to go without his supper," said the Woodpecker. "I will see what I can do."

In the center of the lodge stood a large tamarack tree. Upon this the Woodpecker flew, and commenced going up, turning his head on each side of the tree, and every now and then driving in his bill. At last he pulled something out of the tree and threw it down, when, behold, a fine fat raccoon lay on the ground. He drew out six or seven more, and then came down and told his wife to prepare them.

"Manabozho," he said, "this is the only thing we eat; what else can we give you?"

"It is very good," replied Manabozho.

They smoked their pipes and conversed, and after a while Manabozho got ready to go home, so the Woodpecker said to his wife, "Give him the Other raccoons to take home for his children."

In the act of leaving the lodge Manabozho on purpose dropped one of his mittens, which was soon after observed upon the ground. "Run," said the Woodpecker to his eldest son, "and give it to him; but mind that you do not give it into his hand; throw it at him, for there is no knowing what he may do, he acts so curiously."

The boy did as he was directed. "Grandfather," he said, as he came up to him, "you have left one of your mittens, and here it is."

"Yes," he said, making believe he did not know he had dropped it, "so I did; but don't throw it, you will get it wet on the snow."

The lad, however, threw it, and was about to return when Manabozho cried out, "Bakah! Bakah! Stop, stop; is that all you eat? Do you eat nothing else with your raccoon? Tell me!"

"Yes, that is all, answered the Young Woodpecker; "we have nothing else."

"Tell your father," continued Manabozho, "to come and visit me, and let him bring a sack. I will give him what he shall eat with his raccoon meat."

When the young one returned and reported this message to his father the Old Woodpecker turned up his nose at the invitation. "I wonder," he said "what he thinks he has got, poor fellow!" He was bound, however, to answer the offer of hospitality, and he went accordingly, taking along a cedar-sack, to pay a visit to Manabozho.

Manabozho received the Old Red-Headed Woodpecker with great ceremony. He had stood at the door awaiting his arrival, and as soon as he came in sight Manabozho commenced, while he was yet far off, bowing and opening wide his arms, in token of welcome; all of which the Woodpecker returned in due form, by ducking his bill and hopping to right and left, extending his wings to their full length and fluttering them back to his breast.

When the Woodpecker at last reached the lodge Manabozho made several remarks upon the weather, the appearance of the country, and especially spoke of the scarcity of game. "But we," he added — "we always have enough. Come in, and you shall not go away hungry, my noble birds!"

Manabozho had always prided himself on being able to give as good as he had received; and to be up with the Woodpecker he had shifted his lodge so as to inclose a large dry tamarack tree.

"What can I give you?" said he to the Woodpecker; "as we eat so shall you eat."

With this he hopped forward and, jumping on the tamarack tree, he attempted to climb it just as he had seen the Woodpecker do in his own lodge. He turned his head first on one side and then on the other, as the Woodpecker does, striving to go up the tree, but as often slipping down. Every now and then he would strike the tree with his nose, as if it was a bell, and draw back as if to pull something out of the tree, but he pulled out no raccoons. He dashed his nose so often against the trunk that at last the blood began to flow, and he tumbled down senseless on the ground.

The Woodpecker started up with his drum and rattle to restore him, and by beating them violently he succeeded in bringing him to.

As soon as he came to his senses, Manabozho began to lay the blame of his failure upon his wife, saying to his guest: "Nemesho, it is this woman relation of yours—she is the cause of my not succeeding. She has made me a worthless fellow. Before I married her I also could get raccoons.

The Woodpecker said nothing, but flying on the tree he drew out several fine raccoons. "Here," said he, "this is the way we do" and left him in disdain, carrying his bill high in the air, and stepping over the doorsill as if it were not worthy to be touched by his toes.

THE BOY AND THE WOLVES

Retold by Andrew Lang

Once upon a time an Indian hunter built himself a house in the middle of a great forest, far away from all his tribe; for his heart was gentle and kind and he was weary of the treachery and cruel deeds of those who had been his friends. So he left them and took his wife and three children, and they journeyed on until they found a spot near to a clear stream, where they began to cut down trees and to make ready their wigwam. For many years they lived peacefully and happily in this sheltered place, never leaving it except to hunt the wild animals, which served them both for food and clothes. At last, however, the strong man fell sick, and before long lie knew he must die. So he gathered his family round him and said his last words to them.

"You, my wife, the companion of my days, will follow me ere many moons have waned to the island of the blessed. But for you, 0 my children, whose lives are but newly begun, the wickedness, unkindness, and ingratitude from which I fled are before you. Yet I shall go hence in peace, my children, if you will promise always to love each other and never to forsake your youngest brother."

"Never!" they replied, holding out their hands. And the hunter died content.

Scarcely eight moons had passed when, just as he had said, the wife went forth and followed her husband; but before leaving her children she bade the two elder ones think of their promise never to forsake the younger, for he was a child and weak. And while the snow lay thick upon the ground they tended him and cherished him; but when the earth showed green again the heart of the young man stirred within him, and he longed to see the wigwams of the village where his father's youth was spent.

Therefore he opened all his heart to his sister, who answered: "My brother, I understand your longing for our fellow-men, whom here we cannot see. But remember our father's words. Shall we not seek our own pleasures and forget the little one?"

But he would not listen, and, making no reply, he took his bow and arrows and left the hut. The snows fell and melted, yet he never returned, and at last the heart of the girl grew cold and hard and her little boy became a burden in her eyes, till one day she spoke thus to him: "See, there is food for many days to come. Stay here within the shelter of the hut. I go to seek our brother, and when I have found him I shall return hither."

But when, after hard journeying, she reached the village where her brother dwelt and saw that he had a wife and was happy, and when she, too, was sought by a young brave, then she also forgot the boy alone in the forest and thought only of her husband.

Now as soon as the little boy had eaten all the food which his sister had left him, he went out into the woods and gathered berries and dug up roots, and while the sun shone he was contented and had his fill. But when the snows began and the wind howled, then his stomach felt empty and his limbs cold, and he hid in trees all the night and only crept out to eat what the wolves had left behind. And by and by, having no other friends, he sought their company, and sat by while they devoured their prey, and they grew to know him and gave him food. And without them he would have died in the snow. But at last the snows melted and the ice upon the great lake, and as the wolves went down to the shore the boy went after them. And it happened one day that his big brother was fishing in his canoe near the shore, and he heard the voice of a child singing in the Indian tone:

"My brother, my brother!
I am becoming a wolf,
I am becoming a wolf!"

And when he had so sung he howled as wolves howl. Then the heart of the elder sank and he hastened toward him, crying: "Brother, little brother, come to me;" but he, being half a wolf, only continued his song. And the louder the elder called him, "Brother, little brother, come to me," the swifter he fled after his brothers the wolves and the heavier grew his skin, till, with a long howl, he vanished into the depths of the forest.

So, with shame and anguish in his soul, the elder brother went back to his village, and with his sister mourned the little boy and the broken promise till the end of his life.

THE INDIAN WHO LOST HIS WIFE

Retold by Andrew Lang

Once upon a time there was a man and his wife who lived in the forest far from the rest of the tribe. Very often they spent the day in hunting together, but after awhile the wife found that she had so many things to do that she was obliged to stay at home; so he went alone, though he found that when his wife was not with him he never had any luck. One day, when he was away hunting, the woman fell ill, and in a few days she died. Her husband grieved bitterly and buried her in the house where she had passed her life; but as the time went on he felt so lonely without her that he made a wooden doll about her height amid size for company and dressed it in her clothes. He seated it in front of the fire and tried to think he had his wife back again. The next day he went out to hunt, and when he came home the first thing he did was to go up to the doll and brush off some of the ashes from the fire which had fallen on its face. But he was very busy now, for he had to cook and mend, besides getting food, for there was no one to help him. And so a whole year passed away.

At the end of that time he came back from hunting one night and found some wood by the door and a fire within. The next night there was not only wood and fire, but a piece of meat in the kettle, nearly ready for eating. He searched all about to see who could have done this, but could find no one. The next time he went to hunt he took care not to go far and came in quite early. And while he was still a long way off he saw a woman going into the house with wood on her shoulders. So he made haste and opened the door quickly, and instead of the wooden doll his wife sat in front of the fire. Then she spoke to him and said:

"The Great Spirit felt sorry for you because you would not be comforted, so he let me come back to you, but you must not stretch out your hand to touch me till we have seen the rest of our people. If you do I shall die."

So the man listened to her words, and the woman dwelt there and brought the wood and kindled the fire, till one day her husband said to her:

"It is now two years since you died. Let us now go back to our tribe. Then you will be well and I can touch you."

And with that he prepared food for the journey, a string of deer's flesh for her to carry and one for himself; and so they started. Now, the camp of the tribe was distant six days' journey, and when they were yet one day's journey off it began to snow, and they felt weary and longed for rest. Therefore they made a fire, cooked some food, and spread out their skins to sleep.

Then the heart of the man was greatly stirred and he stretched out his arms to his wife, but she waved her hands and said:

"We have seen no one yet. It is too soon."

But he would not listen to her and caught her to him, and behold! he was clasping the wooden doll. And when he saw it was the doll he pushed it from him in his misery and rushed away to the camp and told them all his story. And some doubted, and they went back with him to the place where he and his wife had stopped to rest, and there lay the doll, and besides, they saw in time snow the steps of two people, and the foot of one was like the foot of the doll. And the man grieved sore all the days of his life.

PUNCHKIN

By E. Frere

Once upon a time there was a Raja who had seven beautiful daughters. They were all good girls; but the youngest, named Balna, was more clever than the rest. The Raja's wife died when they were quite little children, so these seven poor Princesses were left with no mother to take care of them.

The Raja's daughters took it by turns to cook their father's dinner every day, while he was absent deliberating with his Ministers on the affairs of the nation.

About this time the Prudhan died, leaving a widow and one daughter; and every day, when the seven Princesses were preparing their father's dinner, the Prudhan's widow and daughter would come and beg for a little fire from the hearth. Then Balna used to say to her sisters, "Send that woman away; send her away. Let her get the fire at her own house. What does she want with ours? If we allow her to come here, we shall suffer for it some day."

But the other sisters would answer, "Be quiet, Balna; why must you always be quarreling with this poor woman? Let her take some fire if she likes." Then the Prudhan's widow used to go to the hearth and take a few sticks from it; and while no one was looking, she would quickly throw some mud into the midst of the dishes which were being prepared for the Raja's dinner.

Now the Raja was very fond of his daughters. Ever since their mother's death they had cooked his dinner with their own hands, in order to avoid the danger of his being poisoned by his enemies. So, when he found the mud mixed up with his dinner, he thought it must arise from their carelessness, as it did not seem likely that anyone should have put mud there on purpose; but being very kind he did not like to reprove them for it, although this spoiling of the curry was repeated many days.

At last, one day, he determined to hide, and watch his daughters cooking, and see how it all happened; so he went into the next room, and watched them through a hole in the wall.

There he saw his seven daughters carefully washing the rice and preparing the curry, and as each dish was completed, they put it by the fire ready to be cooked. Next he noticed the Prudhan's widow come to the door, and beg for a few sticks from the fire to cook her dinner with. Balna turned to her, angrily, and said, "Why don't you keep fuel in your own house, and not come here every day and take ours? Sisters, don't give this woman any more wood; let her buy it for herself."

Then the eldest sister answered, "Balna, let the poor woman take the wood and the fire; she does us no harm." But Balna replied, "If you let her come here so often, maybe she will do us some harm, and make us sorry for it, some day."

The Raja then saw the Prudhan's widow go to the place where all his dinner was nicely prepared, and, as she took the wood, she threw a little mud into each of the dishes.

At this he was very angry, and sent to have the woman seized and brought before him. But when the widow came, she told him that she had played this trick because she wanted to gain an audience with him; and she spoke so cleverly, and pleased him so well with her cunning words, that instead of punishing her, the Raja married her, and made her his Ranee, and she and her daughter came to live in the palace.

Now the new Ranee hated the seven poor Princesses, and wanted to get them, if possible, out of the way, in order that her daughter might have all their riches, and live in the palace as Princess in their place; and instead of being grateful to them for their kindness to her, she did all she could to make them miserable. She gave them nothing but bread to eat, and very little of that, and very little water to drink; so these seven poor little Princesses, who had been accustomed to have everything comfortable about them, and good food and good clothes all their lives long, were very miserable and unhappy; and they used to go out every day and sit by their dead mother's tomb and cry—and say:

"O mother, mother, cannot you see your poor children, how unhappy we are, and how we are starved by our cruel stepmother?"

One day, while they were thus sobbing and crying, lo and behold! a beautiful pomelo tree grew up out of the grave, covered with fresh, ripe pomeloes, and the children satisfied their hunger by eating some of the fruit, and every day after this, instead of trying to eat the bad dinner their stepmother provided for them, they used to go out to their mother's grave and eat the pommels which grew there on the beautiful tree.

Then the Ranee said to her daughter, "I cannot tell how it is, every day those seven girls say they don't want any dinner, and won't eat any; and yet they never grow thin nor look ill; they look better than you do. I cannot tell how it is." And she bade her watch the seven Princesses, and see if anyone gave them anything to eat.

So next day, when the Princesses went to their mother's grave, and were eating the beautiful pomeloes, the Prudhan's daughter followed them, and saw them gathering the fruit.

Then Balna said to her sisters, "Do you not see that girl watching us? Let us drive her away, or hide the pomeloes, else she will go and tell her mother all about it, and that will be bad for us."

But the other sisters said, "Oh no, do not be unkind, Balna. The girl would never be so cruel as to tell her mother. Let us rather invite her to come and have some of the fruit." And calling her to them, they gave her one of the pomeloes.

No sooner had she eaten it, however, than the Prudhan's daughter went home and said to her mother, "I do not wonder the seven Princesses will not eat the dinner you prepare for them, for by their mother's grave there grows a beautiful pomelo tree, and they go there every day and eat the pomeloes. I ate one, and it was the nicest I have ever tasted."

The cruel Ranee was much vexed at hearing this, and all next day she stayed in her room, and told the Raja that she had a very bad headache. The Raja was deeply grieved, and said to his wife, "What can I do for you?" She answered, "There is only one thing that will make my headache well. By your dead wife's tomb there grows a fine pomelo tree; you must bring that here, and boil it, root and branch, and put a little of the water in which it has been boiled on my forehead, and that will cure my headache." So the Raja sent his servants, and had the beautiful pomelo tree pulled up by the roots, and did as the Ranee desired; and when some of the water, in which it had been boiled, was put on her forehead, she said her headache was gone and she felt quite well.

Next day, when the seven Princesses went as usual to the grave of their mother, the pomelo tree had disappeared. Then they all began to cry very bitterly.

Now there was by the Ranee's tomb a small tank, and as they were crying they saw the tank was filled with a rich cream-like substance, which quickly hardened into a thick white cake. At seeing this all the Princesses were very glad, and they ate some of the cake, and liked it; and next day the same thing happened, and so it went on for many days. Every morning the Princesses went to their mother's grave, and found the little tank filled with the nourishing cream-like cake. Then the cruel stepmother said to her daughter: "I cannot tell how it is, I have had the pomelo tree which used to grow by the Ranee's grave destroyed, and yet the Princesses grow no thinner, nor look more sad, though they never eat the dinner I give them. I cannot tell how it is!"

And her daughter said, "I will watch."

Next day, while the Princesses were eating the cream cake, who should come by but their stepmother's daughter. Balna saw her first, and said, "See, sisters, there comes that girl again. Let us sit round the edge of the tank and not allow her to see it, for if we give her some of our cake, she will go and tell her mother; and that will be very unfortunate for us."

The other sisters, however, thought Balna unnecessarily suspicious, and instead of following her advice, they gave the Prudhan's daughter some of the cake, and she went home and told her mother all about it.

The Ranee, on hearing how well the Princesses fared, was exceedingly angry, and sent her servants to pull down the dead Ranee's tomb, and fill the little tank with the ruins. And not content with this, she next day pretended to be very, very ill—in fact, at the point of death—and when the Raja was much grieved, and asked her whether it was in his power to procure her any remedy, she said to him: "Only one thing can save my life, but I know you will not do it." He replied, "Yes, whatever it is, I will do it." She then said, "To save my life, you must kill the seven daughters of your first wife, and put some of their blood on my forehead and on the palms of my hands, and their death will be my life." At these words the Raja was very sorrowful; but because he feared to break his word, he went out with a heavy heart to find his daughters.

He found them crying by the ruins of their mother's grave.

Then, feeling he could not kill them, the Raja spoke kindly to them, and told them to come out into the jungle with him; and there he made a fire and cooked some rice, and gave it to them. But in the afternoon, it being very hot, the seven Princesses all fell asleep, and when he saw they were fast asleep, the Raja, their father, stole away and left them (for he feared his wife), saying to himself: "It is better my poor daughters should die here, than be killed by their stepmother."

He then shot a deer, and returning home, put some of its blood on the forehead and hands of the Ranee, and she thought then that he had really killed the Princesses, and said she felt quite well.

Meantime the seven Princesses awoke, and when they found themselves all alone in the thick jungle they were much frightened, and began to call out as loud as they could, in hopes of making their father hear; but he was by that time far away, and would not have been able to hear them even had their voices been as loud as thunder.

It so happened that this very day the seven young sons of a neighboring Raja chanced to be hunting in that same jungle, and as they were returning home, after the day's sport was over, the youngest Prince said to his brothers: "Stop, I think I hear some one crying and calling out. Do you not hear voices? Let us go in the direction of the sound, and find out what it is."

So the seven Princes rode through the wood until they came to the place where the seven Princesses sat crying and wringing their hands. At the sight of them the young Princes were very much astonished, and still more so on learning their story; and they settled that each should take one of these poor forlorn ladies home with him, and marry her.

So the first and eldest Prince took the eldest Princess home with him, and married her.

And the second took the second; and third took the third; and the fourth took the fourth; and the fifth took the fifth; and the sixth took the sixth; and the seventh, and the handsomest of all, took the beautiful Balna.

And when they got to their own land, there was great rejoicing throughout the kingdom, at the marriage of the seven young Princes to seven such beautiful Princesses.

About a year after this Balna had a little son, and his uncles and aunts were so fond of the boy that it was as if he had seven fathers and seven mothers. None of the other Princes and Princesses had any children, so the son of the seventh Prince and Balna was acknowledged their heir by all the rest.

They had thus lived very happily for some time, when one fine day the seventh Prince (Balna's husband) said he would go out hunting, and away he went; and they waited long for him, but he never came back.

Then his six brothers said they would go and see what had become of him; and they went away, but they also did not return.

And the seven Princesses grieved very much, for they feared that their kind husbands must have been killed.

One day, not long after this had happened, as Balna was rocking her baby's cradle, and while her sisters were working in the room below, there came to the palace door a man in a long black dress, who said that he was a Fakir, and came to beg. The servant said to him, "You cannot go into the palace—the Raja's sons have all gone away; we think they must be dead, and their widows cannot be interrupted by your begging." But he said, "I am a holy man, you must let me in. Then the stupid servants let him walk through the palace, but they did not know that this was no Fakir, but a wicked Magician named Punchkin.

Punchkin Fakir wandered through the palace, and saw many beautiful things there, till at last he reached the room where Balna sat singing beside her little boy's cradle. The Magician thought her more beautiful than all the other beautiful things he had seen, insomuch that he asked her to go home with him and to marry him. But she said, "My husband, I fear, is dead, but my little boy is still quite young; I will stay here and teach him to grow up a clever man, and when he is grown up he shall go out into the world, and try and learn tidings of his father. Heaven forbid that I should ever leave him, or marry yon." At these words the Magician was very angry, and turned her into a little black dog, and led her away; saying, "Since yon will not come with me of your own free will, I will make you." So the poor Princess was dragged away, without any power of effecting an escape, or of letting her sisters know what had become of her. As Punchkin passed through the palace gate the servants said to him, "Where did yon get that pretty little dog?" And he answered, "One of the Princesses gave it to me as a present." At hearing which they let him go without further questioning.

Soon after this, the six elder Princesses heard the little baby, their nephew, begin to cry, and when they went upstairs they were much surprised to find him all alone, and Balna nowhere to be seen. Then they questioned the servants, and when they heard of the Fakir and the little black dog, they guessed what had happened, and sent in every direction seeking them, but neither the Fakir nor the dog were to be found. What could six poor women do? They gave up all hopes of ever seeing their kind husbands, and their sister, and her husband again, and devoted themselves thenceforward to teaching and taking care of their little nephew.

Thus time went on, till Balna's son was fourteen years old. Then, one day, his aunts told him the history of the family; and no sooner did he hear it, than be was seized with a great desire to go in search of his father and mother and uncles, and if he could find them alive to bring them home again. His aunts, on learning his determination, were much alarmed and tried to dissuade him, saying, "We have lost our husbands, and our sister and her husband, and you are now our sole hope; if you go away, what shall we do?" But he replied, "I pray you not to be discouraged; I will return soon, and if it is possible bring my father and mother and uncles with me." So he set out on his travels; but for some months he could learn nothing to help him in his search.

At last, after he had journeyed many hundreds of weary miles, and become almost hopeless of ever hearing anything further of his parents, he one day came to a country that seemed full of stones, and rocks, and trees, and there he saw a large palace with a tower; hard by was a Malee's little house.

As he was looking about, the Malee's wife saw him, and ran out of the house and said, "My dear boy, who are you that dare venture to this dangerous place?" He answered, "I am a Raja's son, and I come in search of my father, and my uncles, and my mother whom a wicked enchanter bewitched."

Then the Malee's wife said, "This country and this palace belong to a great enchanter; he is all powerful, and if anyone displeases him, he can turn them into stones and trees. All the rocks and trees you see here were living people once, and the Magician turned them to what they now are. Some time ago a Raja's son came here, and shortly afterward came his six brothers, and they were all turned into stones and trees; and these are not the only unfortunate ones, for up in that tower lives a beautiful Princess, whom the Magician has kept prisoner there for twelve years, because she hates him and will not marry him."

Then the little Prince thought, "These must be my parents and my uncles. I have found what I seek at last." So he told his story to the Malee's wife, and begged her to help him to remain in that place awhile and inquire further concerning the unhappy people she mentioned; and she promised to befriend him, and advised his disguising himself lest the Magician should see him, and turn him likewise into stone. To this the Prince agreed. So the Malee's wife dressed him up in a saree, and pretended that he was her daughter.

One day, not long after this, as the Magician was walking in his garden he saw the little girl (as he thought) playing about, and asked her who she was. She told him she was the Malee's daughter, and the Magician said, "You are a pretty little girl, and to-morrow you shall take a present of flowers from me to the beautiful lady who lives in the tower."

The young Prince was much delighted at hearing this, and went immediately to inform the Malee's wife; after consultation with whom he determined that it would be more safe for him to retain his disguise, and trust to the chance of a favorable opportunity for establishing some communication with his mother, if it were indeed she.

Now it happened that at Balna's marriage her husband had given her a small gold ring on which her name was engraved, and she had put it on her little son's finger when he was a baby, and afterward when he was older his aunts had had it enlarged for him, so that he was still able to wear it. The Malee's wife advised him to fasten the well-known treasure to one of the bouquets he presented to his mother, and trust to her recognizing it. This was not to be done without difficulty, as such a strict watch was kept over the poor Princess (for fear of her ever establishing communication with her friends), that though the supposed Malee's daughter was permitted to take her flowers every day, the Magician or one of his slaves was always in the room at the time. At last one day, however, opportunity favored him, and when no one was looking the boy tied the ring to a nosegay, and threw it at Balna's feet. It fell with a clang on the floor, and Balna, looking to see what made the strange sound, found the little ring tied to the flowers. On recognizing it, she at once believed the story her son told her of his long search, and begged him to advise her as to what she had better do; at the same time entreating him on no account to endanger his life by trying to rescue her. She told him that for twelve long years the Magician had kept her shut up in the tower because she refused to marry him, and she was so closely guarded that she saw no hope of release.

Now Balna's son was a bright, clever boy, so he said, "Do not fear, dear mother; the first thing to do is to discover how far the Magician's power extends, in order that we may be able to liberate my father and uncles, whom he has imprisoned in the form of the rocks and trees. You have spoken to him angrily for twelve long years; now rather speak kindly. Tell him you have given up all hopes of again seeing the husband you have so long mourned, and say you are willing to harry him. Then endeavor to find out what his power consists in, and whether he is immortal, or can be put to death."

Balna determined to take her son's advice; and the next day sent for Punchkin, and spoke to him as had been suggested.

The Magician greatly delighted, begged her to allow the wedding to take place as soon as possible.

But she told him that before she married him he must allow her a little more time, in which she might make his acquaintance, and that, after being enemies so long, their friendship could but strengthen by degrees. "And do tell me," she said, "are you quite immortal? Can death never touch you? And are you too great an enchanter ever to feel human suffering?"

"Why do you ask?" said he.

"Because," she replied. "if I am to be your wife, I would fain know all about you, in order, if any calamity threatens you, to overcome, or if possible to avert it."

"It is true," he added, "that I am not as others. Far, far away, hundreds of thousands of miles from this, there lies a desolate country covered with thick jungle. In the midst of the jungle grows a circle of palm trees, and in the center of the circle stand six chattees full of water, piled one above another: below the sixth chattee is a small cage which contains a little green parrot; on the life of the parrot depends my life; and if the parrot is killed I must die. It is. however," he added, "impossible that the parrot should sustain any injury, both on account of the inaccessibility of the country, and because, by my appointment, many thousand genii surround the palm trees, and kill all who approach the place."

Balna told her son what Punchkin had said; but at the same time implored him to give up all idea of getting the parrot.

The Prince, however, replied, "Mother, unless I can get hold of that parrot, you, and my father, and uncles, cannot be liberated: be not afraid, I will shortly return. Do you, meantime, keep the Magician in good humor — still putting off your marriage with him on various pretexts; and before he finds out the cause of delay, I will be here." So saying, he went away.

Many, many weary miles did he travel, till at last he came to a thick jungle; and, being very tired, sat down under a tree and fell asleep. He was awakened by a soft rustling sound, and looking about him, saw a large serpent which was making its way to an eagle's nest built in the tree under which he lay, and in the nest were two young eagles. The Prince seeing the danger of the young birds, drew his sword, and killed the serpent; at the same moment a rushing sound was heard in the air, and the two old eagles, who had been out hunting for food for their young ones, returned. They quickly saw the dead serpent and the young Prince standing over it; and the old mother eagle said to him, "Dear boy, for many' years all our young ones have been devoured by that cruel serpent; you have now saved the lives of our children; whenever you are in need therefore, send to us and we will help you; and as for these little eagles, take them, and let them be your servants."

At this the Prince was very glad, and the two eaglets crossed their wings, on which he mounted; and they carried him far, far away over the thick, jungles, until he came to the place where grew the circle of palm trees, in the midst of which stood the six chattees full of water. It was the middle of the day, and the heat was very great. All round the trees were the genii fast asleep; nevertheless, there were such countless thousands of them, that it would have been quite impossible for anyone to walk through their ranks to the place; down swooped the strong-winged eaglets — down jumped the Prince; in an instant he had overthrown the six chattees full of water, and seized the little green parrot, which he rolled up in his cloak; while, as he mounted again into the air, all the genii below awoke, and finding their treasure gone, set up a wild and melancholy howl.

Away, away flew the little eagles, till they came to their home in the great tree; then the Prince said to the old eagles, "Take back your little ones; they have done me good service; if ever again I stand in need of help, I will not fail to come to you." He then continued his journey on foot till he arrived once more at the Magician's palace, where he sat down at the door and began playing with the Parrot. Punchkin saw him, and came to him quickly, and said, "My boy, where did yon get that parrot? Give it to me, I pray you."

But the Prince answered, "Oh no, I cannot give away my parrot, it is a great pet of mine; I have had it many years."

Then the Magician said, "If it is an old favorite, I can understand your not caring to give it away; but come, what will you sell it for?"

"Sir," said the Prince, "I will not sell my parrot."

Then Punchkin got frightened, and said, "Anything, anything; name what price you will, and it shall be yours." The Prince answered, "Let the seven Raja's sons whom you turned into rocks and trees be instantly liberated."

"It is done as you desire," said the Magician, "only give me my parrot." And With that, by a stroke of his wand, Balna's husband and his brothers resumed their natural shapes. "Now, give me my parrot," repeated Punchkin.

"Not so fast, my master," rejoined the Prince; "I must first beg that you will restore to life all whom you have thus imprisoned."

The Magician immediately waved his wand again; and whilst he cried, in an imploring voice, "Give me my parrot!" the whole garden became suddenly alive: where rocks, and stones, and trees had been before, stood Rajas, and Punts, and Sirdars, and mighty men on prancing horses, and jeweled pages, and troops of armed attendants.

"Give me my parrot!" cried Punchkin. Then the boy took hold of the parrot, and tore off one of its wings; and as he did so the Magician's right arm fell off.

Punchkin then stretched out his left arm, crying, "Give me my parrot!" The Prince pulled off the parrot's second wing, and the Magician's left arm tumbled off.

"Give me my parrot!" cried he, and fell on his knees. The Prince pulled off the parrot's right leg, and the Magician's right leg fell off: the Prince pulled off the parrot's left leg, down fell the Magician's left.

Nothing remained of him save the limbless body and the head; but still he rolled his eyes, and cried "Give me my parrot!" "Take your parrot, then, cried the boy, and with that. he wrung the bird's neck, and threw it at the magician; and as he did so, Punchkin's head twisted round and, with a fearful groan, he died!

Then they let Balna out of the tower; and she, her son, and the seven Princes went to their own country, and lived very happily ever afterward. And as to the rest of the world, everyone went to his own house.

HOW SUN, MOON AND WIND
WENT OUT TO DINNER

By E. Frere

One day Sun, Moon, and Wind went out to dine with their uncle and aunt Thunder and Lightning. Their mother (one of the most distant Stars you see far up in the sky) waited alone for her children's return.

Now both Sun and Wind were greedy and selfish. They enjoyed the great feast that had been prepared for them, without a thought of saving any of it to take home to their mother—but the gentle Moon did not forget her. Of every dainty dish that was brought round, she placed a small portion under one of her beautiful long fingernails, that Star might also have a share in the treat.

On their return, their mother, Who had kept watch for them all night long with her little bright eye, said, "Well, children, what have yon brought home for me?" Then Sun (who was eldest) said, "I have brought nothing home for you. I went out to enjoy myself with my friends—not to fetch dinner for my mother!" And Wind said, "Neither have I brought anything home for you, mother. You could hardly expect me to bring a collection of good things for you, when I merely went out for my own pleasure." But Moon said, "Mother, fetch a plate, see what I have brought you." And shaking her hands she showered down such a choice dinner as never was seen before.

Then Star turned to Sun and spoke thus, "Because you went out to amuse yourself with your friends, and feasted and enjoyed yourself, without any thought of our mother at home—you shall be cursed. Henceforth, your rays shall ever be hot and scorching, and shall burn all that they touch. And men shall hate you, and cover their heads when you appear."

(And that is why the Sun is so hot to this day.)

Then she turned to Wind and said, "You also who forgot your mother in the midst of your selfish pleasures—hear your doom. You shall always blow in the hot, dry weather, and shall parch and shrivel all living things. And men shall detest and avoid you from this very time."

(And that is why the Wind in the hot weather is still so disagreeable.)

But to Moon she said, "Daughter, because you remembered your mother, and kept for her a share in your own enjoyment, from henceforth you shall be ever cool, and calm and bright. No noxious glare shall accompany your pure rays, and men shall always call you 'blessed.'"

(And that is why the Moon's light is so soft, and cool, and beautiful even to this day.)

WHY THE FISH LAUGHED

By Joseph Jacobs

As a certain fisherwoman passed by a palace crying her fish, the queen appeared at one of the windows and beckoned her to come near and show what she had. At that moment a very big fish jumped about in the bottom of the basket.

"Is it a he or a she?" inquired the queen. "I wish to purchase a she fish."

On hearing this the fish laughed aloud.

"It's a he," replied the fisherwoman, and proceeded on her rounds.

The queen returned to her room in a great rage; and on coming to see her in the evening, the king noticed that something had disturbed her.

"Are you indisposed?" he said.

"No; but I am very much annoyed at the strange behavior of a fish. A woman brought me one to-day, and on my inquiring whether it was a male or female, the fish laughed most rudely."

"A fish laugh! Impossible! You must be dreaming."

"I am not a fool. I speak of what I have seen with my own eyes and heard with my own ears."

"Passing strange! Be it so. I will inquire concerning it."

On the morrow the king repeated to his vizier what his wife had told him, and bade him investigate the matter, and be ready with a satisfactory answer within six mouths, on pain of death. The vizier promised to do his best, though he felt almost certain of failure. For live months he labored indefatigably to find a reason for the laughter of the fish. He sought everywhere and from everyone. The wise and learned, and they who were skilled in magic and in all manner of trickery, were consulted. Nobody, however, could explain the matter; and so he returned broken-hearted to his house, and began to arrange his affairs in prospect of certain death, for he had had sufficient experience of the king to know that His Majesty would not go back from his threat. Amongst other things, he advised his son to travel for a time, until the king's anger should have somewhat cooled.

The young fellow, who was both clever and handsome, started off whithersoever Kismet might lead him. He had been gone some days, when he fell in with an old farmer, who also was on a journey to a certain village. Finding the old man very pleasant, he asked him if he might accompany him, professing to be on a visit to the same place. The old farmer agreed, and they walked along together. The day was hot, and the way was long and weary.

"Don't yon think it would be pleasanter if you and I sometimes gave one another a lift?" said the youth.

"What a fool the man is!" thought the old farmer.

Presently they passed through a field of corn ready for the sickle, and looking' like a sea of gold as it waved to and fro in the breeze.

"Is this eaten or not?" said the young man.

Not understanding his meaning, the old man replied, "I don't know."

After a little while the two travelers arrived at a big village, where the young man gave his companion a clasp knife, and said, "Take this, friend, and get two horses with it; but mind and bring it back, for it is very precious."

The old man, looking half amused and half angry, pushed back the knife, muttering something to the effect that his friend was either a fool himself or else tying to play the fool with him. The young man pretended not to notice his reply, and remained almost silent till they reached the city, a short distance outside which was the old farmer's house.

They walked about the bazaar and went to the mosque, but nobody saluted them or invited them to come in and rest.

"What a large cemetery!" exclaimed the young man.

"What does the man mean," thought the old farmer, "calling this largely populated city a cemetery?"

On leaving the city their way led through a cemetery where a few people were praying beside a grave and distributing chupatties and kulchas to Passers-by, in the name of their beloved dead. They beckoned to the two travelers and gave them as much as they would.

"What a splendid city this is!" said the young man.

"Now, the man must surely be demented!" thought the old farmer. "I wonder what he will do next? He will be calling the land water, and the water land; and be speaking of light where there is darkness, and of darkness where it is light." However, he kept his thoughts to himself.

Presently they had to wade through a stream that ran along the edge of the cemetery. The water was rather deep, so the old farmer took off his shoes and pajamas and crossed over; but the young man waded through it with his shoes and pajamas on.

"Well! I never did see such a perfect fool, both in word and in deed, said the old man to himself.

However, he liked the fellow; and thinking that he would amuse his wife and daughter, he invited him to come and stay at his house as long as he had occasion to remain in the village.

"Thank you very much," the young man replied; "but let me first inquire, if you please, whether the beam of your house is strong."

The old farmer left him in despair, and entered his house laughing.

"There is a man in yonder field," he said, after returning their greetings. "He has come the greater part of the way with me, and I wanted him to put up here as long as he had to stay in this village. But the fellow is such a fool that I cannot make anything out of him. He wants to know if the beam of this house is all right. The man must be mad!" and saying this he burst into a fit of laughter.

"Father," said the farmer's daughter, who was a very sharp and wise girl, "this man, whosoever he is, is no fool, as you deem him. He only wishes to know if you can afford to entertain him."

"Oh! of course," replied the farmer. "I see. Well perhaps you can help me to solve some of his other mysteries. While we were walking together he asked whether he should carry me or I should carry him, as he thought that would be a pleasanter mode of proceeding."

"Most assuredly," said the girl. "He meant that one of you should tell a story to beguile the time."

"Oh, yes. Well, we were passing through a cornfield, when he asked me whether it was eaten or not."

"And didn't you know the meaning of this, father? He simply wished to know if the man was in debt or not; because if the owner of the field was in debt, then the produce of the field was as good as eaten to him; that is, it would have to go to his creditors."

"Yes, yes, yes; of course! Then, on entering a certain village, he bade me take his clasp knife and get two horses with it, and bring back the knife again to him."

"Are not two stout sticks as good as two horses for helping one along on the road? He only asked you to cut a couple of sticks and be careful not to lose his knife."

"I see," said time farmer. "While we were walking over the city we did not see anybody that we knew, and not a soul gave us a scrap of anything to eat, till we were passing the cemetery; but there some people called to us and put into our hands some chupatties and kulchas; so my companion called the city a cemetery, and the cemetery a city."

"This also is to be understood, father, if one thinks of the city as the place where everything is to be obtained, and of inhospitable people as worse than the dead. The city, though crowded with people, was as if dead, as far as you were concerned; while, in the cemetery, which is crowded with time dead, you were saluted by kind friends and provided with bread."

"True, true!" said the astonished farmer. "Then, just now, when we were crossing the stream, he waded through it without taking off his shoes and pajamas."

"I admire his wisdom," replied time girl. "I have often thought how stupid people were to venture into that swiftly flowing stream and over those sharp stones with bare feet. The slightest stumble and they would fall, and be wetted from head to foot. This friend of yours is a most wise man. I should like to see him and speak to him."

"Very well," said time farmer; "I will go and find him, and bring him in."

"Tell him, father, that our beams are strong enough, and then he will come in. I'll send on ahead a present to the man, to show him that we can afford to have him for our guest."

Accordingly she called a servant and sent him to the young man with a present of a basin of ghee, twelve chupatties, and a jar of milk, and the following message: "O friend, time moon is full; twelve months make a year, and the sea is overflowing with water."

Half-way the bearer of this present and message met his little son, who, seeing what was in the basket, begged his father to give him some of the food. His father foolishly complied. Presently he saw the young man, and gave him the rest of the present and the message.

"Give your mistress my salaam," he replied, "and tell her that the moon is new, and that I can only find eleven mouths in the year, and the sea is by no means full."

Not understanding the meaning of these words, the servant repeated them word for word, as he had heard them, to his mistress; and thus his theft was discovered, and he was severely punished. After a little while the young man appeared with the old farmer. Great attention was shown to him, and he was treated in every way as it he were the son of a great man, although his humble host knew nothing of his origin. At length be told them everything—

about the laughing of the fish, his father's threatened execution, and his own banishment—and asked their advice as to what he should do.

"The laughing of the fish," said the girl "which seems to have been the cause of all this trouble, indicates that there is a man in the palace who is plotting against the king's life."

"Joy, joy!" exclaimed the vizier's son. "There is yet time for me to return and save my father from an ignominious and unjust death, and the king from danger."

The following day he hastened back to his own country, taking with him the farmer's daughter. Immediately on arrival he ran to the palace and informed his father of what he had heard. The poor vizier, now almost dead from the expectation of death, was at once carried to the king, to whom he repeated the news that his son had just brought.

"Never!" said the king.

"But it must be so, Your Majesty," replied the vizier; "and in order to prove the truth of what I have heard, I pray you call together all the maids in your palace, and order them to jump over a pit, which must be dug. We'll soon find out whether there is any man there."

The king had time pit dug, and commanded all the maids belonging to the palace to try to jump it. All of them tried, but only one succeeded. That one was found to be a man!

Thus was the queen satisfied, and the faithful old vizier saved.

Afterward, as soon as could be, the vizier's son married the old farmer's daughter; and a most happy marriage it was.

THE FARMER AND THE MONEY LENDER

By Joseph Jacobs

There was ounce a farmer who suffered much at time hands of the money lender. Good harvests, or bad, the farmer was always poor, the money lender rich. At the last, when he hadn't a farthing left, the farmer went to the money lender's house, and said, "You can't squeeze water from a stone, and as you have nothing to get by me now, you might tell me the secret of becoming rich."

"My friend," returned the money lender, piously, "riches come from Ram—ask *him*."

"Thank you, I will!" replied the simple farmer; so he prepared three griddle cakes to last him on the journey, and set out to find Ram.

First he met a Brahman, and to him he gave a cake asking him to point out the road to Ram; but the Brahman only took the cake and went on his way without a word. Next the farmer met a Jogi or devotee, and to him he gave a cake, without receiving any help in return. At last, he came upon a poor man sitting under a tree, and finding out he was hungry, the kindly farmer gave him his last cake, and sitting clown to rest beside him, entered into conversation.

"And where are you going?" asked the poor man, at length.

"Oh, I have a long journey before me, for I am going to find Ram!" replied the farmer. "I don't suppose you could tell me which way to go?"

"Perhaps I can," said the poor man, smiling, "for I am Ram! What do you want of me?"

Then the farmer told the whole story, and Rain, taking pity on him, gave him a conch shell, and showed him how to blow it in a particular way, saying, "Remember! whatever you wish for, you have only to blow the conch that way, and your wish will be fulfilled. Only have a care of that money lender, for even magic is not proof against their wiles!"

The farmer went back to his village rejoicing. In fact the money lender noticed his high spirits at once, and said to himself, "Some good fortune must have befallen the stupid fellow, to make him hold his head so jauntily." Therefore he went over to the simple farmer's house, and congratulated him on his good fortune, in such cunning words, pretending to have heard all about it, that before long the farmer found himself telling the whole story – all except the secret of blowing the conch, for, with all his simplicity, the farmer was not quite such a fool as to tell that.

Nevertheless, the money lender determined to have the conch by hook or by crook, and as he was villain enough not to stick at trifles, he waited for a favorable opportunity and stole the conch.

But, after nearly bursting himself with blowing the conch in every conceivable way, he was obliged to give up the secret as a bad job. However, being determined to succeed he went back to the farmer and said, coolly, "Look here; I've got your conch, but I can't use it; you haven't got it, So it's clear you can't use it either. Business is at a standstill unless we make a bargain. Now, I promise to give you back your conch, and never to interfere with your using it, on one condition, which is this – Whatever you get from it, I am to get double."

"Never!" cried the farmer; "that would be the old business all over again!"

"Not at all!" replied time wily money lender; "you will have your share! Now, don't be a dog in the manger, for if you get all you want, what can it matter to you if I am rich or poor?"

At last, though it went sorely against the grain to be of any benefit to a money lender, the farmer was forced to yield, and from that time, no matter what he gained by the power of the couch, time money lender gained double. And the knowledge that this was so preyed upon the farmer's mind day and night, so that he had no satisfaction out of anything.

At last, there came a very dry season – so dry that the farmer's crops withered for want of rain. Then he blew his conch, and wished for a well to water them, and lo! there was the well, but the money lender had two! – two beautiful new wells! This was too much for any farmer to stand: and our friend brooded over it, and brooded over it, till at last a bright idea came into his head. He seized the conch, blew it loudly, and cried out, "Oh Ram! I wish to be blind of one eye!" And so he was in a twinkling, but the money lender of course was blind of both, and in trying to steer his way between the two new wells, he fell into one and was drowned.

Now this true story shows that a farmer once got time better of a money lender-but only by losing one of his eyes.

PRIDE GOETH BEFORE A FALL

By Joseph Jacobs

In a certain village there lived ten cloth merchants who always went about together. Once upon a time they had traveled far afield, and were returning home with a great deal of money which they had obtained by selling their wares. Now there happened to be a dense forest near their village, and this they reached early one morning. In it there lived three notorious robbers, of whose existence the traders had never heard, and while they were still in the middle of it the robbers stood before them, with swords and cudgels in their hands, and ordered them to lay down all they had. The traders had no weapons with them, and so, though they were many more in number, they had to submit themselves to the robbers, who took away everything from them, even the very clothes they wore, and gave to each only a small loin cloth a span in breadth and a cubit in length.

The idea that they had conquered ten men and plundered all their property now took possession of the robbers' minds. They seated themselves like three monarchs before the men they had plundered, and ordered them to dance to them before returning home. The merchants now mourned their fate.

They had lost all they had, except their loin cloth, and still the robbers were not satisfied, but ordered them to dance.

There was, among the ten merchants, one who was very clever. He pondered over the calamity that had come upon him and his friends, the dance they would have to perform, and the magnificent manner in which the three robbers had seated themselves on the grass. At the same time he observed that these last had placed their weapons on the ground, in the assurance of having thoroughly cowed the traders, who were now commencing to dance. So he took the lead in the dance, and, as a song is always sung by the leader on such occasions, to which the rest keep time with hands and feet, he thus began to sing:

We are enty men,
They are erith men:

If each erith man
Surround eno men,
Eno man remains.
Tâ, tai, tôm, tadingana.

The robbers were all uneducated, and thought that the leader was merely singing a song as usual. So it was in one sense: for the leader commenced from a distance, and had sung the song over twice before he and his companions commenced to approach the robbers. They had understood his meaning, because they had been trained in trade.

When two traders discuss the price of an article in the presence of a purchaser, they use a riddling sort of language.

"What is the price of this cloth?" one trader will ask another.

"Enty rupees," another will reply, meaning "ten rupees."

Thus, there is no possibility of the purchaser knowing what is meant unless he be acquainted with trade language. By the rules of this secret language erith means "three," enty means "ten," and eno means "one." So the leader by his song meant to hint to his fellow-traders that they were ten men, the robbers only three, that if three pounced upon each of the robbers, nine of them could hold them down, while the remaining one bound the robbers' hands and feet.

The three thieves, glorying in their victory, and little understanding the meaning of the song and the intentions of the dancers, were proudly seated chewing betel and tobacco. Meanwhile the song was sung a third time. Ta, tai, tom had left the lips of the singer; and, before tadingana was out of them, the traders separated into parties of three, and each party pounced upon a thief. The remaining one—the leader himself—tore up into long narrow strips a large piece of cloth, six cubits long, and tied the hands and feet of the robbers. These were entirely humbled now, and rolled on the ground like three bags of rice!

The ten traders now took back all their property, and armed themselves with the swords and cudgels of their enemies; and when they reached their village, they often amused their friends and relatives by relating their adventure.

HOW THE WICKED SONS WERE DUPED

By Joseph Jacobs

A very wealthy old man, imagining that he was on the point of death, sent for his sons and divided his property among them. However, he did not die for several years afterward, and miserable years many of them were. Besides the weariness of old age, the old fellow had to bear with much abuse and cruelty from his sons. Wretched, selfish ingrates! Previously they vied with one another in trying to please their father, hoping thus to receive more money, but now they had received their patrimony, they cared not how soon he left them—nay, the sooner the better, because he was only a needless trouble and expense. And they let the poor old man know what they felt.

One day he met a friend and related to him all his troubles. The friend sympathized very much with him, and promised to think over the matter, and call in a little while and tell him what to do. He did so; in a few days he visited the old man and put down four bags full of stones and gravel before him.

"Look here, friend," said he. "Your sons will get to know of my coming here to-day, and will inquire about it. You must pretend that I came to discharge a long-standing debt with you, and that you are several thousands of rupees richer than you thought you were. Keep these bags in your own hands, and on no account let your sons get to them as long as you are alive. You will soon find them change their conduct toward you. Salaam, I will come again soon to see how you are getting on."

When the young men got to hear of this further increase of wealth they began to be more attentive and pleasing to their father than ever before. And thus they continued to the day of the old man's demise, when the bags were greedily opened, and found to contain only stones and gravel!

THE TIGER, THE BRAHMAN, AND THE JACKAL

By Flora Annie Steel

Once upon a time a Tiger was caught in a trap. He tried in vain to get out through the bars, and rolled and bit with rage and grief when he failed.

By chance a poor Brahman came by.

"Let me out of this cage, oh pious one!" cried the Tiger.

"Nay, my friend," replied the Brahman mildly, you would probably eat me if I did."

"Not at all!" swore the Tiger with many oaths; "on the contrary, I should be forever grateful, and serve you as a slave!"

Now when the Tiger sobbed and sighed and wept and swore, the pious Brahman's heart softened, and at last he consented to open the door of the cage. Out popped the Tiger, and, seizing the poor man, cried, "What a fool you are! What is to prevent my eating you now, for after being cooped up so long I am terribly hungry!"

In vain the Brahman Pleaded for his life; the most he could gain was a promise to abide by the decision of the first three things he chose to question as to the justice of the Tiger's action.

So the Brahman first asked a Pipal Tree what it thought of the matter, but the Pipal Tree replied coldly, "What have you to complain about? Don't I give shade and shelter to everyone who passes by, and don't they in return tear down my branches to feed their cattle? Don't whimper—be a man!"

Then the Brahman sad at heart, went farther afield till he saw a Buffalo turning a well wheel; but he fared no better from it, for it answered, "You are a fool to expect gratitude! Look at me! While I gave milk they fed me on cottonseed and oil cake, but now I am dry they yoke me here, and give me refuse as fodder!"

The Brahman, still more sad, asked the Road to give him its opinion.

"My dear sir," said the Road, "how foolish you are to expect anything else! Here am I, useful to everybody, yet all, rich and poor, great and small, trample on me as they go past, giving me nothing but the ashes of their pipes and the husks of their grain!"

On this the Brahman turned back sorrowfully, and on the way he met a Jackal, who called out, "Why, what's the matter, Mr. Brahman? You look as miserable as a fish out of water!"

The Brahman told him all that had occurred.

"How very confusing!" said the Jackal, when the recital was ended; "would you mind telling me over again, for everything has got so mixed up?"

The Brahman told it all over again, but the Jackal shook his head in a distracted sort of way, and still could not understand.

"It's very odd," said he, sadly, "but it all seems to go in at one ear and out at the other! I will go to the place where it all happened, and then perhaps I shall be able to give a judgment."

So they returned to the cage, by which the Tiger was waiting for the Brahman, and sharpening his teeth and claws.

"You've been away a long time!" growled the savage beast, "but now let us begin our dinner."

"Our dinner!" thought the wretched Brahman, as his knees knocked together with fright; "what a remarkably delicate way of putting it!"

"Give mime five minutes, my lord!" he pleaded, "in order that I may explain matters to the Jackal here, who is somewhat slow in his wits."

The Tiger consented, and the Brahman began the whole story over again, not missing a single detail, and spinning as long a yarn as possible.

"Oh, my poor brain! oh, my poor brain!" cried the Jackal, wringing its paws. "Let me see! how did it all begin? You were in the cage, and the Tiger came walking by—"

"Pooh!" interrupted the Tiger, "what a fool you are! *I* was in the cage."

"Of course!" cried the Jackal, pretending to tremble with fright; "yes I was in the cage—no I wasn't—dear! dear, where are my wits? Let me see—the Tiger was in the Brahman, and the cage came walking by—no, that's not it, either! Well, don't mind me, but begin your dinner, for I shall never understand!"

"Yes, you shall!" returned the Tiger, in a rage at the Jackal's stupidity; "I'll make you understand! Look here—I am the Tiger—"

"Yes, my lord!"

"And that is the Brahman—"

"Yes, my lord!"

"And that is the cage—"

"Yes, my lord!"

"And I was in the cage—do you understand?"

"Yes—no— Please, my lord—"

"Well?" cried the Tiger impatiently.

"Please, my lord!—how did you get in?"

"How?—why, in the usual way, of course!"

"Oh, dear me!—My head is beginning to whirl again! Please don't get angry, my lord, but what is the usual way?"

At this the Tiger lost patience, and, jumping into the cage, cried, "This way! Now do you understand how it was?"

"Perfectly!" grinned the Jackal, as he dexterously shut the door. "And if you will permit me to say so, I think matters will remain as they were!"

THE LAMBIKIN

By Flora Annie Steel

Once upon a time there was a wee wee Lambikin, who frolicked about on his little tottery legs, and enjoyed himself amazingly.

Now one day he set off to visit his Granny, and was jumping with joy to think of all the good things he should get from her, when who should he meet but a Jackal, who looked at the tender young morsel and said: "Lambikin! Lambikin! I'll EAT YOU!"

But Lambikin only gave a little frisk and said:

"To Granny's house I go,
Where I shall fatter grow,
Then you can eat me so."

The Jackal thought this reasonable, and let Lambikin pass.

By and by he met a Vulture, and the Vulture, looking hungrily at the tender morsel before him, said: "Lambikin! Lambikin! I'll EAT YOU!"

But Lambikin only gave a little frisk, and said:

"To Granny's house I go,
Where I shall fatter grow,
Then you can eat me so."

The Vulture thought this reasonable, and let Lambikin pass.

And by and by he met a Tiger, and then a Wolf, and a Dog, arid an Eagle, and all these, when they saw the tender little morsel, said: "Lambikin! Lambikin! I'll EAT YOU!"

But to all of them Lambikin replied, with a little frisk:

"To Granny's house I go,
Where I shall fatter grow,
Then you can eat me so.

At last he reached his Granny's house, and said, all in a great hurry, "Granny, dear, I've promised to get very fat; so, as people ought to keep their promises, please put me into the corn bin at once."

So his Granny said he was a good boy, and put him into the corn bin, and there the greedy little Lambikin stayed for seven days, and ate, and ate, and ate, until he could scarcely waddle, and his Granny said he was fat enough for anything, and must go home. But cunning little Lambikin said that would never do, for some animal would be sure to eat him on the way back, he was so plump and tender.

"I'll tell you what you must do," said Master Lambikin, "you must make a little drumikin out of the skin of my little brother who died, and then I can sit inside and trundle along nicely, for I'm as tight as a drum myself."

So his Granny made a nice little drumikin out of his brother's skin, with the wool inside, and Lambikin curled himself up snug and warm in the middle, and trundled away gayly. Soon lie met with the Eagle, who called out:

> "Drumikin! Drumikin!
> Have you seen Lambikin?"

And Mr. Lambikin, curled up in his soft warm nest, replied:

> "Fallen into the fire, and so will you
> On little Drumikin. Tum-pa, tum-too!"

"How very annoying!" sighed the Eagle, thinking regretfully of the tender morsel he had let slip.

Meanwhile Lambikin trundled along, laughing to himself, and singing:

> "Tum-pa, tum-too;
> Tum-pa, tum-too!"

Every animal and bird he met asked him the same question:

> "Drumikin! Drumikin!
> Have you seen Lambikin?"

And to each of them the little slyboots replied:

> "Fallen into the fire, and so will you
> On little Drumikin. Tum-pa, tum-too;
> Tum-pa, tum-too; Tum-pa, tum-too!"

Then they all sighed to think of the tender little morsel they had let slip.

At last the Jackal came limping along, for all his sorry looks as sharp as a needle, and he too called out—

"Drumikin! Drumikin!
Have you seen Lambikin?"

And Lambikin, curled up in his snug little nest, replied gayly:

"Fallen into the fire, and so will you
On little Drumikin! Tum-pa—"

But he never got any further, for the Jackal recognized his voice at once, arid cried: "Hullo! you've turned yourself inside out, have you? Just you come out of that!"

Whereupon he tore open Drumikin and gobbled up Lambikin.

THE RAT'S WEDDING

By Flora Annie Steel

Once upon a time a fat, sleek Rat was caught in a shower of rain, and being far from shelter he set to work and soon dug a nice hole in the ground, in which he sat as dry as a bone while the raindrops splashed outside, making little puddles on the road.

Now in the course of digging, he came upon a fine bit of root, quite dry and fit for fuel, which he set aside carefully—for the Rat is an economical creature—in order to take it home with him. So when the shower was over, he set off with the dry root in his mouth. As he went along, daintily picking his way through the puddles, he Saw a Poor Man vainly trying to light a fire, while a little circle of children stood by, and cried piteously.

"Goodness gracious!" exclaimed the Rat, who was both soft-hearted and curious, "What a dreadful noise to make! What is the matter?"

"The children are hungry," answered the Man; "they are crying for their breakfast, but the sticks are damp, the fire won't burn, and so I can't bake the cakes."

"If that is all your trouble, perhaps I can help you," said the good-natured Rat, "you are welcome to this dry root and I'll warrant it will soon make a fine blaze."

The Poor Man, with a thousand thanks, took the dry root, and in his turn presented the Rat with a morsel of dough, as a reward for his kindness and generosity.

"What a remarkably lucky fellow I am!" thought the Rat, as he trotted off gayly with his prize, "and clever, too! Fancy making a bargain like that—food enough to last me five days in return for a rotten old stick! Wah! Wah! Wah! What it is to have brains!"

Going along, hugging his good fortune in this way, he came presently to a Potter's yard, where the Potter, leaving his wheel to spin round by itself, was trying to pacify his three little children, who were screaming arid crying as if they would burst.

"My gracious!" cried the Rat, stopping his ears, "what a noise! do tell me what it is all about."

"I suppose they are hungry," replied the Potter ruefully; "their mother has gone to get flour in the bazaar, for there is none in the house. In the meantime I can neither work nor rest because of them."

"Is that all?" answered the officious Rat; then I can help you. Take this dough, cook it quickly, and stop their mouths with food."

The Potter overwhelmed the Rat with thanks for his obliging kindness, and choosing out a nice well-burned pipkin, insisted on his accepting it as a remembrance.

The Rat was delighted at the exchange, and though the pipkin was just a trifle awkward for him to manage, he succeeded, after infinite trouble, in balancing it on his head and went away gingerly, tink-a-tink, tink-a-tink, down the road, with his tail over his arm for fear he should trip on it. And all the time he kept saying to himself, "What a lucky fellow I am! and clever, too! Such a hand at a bargain!"

By and by he came to where some cowherds were herding their cattle. One of them was milking a buffalo, and having no pail, he used his shoes instead.

"Oh fie! oh fie!" cried the cleanly Rat, quite shocked at the sight. "What a nasty, dirty trick! Why don't you use a pail?"

"For the best of all reasons—we haven't got one!" growled the Cowherd, who did not see why the Rat should put his finger in the pie.

"If that is all," replied the dainty Rat, "oblige me by using this pipkin, for I cannot bear dirt!"

The Cowherd, nothing loath, took the pipkin and milked away until it was brimming over; then turning to the Rat, who stood looking on, said, "Here, little fellow, You may have a drink, in payment."

But if the Rat was good-natured he was also shrewd. "No, no, my friend," said he, "that will not do! As if I could drink the worth of any pipkin at a draft! My dear sir, I couldn't hold it! Besides, I never make a bad bargain, so I expect you, at least to give me the buffalo that gave the milk."

"Nonsense!" cried the Cowherd; "a buffalo for a pipkin! Whoever heard of such a price? And what on earth could you do with a buffalo when you got it? Why, the pipkin was about as much as you could manage."

At this the Rat drew himself up with dignity, for he did not like allusions to his size. "That is my affair, not yours," he retorted; "your business is to hand over the buffalo."

So just for the fun of the thing, and to amuse themselves at the Rat's expense, the cowherds loosened the buffalo's halter and began to tie it to the little animal's tail.

"No! no!" he called, in a great hurry. "If the beast pulled, the skin of my tail would come off, and then where should I be? Tie it around my neck, if you please."

So with much laughter the cowherds tied the halter round the Rat's neck, and he, after a polite leave-taking, set off gayly toward home with his prize; that is to say, he set off with the rope, for no sooner did he come to the end of the tether than be was brought up with a round turn; the buffalo, nose down, grazing away, would not budge until it had finished its tuft of grass, and then seeing another in a different direction marched off toward it, while the Rat, to avoid being dragged, had to trot humbly behind, willy-nilly. He was too proud to confess the truth, of course, and, nodding his head knowingly to the cowherds, said: "Ta-ta, good people! I am going home this way. It may be a little longer, but it's much shadier."

And when the cowherds roared with laughter he took no notice, but trotted on, looking as dignified as possible. "After all," he reasoned to himself, "when one keeps a buffalo one has to look after its grazing. A beast must get a good bellyful of grass if it is to give any milk, and I have plenty of time at my disposal." So all day long he trotted about after the buffalo, making believe; but by evening he was dead tired, and felt truly thankful when the great big beast, having eaten enough, lay down under a tree to chew the cud.

Just then a bridal party came by. The Bridegroom and his friends had evidently gone on to the next village, leaving the Bride's palanquin to follow; so the palanquin bearers, being lazy fellows and seeing a nice shady tree, put down their burden, and began to cook some food.

"What detestable meanness!" grumbled one; "a grand wedding, and nothing but plain rice to eat! Not a scrap of meat in it, neither sweet nor salt! It would serve the skinflints right if we upset the Bride into a ditch!"

"Dear me!" cried the Rat at once, seeing a way out of his difficulty, "that is a shame! I sympathize with your feelings so entirely that if you will allow me, I'll give you my buffalo. You can kill it, and cook it."

"Your buffalo!" returned the discontented bearers. "What rubbish! Whoever heard of a rat owning a buffalo?"

"Not often, I admit," replied the Rat with conscious pride; "but look for yourselves. Can you not see that I am leading the beast by a string?"

"Oh, never mind the string!" cried a great big hungry bearer; master or no master, I mean to have meat for my dinner!" Whereupon they killed the buffalo, and cooking its flesh, ate their dinner with a relish; then, offering the remains to the Rat, said carelessly, "Here, little Rat-skin, that is for you!"

"Now look here!" cried the Rat hotly; "I'll have none of your pottage, or your sauce, either. You don't suppose I am going to give my best buffalo, that gave quarts and quarts of milk—the buffalo I have been feeding all day—for a wee bit of rice? No! I got a loaf for a bit of stick; I got a pipkin for a little loaf; I got a buffalo for a pipkin; and now I'll have the Bride for my buffalo—the Bride, and nothing else!"

By this time the servants, having satisfied their hunger, began to reflect on what they had done, and becoming alarmed at the consequences, arrived at the conclusion it would be wisest to make their escape while they could. So, leaving the Bride in her palanquin, they took to their heels in various directions.

The Rat, being as it were left in possession, advanced to the palanquin, and drawing aside the curtain, with the sweetest of voices and best of bows begged the Bride to descend. She hardly knew whether to laugh or to cry, but as any company, even a Rat's, was better than being quite alone in the wilderness, she did what she was bidden, and followed the lead of her guide, who set off as fast as be could for his hole.

As he trotted along beside the lovely young Bride, who, by her rich dress and glittering jewels, seemed to be some king's daughter, he kept saying to himself, "How clever I am! What bargains I do make, to be sure!"

When they arrived at his hole, the Rat stepped forward with the greatest politeness, and said, "Welcome, madam, to my humble abode! Pray step in, or if you will allow me, and as the passage is somewhat dark, I will show you the way."

Whereupon he ran in first, but after a time, finding the Bride did not follow, he put his nose out again, saying testily, "Well, madam, why don't you follow? Don't you know it's rude to keep your husband waiting?"

"My good sir," laughed the handsome young Bride, "I can't squeeze into that little hole!"

The Rat coughed; then after a moment's thought he replied, "There is some truth in your remark—you *are* overgrown, and I suppose I shall have to build you a thatch somewhere, For to-night you can rest under that wild plum tree."

"But I am so hungry!" said the Bride ruefully.

"Dear, dear! everybody seems hungry to-day!" returned the Rat pettishly; "however, that's easily settled—I'll fetch you Some supper in a trice."

So he ran into his hole, returning immediately with an ear of millet and a dry pea. "There!" said he, triumphantly, "isn't that a fine meal?"

"I can't eat that!" whimpered the Bride; "it isn't a mouthful; and I want rice pottage, and cakes, and sweet eggs, and sugar drops. I shall die if I don't get them!"

"Oh, dear me!" cried the Rat in a rage, "what a nuisance a bride is, to be sure! Why don't you eat the wild plums?"

"I can't live on wild plums!" retorted the weeping Bride; "nobody could; besides, they are only half ripe, and I can't reach them."

"Rubbish!" cried the Rat; "ripe or unripe, they must do you for to-night, and to-morrow you can gather a basketful, sell them in the city, and buy sugar drops and sweet eggs to your heart's content!"

So the next morning the Rat climbed up into the plum tree, and nibbled away at the stalks till the fruit fell down into the Bride's veil. Then, unripe as they were, she carried them into the city, calling out through the streets—

"Green plums I sell! green plums I sell!
Princess am I, Rat's bride as well!"

As she passed by the palace, her mother, the Queen, heard her voice, and running out, recognized her daughter. Great were the rejoicings, for everyone thought the poor Bride had been eaten by wild beasts.

In the midst of the feasting and merriment, the Rat, who had followed the Princess at a distance, and had become alarmed at her long absence, arrived at the door, against which he beat with a big knobby stick, calling out fiercely, "Give me my wife! Give me my wife! She is mine by a fair bargain. I gave a stick and I got a loaf; I gave a loaf and I got a pipkin; I gave a pipkin and I got a buffalo; I gave a buffalo and I got a bride. Give me my wife! Give me my wife!"

"La! son-in-law! What a fuss you do make," said the wily old Queen through the door, "and all about nothing! Who wants to run away with your wife? On the contrary, we are proud to see you, and I only keep you waiting at the door till we can spread the carpets, and receive you in style."

Hearing this, the Rat was mollified, and waited patiently outside while the cunning old Queen prepared for his reception, which she did by cutting a hole in the very middle of a stool, putting a red hot stone underneath, covering it over with a stew-pan lid, and then spreading a beautiful embroidered cloth over all. Then she went to the door, and receiving the Rat with the greatest respect, led him to the stool, praying him to be seated.

"Dear! dear! how clever I am! What bargains I do make, to be sure!" said he to himself as he climbed on to the stool. "Here I am, son-in-law to a real live Queen! What will the neighbors say?"

At first he sat down on the edge of the stool, but even there it was warm, and after a while he began to fidget, saying, "Dear me, mother-in-law, how hot your house is! Everything I touch seems burning!"

"You are out of the wind there, my son," replied the cunning old Queen; "sit more in the middle of the stool, and then you will feel the breeze and get cooler."

But he didn't! for the stewpan lid by this time had become so hot that the Rat fairly frizzled when he sat down on it; and it was not until he had left all his tail, half his hair, and a large piece of his skin behind him, that he managed to escape, howling with pain, and vowing that never, never, never again would he make a bargain!

THE JACKAL AND THE PARTRIDGE

By Flora Annie Steel

A jackal and a partridge swore eternal friendship; but the Jackal was very exacting and jealous. "You don't do half as much for me as I do for you," he used to say, "and yet you talk a great deal of your friendship. Now my idea of a friend is one who is able to make me laugh or cry, give me a good meal, or save my life if need be. You couldn't do that!"

"Let us see," answered the Partridge; "follow me at a little distance, and if I don't make you laugh soon you may eat me!"

So she flew on till she met two travelers trudging along, one behind the other. They were both foot-sore and weary, and the first carried his bundle on a stick over his shoulder, while the second had his shoes in his hand.

Lightly as a feather the Partridge settled on the first traveler's stick. He, none the wiser, trudged on, but the second traveler, seeing the bird sitting so tamely just in front of his nose, said to himself, "What a chance for a supper!" and immediately flung his shoes at it, they being ready to hand. Whereupon the Partridge flew away, and the shoes knocked off the first traveler's turban.

"What a plague do you mean?" cried he, angrily turning on his companion. "Why did you throw your shoes at my head?"

"Brother," replied the other mildly, "do not be vexed. I didn't throw them at you, but at a Partridge that was sitting on your stick."

"On my stick! Do you take me for a fool?" shouted the injured man, in a great rage. "Don't tell me such cock-and-bull stories. First you insult me, and then you lie like a coward; but I'll teach you manners!"

Then he fell upon his fellow traveler without more ado, and they fought until they could not see out of their eyes, till their noses were bleeding, their clothes in rags, and the Jackal had nearly died of laughing.

"Are you satisfied?" asked the Partridge of her friend.

"Well," answered the Jackal, "you have certainly made nine laugh, but I doubt if you could make me cry. It is easy enough to be a buffoon; it is more difficult to excite the highest emotions."

"Let us see," retorted the Partridge, somewhat piqued; "there is a huntsman with his dogs coming along the road. Just creep into that hollow tree and watch me; if you don't weep scalding tears, you must have no feeling in you!"

The Jackal did as he was bid, and watched the Partridge, who began fluttering about the bushes till the dogs caught sight of her, when she flew to the hollow tree where the Jackal was hidden. Of course the dogs smelt him at once, and set up such a yelping and scratching that the huntsman came up, and seeing what it was, dragged the Jackal out by the tail. Whereupon the dogs worried him to their heart's content, and finally left him for dead.

By and by he opened his eyes—for he was only foxing—and saw the Partridge sitting on a branch above him.

"Did you cry?" she asked anxiously. "Did I rouse your high emo—"

"Be quiet, will you!" snarled the Jackal; half dead with fear!"

So there the Jackal lay for some time, getting the better of his bruises, and meanwhile he became hungry.

"Now is the time for friendship!" said he to the Partridge. "Get me a good dinner, and I will acknowledge you a true friend."

"Very well!" replied the Partridge; "only watch me, and help yourself when the time comes."

Just then a troop of women came by, carrying their husbands dinners to the harvest field. The Partridge gave a little plaintive cry, and began fluttering along from bush to bush as if she were wounded.

"A wounded bird! a wounded bird!" cried the women; "we can easily catch it." Whereupon they set off in pursuit, but the cunning Partridge played a thousand tricks, till they became so excited over the chase that they put their bundles on the ground in order to pursue it more nimbly. The Jackal, meanwhile, seizing his opportunity, crept up, and made off with a good dinner.

"Are you satisfied now?" asked the Partridge.

"Well," returned the Jackal, "I confess you have given me a very good dinner; you have also made me laugh—and cry—ahem! But, after all, the great test of friendship is beyond you—you couldn't save my life!"

"Perhaps not," acquiesced the Partridge mournfully, "I am so small and weak. But it grows late—we should be getting home; and as it is a long way round by the ford, let us go across the river. My friend the Crocodile will carry us over."

Accordingly they set off for the river, and the Crocodile kindly consented to carry them across, so they sat on his broad back and he ferried them over.

But just as they were in the middle of the stream the Partridge remarked. "I believe the Crocodile intends to play us a trick. How awkward if he were to drop you into the water!"

"Awkward for you, too!" replied the Jackal, turning pale.

"Not at all! not at all! I have wings, you haven't."

On this the Jackal shivered and shook with fear, and when the Crocodile, in a gruesome growl, remarked that he was hungry and wanted a good meal, the wretched creature hadn't a word to say.

"Pooh!" cried the Partridge airily, "don't try tricks on us—I should fly away, and as for my friend, the Jackal, you couldn't hurt him. He is not such a fool as to take his life with him on these little excursions; he leaves it at home, locked up in the cupboard."

"Is that a fact?" asked the Crocodile, surprised. "Certainly!" retorted the Partridge. Try to eat him if you like, but you will only tire yourself to no purpose.

"Dear me! how very odd!" gasped time Crocodile; and he was so taken aback that he carried the Jackal safe to shore.

"Well, are you satisfied now?" asked the Partridge.

"My dear madam!" quoth the Jackal, "you have made me laugh, you have made me cry, you have given me a good dinner, and you have saved my life; but, upon my honor, I think you are too clever for a friend so good-by!"

And the Jackal never went near the Partridge again.

THE JACKAL AND THE CROCODILE

By Flora Annie Steel

Once upon a time Mr. Jackal was trotting along gayly, when lie caught sight of a wild plum tree laden with fruit on the other side of a broad, deep stream. I could not get across anyhow, so he just sat down on the bank and looked at the ripe, luscious fruit until his mouth watered with desire.

Now it so happened that, just then, Miss Crocodile came floating down stream with her nose in the air.

"Good morning, my dear!" said Mr. Jackal politely; "how beautiful you look to-day, and how charmingly you swim! Now, if I could only swim too, what a fine feast of plums we two friends might have over there together!" And Mr. Jackal laid his paw on his heart, and sighed.

Now Miss Crocodile had a very inflammable heart, and when Mr. Jackal looked at her so admiringly, and spoke so sentimentally, she simpered and blushed, saying, "Oh! Mr. Jackal! how can you talk so? I could never dream of going out to dinner with you, unless — unless — "

"Unless what?" asked the Jackal persuasively.

"Unless we were going to be married!" simpered Miss Crocodile.

"And why shouldn't we be married, my charmer?" returned the Jackal eagerly. "I would go and fetch the barber to begin the betrothal at once, but I am so faint with hunger just at present that I should never reach the village. Now, if the most adorable of her sex would only take pity on her slave, and carry me over the stream, I might refresh myself with those plums, and so gain strength to accomplish the ardent desire of my heart!"

Here the Jackal sighed so piteously, and cast such sheep's eyes at Miss Crocodile, that she was unable to withstand him. So she carried him across to the plum tree, and then sat on the water's edge to think over her wedding dress, while Mr. Jackal feasted on the plums and enjoyed himself.

"Now for the barber, my beauty!" cried the gay Jackal, when he had eaten as much as he could. Then the blushing Miss Crocodile carried him back again, and bade him be quick about his business, like a dear good creature, for really she felt so flustered at the very idea that she didn't know what might happen.

"Now don't distress yourself, my dear!" quoth the deceitful Mr. Jackal, springing to the bank, "because it's not impossible that I may not find the barber, and then, you know, you may have to wait some time, a considerable time in fact, before I return. So don't injure your health for my sake, if you please." With that he blew her a kiss, and trotted away with his tail up.

Of course he never came back, though trusting Miss Crocodile waited patiently for him; at last she understood what a gay, deceitful fellow he was, and determined to have her revenge on him one way or another.

So she hid herself in the water, under the roots of a tree, close to a ford where the Jackal always came to drink. By and by, sure enough, he came lilting along in a self-satisfied way, and went right into the water for a good long draft. Whereupon Miss Crocodile seized him by the right legs and held on. He guessed at once what had happened, and called out, "Oh! my heart's adored! I'm drowning! I'm drowning! If you love me, leave hold of that old root and get a good grip of my leg—it is just next door!"

Hearing this, Miss Crocodile thought she must have made a mistake, and, letting go the Jackal's leg in a hurry, seized an old root close by, and held on. Whereupon Mr. Jackal jumped nimbly to shore, and ran off with his tail up, calling out, "Have a little patience, my beauty! The barber will come some day!"

But this time Miss Crocodile knew better than to wait, and being now dreadfully angry, she crawled away to the Jackal's hole, and, slipping inside, lay quiet.

By and by Mr. Jackal came lilting along with his tail up. "Ho! ho! That is your game, is it?" said he to himself, when he saw the trail of the Crocodile in the sandy soil. So he stood outside, and said aloud, "Bless my stars! What has happened? I don't half like to go in, for whenever I come home my wife always calls out,

> 'Oh, dearest hubby hub!
> What have you brought for grub
> to me and the darling cub?'

and to-day she doesn't say anything!"

Hearing this, Miss Crocodile sang out from inside,

> "Oh, dearest hubby hub!
> What have you brought for grub
> To me and the darling cub?"

The Jackal winked a very big wink, and, stealing in softly, stood at the doorway. Meanwhile Miss Crocodile, hearing him coming, held her breath, and lay, shamming dead, like a big log.

"Bless my stars!" cried Mr. Jackal, taking out his pocket handkerchief, "how very sad! Here's poor Miss Crocodile stone dead, and all for love of me! Dear! dear! Yet it is very odd, and I don't think she can be quite dead, you know—for dead folks always wag their tails!"

On this, Miss Crocodile began to wag her tail very gently, and Mr. Jackal ran off, roaring with laughter, and saying. "Oho! oho! so dead folks always wag their tails!"

THE JACKAL AND THE IGUANA

By Flora Annie Steel

One moonlight night a miserable, half-starved Jackal, skulking through the village, found a worn-out pair of shoes in the gutter. They were too tough for him to eat, so, determined to make some use of them, he strung them to his ears like earrings, and, going down to the edge of the pond, gathered all the old bones he could find together and built a platform of them, plastering it over with mud.

On this he sat in a dignified attitude, and when any animal came to the pond to drink, he cried out in a loud voice, "Hi! stop! You must not taste a drop till you have done homage to me. So repeat these verses which I have composed in honor of the occasion:

'Silver is his dais, plastered o'er with gold;
In his ears are jewels, — some prince I must behold!'"

Now, as most of the animals were very thirsty, and in a great hurry to drink, they did not care to dispute the matter, but gabbled off the words without a second thought. Even the royal tiger, treating it as a jest, repeated the Jackal's rime, in consequence of which the latter became quite a cock-a-hoop, and really began to believe he was a personage of great importance.

By and by an Iguana, or big lizard, came waddling down to the water, looking for all the world like a baby alligator.

"Hi! you there!" sang out the Jackal; "you mustn't drink until you have said —

'Silver is his dais, plastered o'er with gold;
In his ears are jewels, — some prince I must behold!'"

"Pouf! pouf! pouf!" gasped the Iguana. "Mercy on us, how dry my throat is! Mightn't I have just a wee sip of water first? and then I could do justice to your admirable lines; at present I am as hoarse as a crow!"

"By all means," replied the Jackal, with a gratified smirk. "I flatter myself the verses are good, especially when well recited."

So the Iguana, nose down in the water, drank away until the Jackal began to think he would never leave off, and was quite taken aback when he finally came to an end of his draft, and began to move away.

"Hi! hi!" cried the Jackal, recovering his presence of mind, "stop a bit, and say —

'Silver is his dais, plastered o'er with gold;
In his ears are jewels, — some prince I must behold!'"

"Dear me!" replied the Iguana, politely, "I was very near forgetting! Let me see — I must try my voice first — do, re, me, fa, sol, la, si — that is right! Now, how does it run?"

"Silver is his dais, plastered o'er with gold;
In his ears are jewels, — some prince I must behold!"

repeated the Jackal, not observing that the Lizard Was carefully edging farther and farther away.

"Exactly so," returned the Iguana; "I think I could say that!" Whereupon he sang out at the top of his voice —

"Bones made up his dais, with mud it's plastered o'er,
Old shoes are his eardrops; a jackal, nothing more!"

And turning round, he bolted for his hole as hard as he could.

The Jackal could scarcely believe his ears, and sat dumb with astonishment. Then, rage lending him wings, he flew after the Lizard, who, despite his short legs and scanty breath, put his best foot foremost, and scuttled away at a great rate.

It was a near race, however, for just as he popped into his hole, the Jackal caught him by the tail, and held on. Then it was a case of "pull, butcher; pull, baker," until the Lizard made certain his tail must come off, and he felt as if his front teeth would come out. Still not an inch did either budge, one way or the other, and there they might have remained till the present day, had not the Iguana called out, in his sweetest tones, "Friend, I give in! Just leave hold of my tail, will you? then I can turn round and come out."

Whereupon the Jackal let go, and the tail disappeared up the hole in a twinkling; while all the reward the Jackal got for digging away until his nails were nearly worn out was hearing the Iguana sing softly —

"Bones made up his dais, with mud it's plastered o'er,
Old shoes are his eardrops; a jackal, nothing more

THE BEAR'S BAD BARGAIN

By Flora Annie Steel

Once upon a time a very old Woodman lived with his very old Wife in a tiny hut close to the orchard of a very rich man, so close that the boughs of a pear tree hung right over the cottage yard. Now it was agreed between the rich man and the Woodman that if any of the fruit fell into the yard, the old couple were to be allowed to eat it; so you may imagine with what hungry eyes they watched the pears ripening, and prayed for a storm of wind, or a flock of flying foxes, or anything which would cause the fruit to fall. But nothing came, and the old Wife, who was a grumbling, scolding old thing, declared they would infallibly become beggars. So she took to giving her husband nothing but dry bread to eat, and insisted on his working harder than ever, till the poor soul got quite thin; and all because the pears would not fall down!

At last the Woodman turned round and declared he would not work more unless his Wife gave him Khichri for his dinner; so with a very bad grace the old woman took some rice and pulse, some butter and spices, and began to cook a savory Khichri. What an appetizing smell it had, to be sure! The Woodman was for gobbling it up as soon as ever it was ready. "No, no," cried the greedy old Wife, not till you have brought me in another load of Wood; and mind it is a good one. You must work for your dinner."

So the old man set off to the forest and began to hack and to hew with such a will that he soon had quite a large bundle, and with every faggot he cut he seemed to smell the savory Khichri and think of the feast that was coming.

Just then a Bear came swinging by, with its great black nose tilted in the air, and its little keen eyes peering about; for bears, though good enough fellows on the whole, are just dreadfully inquisitive.

"Peace be with you, friend," said the Bear, "and what may you be going to do with that remarkably large bundle of wood?"

"It is for my Wife," returned the Woodman. "The fact is," he added confidentially, smacking his lips, "she has made such a Khichri for dinner! and if I bring in a good bundle of wood she is pretty sure to give me a plentiful portion. Oh, my dear fellow, you should just smell that Khichri."

At this the Bear's mouth began to water, for, like all bears, he was a dreadful glutton.

"Do you think your Wife would give mite some, too, if I brought her a bundle of wood?" he asked anxiously.

"Perhaps; if it is a very big load," answered the Woodman craftily.

"Would—would four hundredweight be enough?" asked the Bear.

"I'm afraid not," returned the Woodman, shaking his head; "you see Khichri is an expensive dish to make—there is rice in it, and plenty of butter, and pulse, and—"

"Would—would eight hundredweight do?"

"Say half a ton, and it's a bargain!" quoth the Woodman.

"Half a ton is a large quantity!" sighed the Bear.

"There is saffron in the Khichri," remarked the Woodman, casually.

The Bear licked his lips, and his little eyes twinkled with greed and delight.

"Well it's a bargain! Go home sharp and tell your Wife to keep the Khichri hot; I'll be with you in a trice."

Away went the Woodman in great glee to tell his Wife how the Bear had agreed to bring half a ton of wood in return for a share of the Khichri.

Now the wife could not help allowing that her husband had made a good bargain, but being by nature a grumbler, she was determined not to be pleased, so she began to scold the old man for not having settled exactly the share the Bear was to have. "For," said she, "he will gobble up the potful before we have finished our first helping."

On this the Woodman became quite pale. "In that case," he said, "we had better begin now, and have a fair start." So without more ado they squatted down on the floor, with the brass pot full of Khichri between them, and began to eat as fast as they could.

"Remember to leave some for the Bear, Wife," said the Woodman, speaking with his mouth crammed full.

"Certainly, certainly," she replied, helping herself to another handful.

"My dear," cried the old woman in her turn, with her mouth so full she could hardly speak, "remember the poor Bear!"

"Certainly, certainly, my love!" returned the old man, taking another mouthful.

So it went on, till there was not a single grain left in the pot.

"What's to be done now?" said the Woodman; "it is all your fault, Wife, for eating so much."

"My fault!" retorted his Wife scornfully, "why, you ate twice as much as I did!"

"No, I didn't!"

"Yes, you did! Men always eat more than women."

"No, they don't!"

"Yes, they do!"

"Well, it's no use quarreling about it now," said the Woodman, "the Khichri's gone, and the Bear will be furious."

"That wouldn't matter much if we could get the wood," said the greedy old woman. "I'll tell you what we must do—we must lock up everything there is to eat in the house, leave the Khichri pot by the fire, and hide in the garret. When the Bear comes he will think we have gone out and left his dinner for him. Then he will throw down his bundle and come in. Of course he will rampage a little when he finds the pot is empty, but he can't do much mischief, and I don't think he will take the trouble of carrying the wood away."

So they made haste to lock up all the food and hide themselves in the garret.

Meanwhile the Bear had been toiling and moiling away at his bundle of wood, which took him much longer to collect than he expected; however, at last he arrived quite exhausted at the woodcutter's cottage. Seeing the brass Khichri pot by the fire, he threw down his load and went in. And then— mercy! wasn't he angry when he found nothing in it—not even a grain of rice, nor a tiny wee bit of pulse, but only a smell that was so uncommonly nice that he actually cried with rage and disappointment. He flew into the most dreadful temper, but though he turned the house topsy-turvy, he could not find a morsel of food. Finally, he declared he would take the wood away again, but, as the crafty old woman had imagined, when he came to the task, he did not care, even for the sake of revenge, to carry so heavy a burden.

"I won't go away empty-handed," said he to himself, seizing the Khichri pot; "if I can't get the taste I'll have the smell!"

Now, as he left the cottage, he caught sight of the beautiful golden pears hanging over into the yard. His mouth began to water at once, for he was desperately hungry, and the pears were the best of the season. In a trice he was on the wall, up the tree, and gathering the biggest and ripest one he could find, was just putting it into his mouth when a thought struck him.

"If I take these pears home I shall be able to sell them for ever so much to the other bears, and then with the money I shall be able to buy some Khichri. Ha, ha! I shall have the best of the bargain after all!"

So saying, he began to gather the ripe pears as fast as he could and put them in the Khichri pot, but whenever he came to an unripe one he would shake his head and say, "No one would buy that, yet it is a pity to waste it." So he would pop it into his mouth and eat it, making wry faces if it was very sour.

Now all this time the Woodman's Wife had been watching the Bear through a crevice, and holding her breath for fear of discovery; but, at last, what with being asthmatic, and having a cold in her head, she could hold it no longer, and just as the Khichri pot was quite full of golden ripe pears, out she came with the most tremendous sneeze you ever heard—"A-h-che-u!"

The Bear, thinking some one had fired a gun at him, dropped the Khichri pot into the cottage yard, and fled into the forest as fast as his legs would carry him.

So the Woodrnan and his Wife got the Khichri, the wood, and the coveted pears, but the poor bear got nothing but a very bad stomachache from eating unripe fruit.

THE THIEF AND THE FOX

By Ramaswarni Raju

A man tied his horse to a tree and went into an inn. A Thief hid the horse in a wood, and stood near the tree as if he had not done it.

"Did you see my horse?" said the man.

"Yes," said the Thief, "I saw the tree eat up your horse."

"How could the tree eat up my horse?" said the man.

"Why it did so," said the Thief.

The two went to a Fox and told him of the case. The Fox said. "I am dull. All last night the sea was on fire; I had to throw a great deal of hay into it to quench the flames; so come to-morrow, and I shall hear your case.

"Oh, you lie," said the Thief. "How could the sea burn? How could hay quench the flames?"

"Oh, you lie," said the Fox, with a loud laugh; "how could a tree eat up a horse?"

The Thief saw his lie had no legs, and gave the man his horse.

THE FARMER AND THE FOX

By Ramaswami Raju

A farmer was returning from a fair which he had attended the previous day at a neighboring market town. He had a quantity of poultry which he had purchased. A Fox observed this, and approaching the Farmer, said, "Good morning, my friend."

"What cheer, old fellow?" said the Farmer.

"I am just coming from the wood, through which you mean to go with your poultry. A band of highwaymen has been tarrying there since daybreak."

"Then what shall I do?" said the Farmer.

"Why," said the Fox, "if I were you I should stay here a while, and after breakfast enter the wood, for by that time the robbers will have left the place."

"So be it," said the Farmer, and had a hearty breakfast, with Reynard for his guest.

They kept drinking for a long time. Reynard appeared to have lost his wits; he stood up and played the drunkard to perfection. The Farmer, who highly admired the pranks of his guest, roared with laughter, and gradually fell into a deep slumber. It was some time after noon when he awoke. To his dismay he found that the Fox was gone, and that the poultry had all disappeared!

"Alas!" said the Farmer, as he trudged on his way home with a heavy heart, "I thought the old rogue was quite drowned in liquor, but I now see it was all a pretense. One must indeed be very sober to play the drunkard to perfection."

THE FOOLS AND THE DRUM

By Ramaswami Raju

Two fools heard a Drum sounding, and said to themselves, There is some one inside it who makes the noise."

So, watching a moment, when the drummer was out, they pierced a hole in each side of it, and pushed their hands in. Each felt the hand of the other within the Drum, and exclaimed, "I have caught him!"

Then one said to the other, "Brother, the fellow seems to be a stubborn knave; come what will, we should not give in."

"Not an inch, brother," said the other.

So they kept pulling each other's hand, fancying it was the man in the Drum. The drummer came up, and finding them in such an awkward plight showed them with his fist who the man in the Drum really was. But as his fine Drum was ruined, he said, with a sigh, "Alas! Fools have fancies with a triple wing!"

THE LION AND THE GOAT

By Ramaswami Raju

A lion was eating up one after another the animals of a certain country. One day an old Goat said, "We must put a stop to this. I have a plan by which he may be sent away from this part of the country."

"Pray act up to it at once," said the other animals.

The old Goat laid himself down in a cave on the roadside, with his flowing beard and long curved horns. The Lion, on his way to the village, saw him, and stopped at the mouth of the cave.

"So you have come, after all," said the Goat.

"What do you mean?" said the Lion.

"Why, I have long been lying in this cave. I have eaten up one hundred elephants, a hundred tigers, a thousand wolves, and ninety-nine lions. One more lion has been wanting. I have waited long and patiently. Heaven has, after all, been kind to me," said the Goat, and shook his horns and his beard, and made a start as if he were about to spring upon the Lion.

The latter said to himself, "This animal looks like a Goat, but it does not talk like one. So it is very likely some wicked spirit in this shape. Prudence often serves us better than valor, so for the present I shall return to the wood," and he turned back.

The Goat rose up, and, advancing to the mouth of the cave, said, "Will you come back tomorrow?"

"Never again," said the Lion.

"Do you think I shall be able to see you, at least, in the wood to-morrow?"

"Neither in the wood nor in this neighborhood any more," said the Lion, and running to the forest, soon left it with his kindred.

The animals in the country, not hearing him roar any more, gathered round the Goat, and said, "The wisdom of one doth save a host."

THE GLOWWORM AND THE JACKDAW

By Ramaswami Raju

Jackdaw once ran up to a Glowworm and was about to seize him. "Wait a moment, good friend," said the Worm, "and you shall hear something to your advantage."

"Ah! what is it?" said the Daw.

"I am but one of the many glowworms that live in this forest. If you wish to have them all, follow me," said the Glowworm.

"Certainly!" said the Daw.

Then the Glowworm led him to a place in the wood where a fire had been kindled by some woodmen, and pointing to the sparks flying about, said, "There you find the glowworms warming themselves round a fire. When you have done with them I shall show you some more, at a distance from this place."

The Daw darted at the sparks and tried to swallow some of them, but his mouth being burned by the attempt, he ran away exclaiming, "Ah, the Glowworm is a dangerous little creature!"

THE CAMEL AND THE PIG

By Ramaswami Raju

A camel said, "Nothing like being tall! Look how tall I am!"

A Pig, who heard these words, said, "Nothing like being short! Look how short I am!"

The Camel said, "Well, if I fail to prove the truth of what I said. I shall give up my hump."

The Pig said, "If I fail to prove the truth of what I have said, I shall give up my snout."

"Agreed!" said the Camel.

"Just so!" said the Pig.

They came to a garden, inclosed by a low wall without any opening. The Camel stood on this side of the wall, and reaching the plants within by means of his long neck, made a breakfast on them. Then he turned, jeeringly to the Pig, who had been standing at the bottom of the wall, without even having a look at the good things in the garden, and said, "Now, would you be tall or short?"

Next they came to a garden, inclosed by a high wall, with a wicket gate at one end. The Pig entered by the gate, and, after having eaten his fill of the vegetables within, came out, laughing at the poor Camel, who had had to stay outside because he was too tall to enter the garden by the gate, and said, "Now, would you be tall or short?"

Then they thought the matter over and came to the conclusion that the Camel should keep his hump and the Pig his snout, observing, "Tall is good, where tall would do; of short, again, 'tis also true!"

THE DOG AND THE DOG DEALER

By Ramaswami Raju

A dog was standing by the cottage of a peasant. A man who dealt in dogs passed by the way. The Dog said, "Will you buy me?"

The man said, "Oh, you ugly little thing! I would not give a quarter of a penny for you!"

Then the Dog went to the palace of the king and stood by the portal. The sentinel caressed it, and said, "You are a charming little creature!"

Just then the Dog Dealer came by. The Dog said, "Will you buy me?"

"Oh," said the man, "you guard the palace of the king, who must have paid a high price for you. I cannot afford to pay the amount, else I would willingly take you."

"Ah!" said the Dog, "how place and position affect people!"

THE TIGER, THE FOX, AND THE HUNTERS

By Ramaswami Raju

A fox was once caught in a trap. A hungry Tiger saw him and said, "So you are here!"

"Only on your account," said the Fox in a whisper.

"How so?" said the Tiger.

"Why, you were complaining you could not get men to eat, so I got into this net to-day, that you may have the men when they come to take me," said the Fox, and gave a hint that if he would wait a while in a thicket close by he would point out the men to him.

"May I depend upon your word?" said the Tiger.

"Certainly," said the Fox.

The Hunters came, and seeing the Fox in the net, said, "So you are here!"

"Only on your account," said the Fox, in a whisper.

"How so?" said the men.

"Why, you were complaining you could not get at the Tiger that has been devouring your cattle; I got into this net to-day that you may have him. As I expected, he came to eat me up, and is in yonder thicket," said the Fox, and gave a hint that if they would take him out of the trap he would point out the Tiger.

"May we depend upon your word?" said the men.

"Certainly," said the Fox, while the men went with him in a circle to see that he did not escape.

Then the Fox said to the Tiger and the men, "Sir Tiger, here are the men; gentlemen, here is the Tiger."

The men left the Fox and turned to the Tiger. The former beat a hasty retreat to the wood, saying, "I have kept my promise to both; now you may settle it between yourselves."

The Tiger exclaimed, when it was too late, "Alas! what art for a double part!"

THE SEA, THE FOX, AND THE WOLF

By Ramaswami Raju

A fox that lived by the seashore once met a Wolf that had never seen the Sea. The Wolf said, "What is the Sea?"

"It is a great piece of water by my dwelling," said the Fox.

"Is it under your control?" said the Wolf.

"Certainly," said the Fox.

"Will you show me the Sea, then?" said the Wolf.

"With pleasure," said the Fox. So the Fox led the Wolf to the Sea and said to the waves, "Now go back"—they went back! "Now come up"—and they came up! Then the Fox said to the waves, "My friend, the Wolf, has come to see you, so you will come up and go back till I bid you stop; and the Wolf saw with wonder the waves coming up and going back.

He said to the Fox, "May I go into the Sea?"

"As far as you like. Don't be afraid, for at a word, the Sea would go or come as I bid, and as you have already seen."

The Wolf believed the Fox, and followed the waves rather far from the shore. A great wave soon upset him, and threw his carcass on the shore. The Fox made a hearty breakfast on it.

THE FOX IN THE WELL

By Ramaswami Raju

A fox fell into a well and was holding hard to some roots at the side of it, just above the water. A Wolf, who was passing by, saw him, and said, "Hello, Reynard, after all you have fallen into a well!"

"But not without a purpose, and not without the means of getting out of it," said the Fox.

"What do you mean?" said the Wolf.

"Why," said the Fox, "there is a drought all over the country now, and the water in this well is the only means of appeasing the thirst of the thousands that live in this neighborhood. They held a meeting, and requested me to keep the water from going down lower; so I am holding it up for the public good."

"What will be your reward?" said the Wolf.

"They will give me a pension, and save me the trouble of going about every day in quest of food, not to speak of innumerable other privileges that will be granted me. Further, I am not to stay here all day. I have asked a kinsman of mine, to whom I have communicated the secret of holding up the water, to relieve me from time to time. Of course he will also get a pension, and have other privileges. I expect him here shortly."

"Ah, Reynard, may I relieve you, then? May I hope to get a pension and other privileges? You know what a sad lot is mine, especially in winter."

"Certainly," said the Fox; "but you must get a long rope, that I may come up and let you in.

So the Wolf got a rope. Up came the Fox and down went the wolf, when the former observed, with a laugh, "My dear sir, you may remain there till doomsday, or till the owner of the well throws up your carcass," and left the place.

ASHIEPATTLE AND HIS GOODLY CREW

By P. C. Asbjörnsen

Once upon a time there was a king, and this king had heard about a ship which went just as fast by land as by water; and as he wished to have one like it, he promised his daughter and half the kingdom to anyone who could build one for him. And this was given out at every church all over the country. There were many who tried, as you can imagine; for they thought it would be a nice thing to have half the kingdom, and the princess wouldn't be a bad thing into the bargain. But they all fared badly.

Now there were three brothers, who lived far away on the borders of a forest; the eldest was called Peter, the second Paul, and the youngest Espen Ashiepattle, because he always sat in the hearth, raking and digging in the ashes.

It so happened that Ashiepattle was at church on the Sunday when the proclamation about the ship, which the king wanted, was read. When he came home amid told his family, Peter, the eldest, asked his mother to get some food ready for him, for now he was going away to try if he could build the ship and win the princess and half the kingdom. When the bag was ready lie set out. On the way he met an old man who was very crooked and decrepit.

"Where are you going?" said the man.

"I'm going into the forest to make a trough for my father. He doesn't like to eat at table in our company," said Peter.

"Trough it shall he!" said the man. "What have you got in that bag of yours?" he added.

"Stones," said Peter.

"Stones it shall be," said the man. Peter then went into the forest and began to cut and chop away at the trees and work away as hard as he could, but in spite of all his cutting and chopping he could only turn out troughs. Toward dinner time he wanted something to eat and opened his bag. But there was not a crumb of food in it. As he had nothing to live upon, and as he did not turn out anything but troughs, he became tired of the work, took his ax and bag on his shoulder, and went home to his mother.

Paul then wanted to set out to try his luck at building the ship and winning the princess and half the kingdom. He asked his mother for provisions, and when the bag was ready he threw it over his shoulder and went on his way to the forest. On the road he met the old man, who was very crooked and decrepit.

"Where are you going?" said the man.

"Oh, I am going into the forest to make a trough for our sucking pig," said Paul.

"Pig trough it shall be," said the man. "What have you got in that bag of yours?" added the man.

"Stones," said Paul.

"Stones it shall be," said the man.

Paul then began felling trees and working away as hard as he could, but no matter how he cut and how he worked he could only turn out pig troughs. He did not give in, however, but worked away till far into the afternoon before he thought of taking any food; then all at once he became hungry and opened his bag, but not a crumb could he find. Paul became so angry he turned the bag inside out and struck it against the stump of a tree; then lie took his ax, went out of the forest, and set off homeward.

As soon as Paul returned, Ashiepattle wanted to set out and asked his mother for a bag of food.

"Perhaps I can manage to build the ship and win the princess and half the kingdom," said he.

"Well, I never heard the like," said his mother. "Are you likely to win the princess, you, who never do anything but root and dig in the ashes? No, you shan't have any bag with food!"

Ashiepattle did not give in, however, but he prayed and begged till he got leave to go. He did not get any food, not he; but he stole a couple of oatmeal cakes and some flat beer and set out.

When he had walked a while he met the same old man, who was so crooked and tattered and decrepit.

"Where are you going?" said the man.

"Oh, I was going into the forest to try if it were possible to build a ship which can go as fast by land as by water," said Ashiepattle, "for the king has given out that anyone who can build such a ship shall have the princess and half the kingdom."

"What have you got in that bag of yours?" said the man.

"Not much worth talking about; there ought to be a little food in it," answered Ashiepattle.

"If you'll give me a little of it I'll help you, said the man.

"With all my heart," said Ashiepattle, "but there is nothing but some oatmeal cakes and a drop of flat beer."

It didn't matter what it was, the man said; if he only got some of it he would be sure to help Ashiepattle.

When they came up to an old oak in the wood the man said to the lad, "Now you must cut off a chip and then put it back again in exactly the same place, and when you have done that you can lie down and go to sleep."

Ashiepattle did as he was told and then lay down to sleep, and in his sleep he thought he heard somebody cutting and hammering and sawing and carpentering, but he could not wake up till the man called him; then the ship stood quite finished by the side of the oak.

"Now you must go on board and everyone you meet you must take with you," said the man. Espen Ashiepattle thanked him for the ship, said he would do so, and then sailed away.

When he had sailed some distance he came to a long, thin tramp, who was lying near some rocks, eating stones.

"What sort of a fellow are you, that you lie there eating stones?" asked Ashiepattle. The tramp said he was so fond of meat he could never get enough, therefore he was obliged to eat stones. And then he asked if he might go with him in the ship.

"If you want to go with us, you must make haste and get on board," said Ashiepattle.

Yes, that he would, but he must take with him some large stones for food.

When they had sailed some distance they met one who was lying on the side of a sunny hill, sucking at a bung.

"Who are you," said Ashiepattle, "and what is the good of lying there sucking that bung?"

"Oh, when one hasn't got the barrel, one must be satisfied with the bung," said the man. "I'm always so thirsty, I can never get enough beer and wine." And then he asked for leave to go with him in the ship.

"If you want to go with me you must make haste and get on board," said Ashiepattle.

Yes, that he would. And so he went on board and took the bung with him to allay his thirst.

When they had sailed a while again they met one who was lying with his ear to the ground, listening.

"Who are you, and what is the good of lying there on the ground listening?" said Ashiepattle.

"I'm listening to the grass, for I have such good ears that I can hear the grass growing," said the man. And then he asked leave to go with him in the ship. Ashiepattle could not say nay to that, so he said:

"If you want to go with me, you must make haste and get on board."

Yes, the man would. And he also went on board.

When they had sailed some distance they came to one who was standing taking aim with a gun.

"Who are you, and what is the good of standing there aiming like that?" asked Ashiepattle.

So the man said: "I have such good eyes that I can hit anything, right to the end of the world." And then he asked for leave to go with him in the ship.

"If you want to go with me, you must make haste and get on board," said Ashiepattle.

Yes, that he would. And he went on board.

When they had sailed some distance again they came to one who was hopping and limping about on one leg, and on the other he had seven ton weights.

"Who are you, said Ashiepattle, "and what is the good of hopping and limping about on one leg with seven ton weights on the other?"

"I am so light," said the man, "that if I walked on both my legs I should get to the end of the world in less than five minutes." And then he asked for leave to go with him in the ship.

"If you want to go with us, you must make haste and get on board," said Ashiepattle.

Yes, that he would. And so he joined Ashiepattle and his crew on the ship.

When they had sailed on some distance they met one who was standing holding his hand to his mouth.

"Who are you?" said Ashiepattle, "and what is the good of standing there, holding your mouth like that?"

"Oh, I have seven summers and fifteen winters in my body," said the man; "so I think I ought to keep my mouth shut, for if they get out all at the same time they would finish off the world altogether." And then he asked for leave to go with him in the ship.

"If you want to go with us you must make haste and get on board," said Ashiepattle.

Yes, that he would, and then he joined the others on the ship.

When they had sailed a long time they came to the king's palace.

Ashiepattle went straight in to the king and said the ship stood ready in the courtyard outside; and now he wanted the princess, as the king had promised.

The king did not like this very much, for Ashiepattle did not cut a very fine figure; he was black and sooty, and the king did not care to give his daughter to such a tramp, so he told Ashiepattle that he would have to wait a little.

"But you can have her all the same, if by this time to-morrow you can empty my storehouse of three hundred barrels of meat," said the king.

"I suppose I must try," said Ashiepattle; "but perhaps you don't mind my taking one of my crew with me?"

"Yes, you can do that, and take all six if you like," said the king, for he was quite sure that even if Ashiepattle took six hundred with him, it would be impossible. So Ashiepattle took with him the one who ate stones and always hungered after meat.

When they came next morning and opened the storehouse they found he had eaten all the meat, except six small legs of mutton, one for each of his companions. Ashiepattle then went to the king and said the storehouse was empty, and he supposed he could now have the princess.

The king went into the storehouse and, sure enough, it was quite empty; but Ashiepattle was still black and sooty, and the king thought it was really too bad that such a tramp should have his daughter. So he said he had a cellar full of beer and old wine, three hundred barrels of each kind, which he would have him drink first.

"I don't mind your having my daughter if you can drink them up by this time to-morrow," said the king.

"I suppose I must try," said Ashiepattle, "but perhaps you don't mind my taking one of my crew with me?"

"Yes, you may do that," said the king, for he was quite sure there was too much beer and wine even for all seven of them. Ashiepattle took with him the one who was always sucking the bung and was always thirsty; and the king then shut them down in the cellar.

There the thirsty one drank barrel after barrel, as long as there was any left, but in the last barrel he left a couple of pints to each of his companions.

In the morning the cellar was opened and Ashiepattle went at once to the king and said he had finished the beer and wine, and now he supposed he could have the princess as the king had promised.

"Well, I must first go down to the cellar and see," said the king, for he could not believe it; but when he got there he found nothing but empty barrels.

But Ashiepattle was both black and sooty and the king thought it wouldn't do for him to have such a son in law. So he said that if Ashiepattle could get water from the end of the world in ten minutes for the princess's tea, he could have both her and half the kingdom; for he thought that task would be quite impossible.

"I suppose I must try," said Ashiepattle, and sent for the one of his crew who jumped about on one leg and had seven ton weights on the other, and told him he must take off the weights and use his legs as quickly as he could, for he must have water from the end of the world for the princess's tea in ten minutes.

So he took off the weights, got a bucket, and set off, and the next moment he was out of sight. But they waited and waited and still he did not return. At last it wanted but three minutes to the time and the king became as pleased as if he had won a big wager.

Then Ashiepattle called the one who could hear the grass grow and told him to listen and find out what had become of their companion.

"He has fallen asleep at the well'," said he who could hear the grass grow; "I can hear him snoring, and a troll is scratching his head." Ashiepattle then called the one who could shoot to the end of the world and told him to send a bullet into the troll; he did so and hit the troll right in the eye. The troll gave such a yell that he woke the man who had come to fetch the water for the tea, and when he returned to the palace there was still one minute left out of the ten.

Ashiepattle went straight to the king and said: "Here is the water;" and now he supposed he could have the princess, for surely the king would not make any more fuss about it now. But the king thought that Ashiepattle was just as black and sooty as ever, and did not like to have him for a son-in-law; so he said he had three hundred fathoms of wood with which he was going to dry corn in the bakehouse, and he wouldn't mind Ashiepattle having his daughter if he would first sit in the bakehouse and burn all the wood; he should then have the princess, and that without fail.

"I suppose I must try," said Ashiepattle; "but perhaps you don't mind my taking one of my crew with me?"

"Oh, no, you can take all six," said the king, for he thought it would be warm enough for all of them.

Ashiepattle took with him the one who had fifteen winters and seven summers in his body, and in the evening he went across to the bakehouse: but the king had piled up so much wood on the fire that you might almost have melted iron in the room. They could not get out of it, for no sooner were they inside than the king fastened the bolt and put a couple of padlocks on the door besides. Ashiepattle then said to his companion:

"You had better let out six or seven winters, so that we may get something like summer weather here."

They were then just able to exist, but during the night it got cold again and Ashiepattle then told the man to let out a couple of summers, and so they slept far into the next day. But when they heard the king outside Ashiepattle said:

"You must let out a couple more winters, but you must manage it so that the last winter you let out strikes the king right in the face."

He did so, and when the king opened the door, expecting to find Ashiepattle and his companion burned to cinders, he saw them huddling together and shivering with cold till their teeth chattered. The same instant Ashiepattle's companion with the fifteen winters in his body let loose the last one right in the king's face, which swelled up into a big chilblain.

"Can I have the princess now?" asked Ashiepattle

"Yes, take her and keep her and the kingdom into the bargain," said the king, who dared not refuse any longer. And so the wedding took place and they feasted and made merry and fired off guns and powder.

While the people were running about searching for wadding for their guns, they took me instead, gave me some porridge in a bottle and some milk in a basket, and fired me right across here, so that I could tell you how it all happened.

THE SQUIRE'S BRIDE

By P. C. Asbjörnsen

Once upon a time there was a rich squire who owned a large farm, and had plenty of silver at the bottom of his chest and money in the bank besides; but he felt there was something wanting, for he was a widower.

One day the daughter of a neighboring farmer was working for him in the hayfield. The squire saw her and liked her very much, and as she was the child of poor parents he thought if he only hinted that he wanted her she would be ready to marry him at once.

So he told her he had been thinking of getting married again.

"Aye! one may think of many things," said the girl, laughing slyly.

In her opinion the old fellow ought to be thinking of something that behooved him better than getting married.

"Well, you see, I thought that you should be my wife!"

"No, thank you all the same," said she, "that's not at all likely."

The squire was not accustomed to be gainsaid, and the more she refused him the more determined he was to get her.

But as he made no progress in her favor he sent for her father and told him that if he could arrange the matter with his daughter he would forgive him the money he had lent him, and he would also give him the piece of land which lay close to his meadow into the bargain.

"Yes, you may be sure I'll bring my daughter to her senses," said the father. "She is only a child, and she doesn't know what's best for her." But all his coaxing and talking did not help matters. She would not have the squire, she said, if he sat buried in gold up to his ears.

The squire waited day after day, but at last he became so angry and impatient that he told the father, if he expected him to stand by his promise, he would have to put his foot down and settle the matter now, for he would not wait any longer.

The man knew no other way out of it but to let the squire get everything ready for the wedding; and when the parson and the wedding guests had arrived the squire should send for the girl as if she were wanted for some work on the farm. When she arrived she would have to be married right away, so that she would have no time to think it over.

The squire thought this was well and good, and so he began brewing and baking and getting ready for the wedding in grand style. When the guests had arrived the squire called one of his farm lads and told him to run down to his neighbor and ask him to send him what he had promised.

"But if you are not back in a twinkling," he said, shaking his fist at him, "I'll—"

He did not say more, for the lad ran off as if he had been shot at.

"My master has sent me to ask for that you promised him," said the lad, when he got to the neighbor, "but there is no time to be lost, for he is terribly busy to-day."

"Yes, yes! Run down into the meadow and take her with you. There she goes!" answered the neighbor.

The lad ran off and when he came to the meadow he found the daughter there raking the hay.

"I am to fetch what your father has promised my master," said the lad.

"Ah, ha!" thought she. "Is that what they are up to?"

"Ah, indeed!" she said. "I suppose it's that little bay mare of ours. You had better go and take her. She stands there tethered on the other side of the pea field," said the girl.

The boy jumped on the back of the bay mare and rode home at full gallop.

"Have you got her with you?" asked the squire.

"She is down at the door," said the lad.

"Take her up to the room my mother had," said the squire.

"But master, how can that be managed?" said the lad.

"You must just do as I tell you," said the squire. "If you cannot manage her alone you must get the men to help you," for he thought the girl might turn obstreperous.

When the lad saw his master's face he knew it would be no use to gainsay him. So he went and got all the farm tenants who were there to help him. Some pulled at the head and the forelegs of the mare and others pushed from behind, and at last they got her up the stairs and into the room. There lay all the wedding finery ready.

"Now, that's done master!" said the lad; "but it was a terrible job. It was the worst I have ever had here on the farm.

"Never mind, you shall not have done it for nothing," said his master. "Now send the women up to dress her."

"But I say master—!" said the lad.

"None of your talk!" said the squire. "Tell them they must dress her and mind and not forget either wreath or crown.

The lad ran into the kitchen.

"Look here, lasses," he said; "you must go upstairs and dress up the bay mare as bride. I expect the master wants to give the guests a laugh."

The women dressed the bay mare in everything that was there, and then the lad went and told his master that now she was ready dressed, with wreath and crown and all.

"Very well, bring her down!" said the squire. "I will receive her myself at the door," said he.

There was a terrible clatter on the stairs; for that bride, you know, had no silken shoes on.

When the door was opened and the squire's bride entered the parlor you can imagine there was a good deal of tittering and grinning.

And as for the squire you may he sure line had had enough of that bride, and they say he never went courting again.

THE DOLL IN THE GRASS

By P. C. Asbjörnsen

Once upon a time there was a king who had twelve sons. When they were grown up he told them they must go out into the world and find themselves wives, who must all be able to spin and weave and make a shirt in one day, else he would not have them for daughters-in-law. He gave each of his sons a horse and a new suit of armor, and so they set out in the world to look for wives.

When they had traveled a bit on the way they said they would not take Ashiepattle with them, for he was good for nothing. Ashiepattle must stop behind; there was no help for it. He did not know what he should do or which way he should turn; he became so sad that he got off the horse and sat down on the grass and began to cry.

When he had sat a while one of the tussocks among the grass began to move, and out of it came a small white figure; as it came nearer Ashiepattle saw that it was a beautiful little girl, but she was so tiny, so very, very tiny.

She went up to him and asked him if he would come below and pay a visit to the doll in the grass.

Yes, that he would; and so he did. When he came down below, the doll in the grass was sitting in a chair dressed very finely and looking still more beautiful. She asked Ashiepattle where he was going and what was his errand.

He told her they were twelve brothers, and that the king had given them each a horse and a suit of armor, and told them to go out in the world and find themselves wives, but they must all be able to spin and weave and make a shirt in a day.

"If you can do that and will become my wife, I will not travel any farther," said Ashiepattle to the doll in the grass.

Yes, that she would, and she set to work at once to get the shirt spun, woven, and made; but it was so tiny, so very, very tiny, no bigger than—so!

Ashiepattle then returned home, taking the shirt with him; but when he brought it out he felt very shy because it was so small. But the king said he could have her for all that, and you can imagine how happy and joyful Ashiepattle became.

The road did not seem long to him as he set out to fetch his little sweetheart. When he came to the doll in the grass he wanted her to sit with him on his horse; but no, that she wouldn't; she said she would sit and drive in a silver spoon, and she had two small while horses which would draw her. So they set out, he on his horse and she in the silver spoon; and the horses which drew her were two small white mice.

Ashiepattle always kept to one side of the road, for he was so afraid he should ride over her; she was so very, very tiny.

When they had traveled a bit on the way they came to a large lake; there Ashiepattle's horse took fright and shied over to the other side of the road, and upset the spoon, so that the doll in the grass fell into the water. Ashiepattle became very sad, for he did not know how he should get her out again; but after a while a merman brought her up.

But now she had become just as big as any other grown-up being and was much more beautiful than she was before. So he placed her in front of him on the horse and rode home.

When Ashiepattle got there all his brothers had also returned, each with a sweetheart; but they were so ugly and ill-favored and bad-tempered that they had come to blows with their sweethearts on their way home. On their heads they had hats which were painted with tar and soot, and this had run from their hats down their faces, so that they were still uglier and more ill-favored to behold.

When the brothers saw Ashiepattle's sweetheart they all became envious of him, but the king was so pleased with Ashiepattle and his sweetheart that he drove all the others away, and so Ashiepattle was married to the doll in the grass; and afterward they lived happy and comfortable for a long, long while; and if they are not dead, they must be still alive.

THE BEAR AND THE FOX

By P. C. Asbjörnsen

Once upon a time there was a bear, who sat on a sunny hillside taking a nap. Just then a fox came slinking by and saw him.

"Aha! have I caught you napping, grandfather? See if I don't play you a trick this time!" said Reynard to himself.

He then found three wood mice and laid them on a stump of a tree just under the bear's nose.

"Boo! Bruin! Peter the hunter is just behind that stump!" shouted the fox right into the bear's ear, and then took to his heels and made off into the wood.

The bear woke at once, and when he saw the three mice he became so angry that he lifted his paw and was just going to strike them, for he thought it was they who had shouted in his ear.

But just then he saw Reynard's tail between the bushes and he set off at such a speed that the branches crackled under him, and Bruin was soon so close upon Reynard that he caught him by the right hind leg just as be was running into a hole under a pine tree.

Reynard was now in a fix; but he was not to be outwitted, and he cried:

"Slip pine root, grip fox foot," and so the bear let go his hold; but the fox laughed far down in the hole and said:

"I sold you that time, also, grandfather!"

"Out of sight is not out of mind!" said the bear, who was in a fine fury.

The other morning, when Bruin came trudging across the moor with a fat pig, Master Reynard was lying on a stone by the moorside.

"Good-day, grandfather!" said the fox. "What nice thing have you got there?"

"Pork," said the bear.

"I have got something tasty as well," said the fox.

"What's that?" said the bear.

"It's the biggest bees' nest I ever found," said Reynard.

"Ah, indeed," said the bear, grinning, and his mouth began to water, he thought a little honey would be so nice. "Shall we change victuals?" he said.

"No, I won't do that," said Reynard. But they made a wager about naming three kinds of trees. If the fox could say them quicker than the bear he was to have one bite at the pig; but if the bear could say them quicker he was to have one suck at the bee's nest. The bear thought he would be able to suck all the honey up at one gulp.

"Well said the fox, "that's all well and good but if I win you must promise to tear off the bristles where I want to have a bite," he said.

"Well, I suppose I must, since you are too lazy yourself," said the bear.

Then they began to name the trees.

"Spruce, fir, pine," growled the bear. His voice was very gruff. But all these were only different names of one kind of tree.

"Ash, aspen, oak," screeched the fox, so that the forest resounded. He had thus won the bet, and so he jumped down, took the heart out of the pig at one bite, and tried to run off. But the bear was angry, because he had taken the best bit of the whole pig, and seized hold of him by his tail and held him fast.

"Just wait a bit," said the bear, who was furious.

"Never mind, grandfather; if you'll let me go you shall have a taste of my honey," said the fox.

When the bear heard this he let go his hold and the fox jumped up on the stone after the honey.

"Over this nest," said Reynard, "I'll put a leaf, and in the leaf there is a hole, through which you can suck the honey." He then put the nest right up under the bear's nose, pulled away the leaf, jumped on to the stone, and began grinning and laughing; for there was neither honey nor honeycomb in the nest. It was a wasp's nest as big as a man's head, full of wasps, and out they swarmed and stung the bear in his eyes and ears and on his mouth and snout. He had so much to do with scratching them off him that he had no the to think of Reynard.

Ever since the bear has been afraid of wasps.

Once the fox and the bear made up their minds to have a field in common. They found a small clearing far away in the forest, where they sowed rye the first year.

"Now we must share and share alike," said Reynard; "if you will have the roots I will have the tops," he said.

Yes, Bruin was quite willing; but when they had thrashed the crop the fox got all the corn, while the bear got nothing but the roots and tares.

Bruin didn't like this, but the fox said it was only as they had agreed.

"This year I am the gainer," said the fox; "another year it will be your turn; you can then have the tops and I will be satisfied with the roots."

Next spring the fox asked the bear if he didn't think turnips would be the right thing for that year.

"Yes, that's better food than corn," said the bear; and the fox thought the same.

When the autumn came the fox took the turnips, but the bear only got the tops.

The bear then became so angry that he parted company then and there with Reynard.

One day the bear was lying eating a horse which he had killed. Reynard was about again and came slinking along, his mouth watering for a tasty bit of the horseflesh.

He sneaked in and out and round about till he came up behind the bear, when he made a spring to the other side of the carcass, snatching a piece as he jumped across.

The bear was not slow either; he made a dash after Reynard and caught the tip of his red tail in his paw. Since that time the fox has always had a white tip to his tail.

"Wait a bit Reynard, and come here," said the bear, "and I'll teach you how to catch horses."

Yes, Reynard was quite willing to learn that, but he didn't trust himself too near the bear.

"When you see a horse lying asleep in a sunny place," said the bear, "you must tie yourself fast with the hair of his tail to your brush, and then fasten your teeth in his thigh," he said.

Before long the fox found a horse lying asleep on a sunny hillside; and so he did as the bear had told him; he knotted and tied himself well to the horse with the hair of the tail and then fastened his teeth into his thigh.

Up jumped the horse and began to kick and gallop so that Reynard was dashed against stock and stone, and was so bruised and battered that he nearly lost his senses.

All at once a hare rushed by. "Where are you off to in such a hurry, Reynard?" said the hare.

"I'm having a ride, Bunny!" said the fox.

The hare sat up on his hind legs and laughed till the sides of his mouth split right up to his ears, at the thought of Reynard having such a grand ride; but since then the fox has never thought of catching horses again.

That time it was Bruin who for once had the better of Reynard; otherwise they say the bear is as simple-minded as the trolls.

THE LAD WHO WENT TO THE NORTH WIND

By Sir George Webbe Dasent

Once upon a time there was an old widow who had one son, and she was poorly and weak, her son had to go up into the safe to fetch meal for cooking; but when he got outside the safe, and was just going down the steps, there came the North Wind, puffing and blowing, caught up the meal, and so away with it through the air. Then the lad went back into the safe for more; but when he came out again on the steps, if the North Wind didn't come again and carry off the meal with a puff; and more than that, he did so the third time. At this the lad got very angry; and as he thought it hard that the North Wind should behave so, he thought he'd just look him up and ask him to give up his meal.

So off he went, but the way was long, and he walked and walked; but at last he came to the North Wind's house.

"Good day!" said the lad, and "thank you for coming to see us yesterday."

"GOOD DAY!" answered the North Wind, for his voice was loud and gruff, "AND THANKS FOR COMING TO SEE ME. WHAT DO YOU WANT?"

"Oh!" answered the lad, "I only wished to ask you to be so good as to let me have back that meal you took from me on the safe steps, for we haven't much to live on; and if you're to go on snapping up the morsel we have there'll be nothing for it but to starve."

"I haven't got your meal," said the North Wind; "but if you are in such need, I'll give you a cloth which will get you everything you want, if you only say, 'Cloth, spread yourself, and serve up all kinds of good dishes!'"

With this the lad was well content. But, as the way was so long he couldn't get home in one day, he stopped at an inn on the way; and when they were going to sit down to supper, he laid the cloth on a table which stood in the corner and said:

"Cloth, spread yourself, and serve up all kinds of good dishes."

He had scarce said so before the cloth did as it was bid; and all who stood by thought it a fine thing, but most of all the landlady. So, when all were fast asleep, at dead of night, she took the lad's cloth, and put another in its stead, just like the one he had got from the North Wind, but which couldn't so much as serve up a bit of dry bread.

So when the lad awoke, he took his cloth and went off with it, and that day he got home to his mother.

"Now," said he, "I've been to the North Wind's house, and a good fellow he is, for he gave me this cloth, and when I only say to it, 'Cloth, spread yourself, and serve up all kinds of good dishes,' I get any sort of food I please."

"All very true, I dare say," said his mother, "but seeing is believing, and I shan't believe it till I see it."

So the lad made haste, drew out a table, laid the cloth on it, and said—"Cloth, spread yourself, and serve up all kinds of good dishes."

But never a bit of dry bread did the cloth serve

"Well," said the lad, "there's no help for it but to go to the North Wind again;" and away he went.

So late in the afternoon he came to where the North Wind lived.

"Good evening!" said the lad.

"Good evening!" said the North Wind. "I want my rights for that meal of ours which you took," said the lad; "for, as for that cloth I got, it isn't worth a penny."

"I've got no meal," said the North Wind; "but yonder you have a ram which coins nothing but golden ducats as soon as you say to it—

"'Ram, ram! Make money!'"

So the lad thought this a fine thing; but as it was too far to get home that day, he stopped for the night at the same inn where he had slept before.

Before he called for anything, he tried the truth of what the North Wind had said of the ram, and found it all right; but when the landlord saw that, he thought it was a famous ram, and, when the lad had fallen asleep, he took another which couldn't coin gold ducats, and changed the two.

Next morning off went the lad; and when he got home to his mother, he said—"After all, the North Wind is a jolly fellow; for now he has given me a ram which can coin golden ducats if I only say, 'Ram, ram! Make money!'"

"All very true, I dare say," said his mother; "but I shan't believe any such stuff until I see the ducats made."

"Ram, ram! Make money!" said the lad; but the ram made no money.

So the lad went back again to the North Wind, and blew him up, and said the ram was worth nothing, and he must have his rights for the meal.

"Well," said the North Wind, "I've nothing else to give you but that old stick in the corner yonder; but it's a stick of that kind that if you say — 'Stick, stick! lay on!' it lays on till you say, 'Stick, stick! now stop!'

So, as the way was long the lad turned in this night, too, to the landlord; but as he could pretty well guess how things stood as to the cloth and the ram, he lay down at once on the bench and began to snore, as if he were asleep.

Now the landlord, who easily saw that the stick must be worth something, hunted up one which was like it, and when he heard the lad snore, was going to change the two, but just as the landlord was about to take it, the lad bawled out — "Stick, stick! lay on!"

So the stick began to beat the landlord till he jumped over chairs, and tables, and benches, and yelled and roared, — "Oh my! oh my! bid the stick be still, else it will beat me to death, and you shall have back your cloth and your ram,

When the lad thought the landlord had got enough, he said — "Stick, stick! now stop!"

Then he took the cloth and put it into his pocket, and went home with his stick in his hand, leading the ram by a cord round its horns; and so he got his rights for the meal he had lost.

THE HUSBAND WHO WAS TO MIND THE HOUSE

By Sir George Webbe Dasent

Once upon a time there was a man, so surly and cross, he never thought his wife did anything right in the house. So one evening in haymaking time, he came home, scolding and swearing, and showing his teeth and making a dust.

"Dear love, don't be so angry; there's a good man," said his goody; "tomorrow let's change our work. I'll go out with the mowers and mow, and you shall mind the house at home."

Yes, the husband thought that would do very well. He was quite willing, he said.

So early next morning his goody took a scythe over her neck, and went out into the hayfield with the mowers and began to mow; but the man was to mind the house, and do the work at home.

First of all he wanted to churn the butter; but when he had churned a while, he got thirsty, and went down to the cellar to tap a barrel of ale. So, just when he had knocked in the bung, and was putting the tap into the cask, he heard overhead the pig come into the kitchen. Then off he ran up the cellar steps, with the tap in his hand, as fast as he could, to look after the pig, lest it should upset the churn; but when he got up, and saw that the pig had already knocked the churn over, and stood there, routing and grunting amid the cream which was running all over the floor, he got so wild with rage that he quite forgot his ale barrel and ran at the pig as hard as he could. He caught it, too, just as it ran out of doors, and gave it such a kick that piggy lay for dead on the spot. Then all at once he remembered he had the tap in his hand, but when he got down to the cellar, every drop of ale had run out of the cask.

Then he went into the dairy and found enough cream left to fill the churn again, and so he began to churn, for butter they must have for dinner. When he had churned a bit, he remembered that their milking cow was still shut up in the brye, and hadn't had a bit to eat or a drop to drink all the morning, though the sun was high. Then all at once he thought 'twas too far to take her down to the meadow, so he'd just get her up on the housetop—for the house, you must know, was thatched with sods, and a fine crop of grass was growing there.

Now their house lay close up against a steep down, and he thought if he laid a plank across to the thatch at the back he'd easily get the cow up.

But still he couldn't leave the churn, for there was his little babe crawling about the floor, and "if I leave it," he thought, "the child is sure to upset it!" So he took the churn on his back, and went out with it; but then he thought he'd better first water the cow before he turned her out on the thatch; so he took up a bucket to draw water out of the well; but, as he stooped down at the well's brink, all the cream ran out of the churn over his shoulders, and so down into the well.

Now it was near dinner time, and he hadn't even got the butter yet; so he thought he'd best boil the porridge, and filled the pot with water, and hung it over the fire. When he had done that, he thought the cow might perhaps fall off the thatch and break her legs or her neck. So he got up on the house to tie her up. One end of the rope he made fast to the cow's neck, and the other he slipped down the chimney and tied round his own thigh; and he had to make haste, for the water now began to boil in the pot, and he had still to grind the oatmeal.

So he began to grind away; but while he was hard at it, down fell the cow off the housetop after all, and as she fell, she dragged the man up the chimney by the rope. There he stuck fast; and as for the cow, she hung halfway down the wall, swinging between heaven and earth, for she could neither get down nor up.

And now the goody had waited seven lengths and seven breadths for her husband to come and call them home to dinner; but never a call they had. At last she thought she'd waited long enough, and went home. But when she got there and saw the cow hanging in such an ugly place, she ran up and cut the rope in two with her scythe. But as she did this, down came her husband out of the chimney; and so when his old dame came inside the kitchen, there she found him standing on his head in the porridge pot.

HOW ONE WENT OUT TO WOO

By Sir George Webbe Dasent

Once upon a time there was a lad who went out to woo him a wife. Among other places he came to a farmhouse, where the household were little better than beggars; but when the wooer came in they wanted to make out that they were well to do, as you may guess. Now the husband had got a new arm to his coat.

"Pray, take a seat," he said to the wooer; "but there's a shocking dust in the house."

So he went about rubbing and wiping all the benches and tables with his new arm, but he kept the other all the while behind his back.

The wife she had got one new shoe, and she went stamping and sliding with it up against the stools and chairs saying, "How untidy it is here! Everything is out of place!"

Then they called out to their daughter to come down and put things to rights; but the daughter she had got a new cap; so she put her head in at the door, and kept nodding and nodding, first to this side and then to that.

"Well! For my part, She said, I can't be everywhere at once."

Aye! Aye! That was a well-to-do household the wooer had come to.

WHY THE BEAR IS STUMPY-TAILED

By Sir George Webbe Dasent

One day the Bear met the Fox, who came slinking along with a string of fish he had stolen.

"Whence did you get these from?" asked the Bear.

"Oh! My Lord Bruin, I've been out fishing and caught them," said the Fox.

So the Bear had a mind to learn to fish too, and bade the Fox tell him how he was to set about it.

"Oh! It's an easy craft for you", answered the Fox, "and soon learned. You've only got to go upon the ice, and cut a hole and stick your tail down into it; and so you must go on holding it there as long as you can. You're not to mind if your tail smarts a little; that's when the fish bite. The longer you hold it there the more fish you'll get; and then all at once out with it, with a cross pull sideways, and with a strong pull too."

Yes; the Bear did as the Fox had said, and held his tail a long, long time down in the hole, till it was fast frozen in. Then he pulled it out with a cross pull, and it snapped short off. That's why Bruin goes about with a stumpy tail this very day.

BOOTS WHO MADE THE PRINCESS SAY "THAT'S A STORY"

By Sir George Webbe Dasent

Once upon a time there was a King who had a daughter, and she was such a dreadful storyteller that the like of her was not to be found far or near. So the King gave out, that if anyone could tell such a string of lies as would get her to say, "That's a story," he should have her to wife, and half the kingdom besides. Well, many came, as you may fancy, to try their luck, for everyone would have been very glad to have the Princess, to say nothing of the kingdom; but they all cut a sorry figure, for the Princess was so given to storytelling, that all their lies went in at one ear and out of the other. Among the rest came three brothers to try their luck, and the two elder went first, but they fared no better than those that had gone before them. Last of all, the third, Boots, set off and found the Princess in the farmyard.

"Good morning," he said, "and thank you for nothing." "Good morning," said she, "and the same to you." Then she went on—

"You haven't such a fine farmyard as ours, I'll be bound; for when two shepherds stand, one at each end of it, and blow their ram's horns, the one can't hear the other."

"Haven't we though!" answered Boots; "ours is far bigger; for when a calf starts to cross a field, it is a full-grown cow when it reaches the other end."

"I dare say," said the Princess. "Well, but you haven't such a big ox, after all, as ours yonder; for when two men sit, one on each horn, they can't touch each other with a tweny-foot rule."

"Stuff!" said Boots; "is that all? Why, we have an ox who is so big, that when two men sit, one on each horn, and each blows his great mountain-trumpet, they can't hear one another."

"I dare say," said the Princess; "but you haven't so much milk as we, I'll be bound; for we milk our cows into great pails, and carry them indoors, and empty them into great tubs, and so we make great, great cheeses."

"Oh! you do, do you?" said Boots. "Well, we milk ours into great tubs, and then we put them in carts and drive them indoors, and then we turn them out into great brewing vats, and so we make cheeses as big as a great house. We had, too, a dun mare to tread the cheese well together when it was making; but once she tumbled down into the cheese, and we lost her; and after we had eaten at this cheese seven years, we came upon a great dun mare, alive and kicking. Well, once after that I was going to drive this mare to the mill, and her backbone snapped in two; but I wasn't put out, not I; for I took a spruce sapling, and put it into her for a backbone, and she had no other backbone all the while we had her. But the sapling grew up into such a tall tree, that I climbed right up to the sky by it, and when I got there I saw a lady sitting and spinning the foam of the sea into pigs' — bristle ropes; but just then the spruce-fir broke short off, and I couldn't get down again; so the lady let me down by one of the ropes, and down I slipped straight into a fox's hole, and who should sit there but my mother and your father cobbling shoes; and just as I stepped in, my mother gave your father such a box on the ear that it made his whiskers curl."

"That's a story!" said the Princess, "my father never did any such thing in all his born days!"

So Boots got the Princess to wife, and half the kingdom besides.

THE WITCH IN THE STONE BOAT

Retold by Andrew Lang

There was once a king and queen, and they had a son called Sigurd, who was very strong and active and good-looking. When the king came to be bowed down with the weight of years he spoke to his son, and said that now it was time for him to look out for a fitting match for himself, for he did not know how long he might last now, and he would like to see him married before he died.

Sigurd was not averse to this and asked his father where he thought it best to look for a wife. The king answered that in a certain country there was a king who had a beautiful daughter, and he thought it would be most desirable if Sigurd could get her. So the two parted, and Sigurd prepared for the journey and went to where his father had directed him.

He came to the king and asked his daughters hand, which was readily granted him, but only on the condition that he should remain there as long as he could, for the king himself was not strong and not very able to govern his kingdom. Sigurd accepted this condition, but added that he would have to get leave to go home again to his own country when he heard news of his father's death. After that Sigurd married the princess and helped his father-in-law to govern the kingdom. He and the princess loved each other dearly, and after a year a son came to them, who was two years old when word came to Sigurd that his father was dead. Sigurd now prepared to return home with his wife and child and went on board ship to go by sea.

They had sailed for several days, when the breeze suddenly fell and there came a dead calm at a time when they needed only one day's voyage to reach home. Sigurd and his queen were one day on deck when most of the others on the ship had fallen asleep. There they sat and talked for a while, and had their little son along with them. After a time Sigurd became so heavy with sleep that he could no longer keep awake, so he went below and lay down, leaving the queen alone on the deck playing with her son.

A good while after Sigurd had gone below the queen saw something black on the sea which seemed to be coming nearer. As it approached she could make out that it was a boat and could see the figure of some one sitting in it and rowing it. At last the boat came alongside the ship, and now the queen saw that it was a stone boat, out of which there came on board the ship a fearfully ugly witch. The queen was more frightened than words can describe, and could neither speak a word nor move from the place so as to awaken the king or the sailors. The witch came right up to the queen, took the child from her, and laid it on the deck; then she took the queen and stripped her of all her fine clothes, which she proceeded to put on herself and looked then like a human being. Last of all she took the queen, put her into the boat and said:

"This spell I lay upon you, that you slacken not your course until you come to my brother in the under world."

The queen sat stunned and motionless, but the boat at once shot away from the ship with her, and before long she was out of sight.

When the boat could no longer be seen the child began to cry, and though the witch tried to quiet it she could not manage it; so, with the child on her arm, she went below to where the king was sleeping, and awakened him, scolding him for leaving them alone on deck while he and all the crew were asleep. It was great carelessness of him, she said, to leave no one to watch the ship with her.

Sigurd was greatly surprised to hear his queen scold him so much, for she had never said an angry word to him before; but he thought it was quite excusable in this case, and tried to quiet the child along with her but it was no use. Then he went and wakened the sailors and bade them hoist the sails, for a breeze had sprung up and was blowing straight toward the harbor.

They soon reached the land which Sigurd was to rule over, and found all the people sorrowful for the old king's death, but they became glad when they got Sigurd back to the court, and made him king over them.

The king's son, however, hardly ever stopped crying from the time he had been taken from his mother on the deck of the ship, although he had always been such a good child before, so that at last the king had to get a nurse for him — one of the maids of the court. As soon as the child got into her charge he stopped crying and behaved as well as before.

After the sea voyage it seemed to the king that the queen had altered very much in many ways, and not for the better. He thought her much more haughty and stubborn and difficult to deal with than she used to be. Before long others began to notice this as well as the king. In the court there were two young fellows, one of eighteen years old, the other of nineteen, who were very fond of playing chess and often sat long inside playing at it. Their room was next the queen's, and often during the day they heard the queen talking.

One day they paid more attention than usual when they heard her talk, and put their ears close to a crack in the wall between the rooms, and heard the queen say quite plainly: "When I yawn a little, then I am a nice little maiden: when I yawn halfway, then I am half a troll; and when I yawn fully then I am a troll altogether."

As she said this she yawned tremendously, and in a moment had put on the appearance of a fearfully ugly troll. Then there came up through the floor of the room a three-headed giant with a trough full of meat, who saluted her as his sister and set down the trough before her. She began to eat out of it and never stopped till she had finished it. The young fellows saw all this going on, but did not hear the two of them say anything to each other. They were astonished, though, at how greedily the queen devoured the meat and how much she ate of it, and were no longer surprised that she took so little when she sat at table with the king. As soon as she had finished it the giant disappeared with the trough by the same way as he had come, and the queen returned to her human shape.

Now we must go back to the king's son after he had been put in charge of the nurse. One evening. after she had lit a candle and was holding the child, several planks sprang up in the floor of the room, and out at the opening came a beautiful woman dressed in white, with an iron belt round her waist, to which was fastened an iron chain that went down into the ground. The woman came up to the nurse, took the child from her, and pressed it to her breast; then she gave it back to the nurse and returned by the same way as she had come, and the floor closed over her again. Although the woman had not spoken a single word to her, the nurse was very much frightened, but told no one about it.

Next evening the same thing happened again, just as before, but as the woman was going away she said in a sad tone, "Two are gone and one only is left," and then disappeared as before. The nurse was still more frightened when she heard the woman say this, and thought that perhaps some danger was hanging over the child, though she had no ill opinion of the unknown woman, who, indeed, had behaved toward the child as if it were her own. The most mysterious thing was the woman saying "and only one is left"; but the nurse guessed that this must mean that only one day was left, since she had come for two days already.

At last the nurse made up her mind to go to the king. She told him the whole story and asked him to be present in person the next day about the time when the woman usually came. The king promised to do so, and came to the nurse's room a little before the time and sat down on a chair with his drawn sword in his hand. Soon after the planks in the floor sprang up as before, and the woman came up, dressed in white, with the iron belt and chain. The king saw at once that it was his own queen, and immediately hewed asunder the iron chain that was fastened to the belt. This was followed by such noises and crashings down in the earth that all the king's palace shook, so that no one expected anything else than to see every bit of it shaken to pieces. At last the noises and shaking stopped, and they began to come to themselves again.

The king and queen embraced each other, and she told him the whole story — how the witch came to the ship when they were all asleep and sent her off in the boat. After she had gone so far that she could not see the ship, she sailed on through darkness until she landed beside a three-headed giant. The giant wished her to marry him, but she refused; whereupon he shut her up by herself and told her she would never get free until she consented. After a time she began to plan how to get her freedom, and at last told him that she would consent if he would allow her to visit her son on earth three days on end. This he agreed to, but put on her this iron belt and chain, the other end of which he fastened around his, own waist, and the great noises that were heard when the king cut the chain must have been caused by the giant's falling down the underground passage when the chain gave way so suddenly. The giant's dwelling, indeed, was right under the palace, and the terrible shakings must have been caused by him in his death throes.

The king now understood how the queen he had had for some time past had been so ill-tempered. He at once had a sack drawn over her head and made her be stoned to death, and after that torn in pieces by untamed horses. The two young fellows also told now what they had heard and seen in the queen's room, for before this they had been afraid to say anything about it, on account of the Queen's power.

The real queen was now restored to all her dignity and was beloved by all. The nurse was married to a nobleman and the king and queen gave her splendid presents.

THE SNUFFBOX

By Paul Sébillot

As often happens in this world, there was once a young man who spent all his time in traveling. One day, as he was walking along, he picked up a snuffbox. He opened it, and the snuffbox said to him in the Spanish language: "What do you want?" He was very much frightened, but, luckily, instead of throwing the box away he only shut it tight and put it in his pocket. Then he went on, away, away, away, and as he went he said to himself, "if it says to me again, 'What do you want?' I shall know better what to say this time." So he took out the snuffbox and opened it, and again it asked: "What do you want?" "My hat full of gold," answered the youth, and immediately it was full.

Our young man was enchanted. Henceforth he should never be in need of anything. So on he traveled, away, away, away, through thick forests, till at last he came to a beautiful castle. In the castle there lived a king. The young man walked round and round the castle, not caring who saw him, till the king noticed him and asked what he was doing there. "I was just looking at your castle." "You would like to have one like it, wouldn't you?" The young man did not reply, but when it grew dark he took out his snuffbox and opened the lid." What do you want?" "Build me a castle with laths of gold and tiles of diamond and the furniture all of silver and gold." He had scarcely finished speaking when there stood in front of him, exactly opposite the king's palace, a castle built precisely as he had ordered. When the king awoke he was struck dumb at the sight of the magnificent house shining in the rays of the sun. The servants could not do their work for stopping to stare at it. Then the king dressed himself and went to see the young man. And he told him plainly that he was a very powerful prince, and that he hoped that they might all live together in one house or the other, and that the king would give him his daughter to wife. So it all turned out just as the king wished. The young man married the princess and they lived happily in the palace of gold.

But the king's wife was jealous both of the young man and of her own daughter. The princess had told her mother about the snuffbox, which gave them everything they wanted, and the queen bribed a servant to steal the snuffbox. They noticed carefully where it was put away every night, and one evening, when the whole world was asleep, the woman stole it and brought it to her old mistress. Oh, how happy the queen was! She opened the lid and the snuffbox said to her: "What do you want?" And she answered at once: "I want you to take me and my husband and my servants and this beautiful house and set us down on the other side of the Red Sea, but my daughter and her husband are to stay behind."

When the young couple woke up they found themselves back in the old castle, without their snuffbox. They hunted for it high and low, but quite vainly. The young man felt that no time was to be lost, and he mounted his horse and filled his pockets with as much gold as he could carry. On he went, away, away, away, but he sought the snuffbox in vain all up and down the neighboring countries, and very soon he came to the end of all his money. But still he went on, as fast as the strength of his horse would let him, begging his way.

Some one told him that he ought to consult the moon, for the moon traveled far and might be able to tell him something. So he went away, away, away, and ended, somehow or other, by reaching the land of the moon. There he found a little old woman who said to him: "What are you doing here? My son eats all living things he sees, and if you are wise you will go away without coming any farther." But the young man told her all his sad tale, and how he possessed a wonderful snuffbox, and how it had been stolen from him, and how he had nothing left now that he was parted from his wife and was in need of everything. And he said that perhaps her son, who traveled so far, might have seen a palace with laths of gold and tiles of diamond and furnished all in silver and gold. As he spoke these last words the moon came in and said he smelled mortal flesh and blood. But his mother told him that it was an unhappy man who had lost everything and had come all this way to consult him, and bade the young man not to be afraid, but to come forward and show himself. So he went boldly up to the moon, and asked if by any accident he had seen a palace with the laths of gold and the tiles of diamond and all the furniture of silver and gold. Once this house belonged to him, but now it was stolen. And the moon said no, but that the sun traveled farther than he did, and that the young man had better go and ask him.

So the young man departed and went away, away, away, as well as his horse would take him, begging his living as he rode along, and somehow or other at last he got to the land of the sun. There he found a little old woman, who asked him: "What are you doing here? Go away. Have you not heard that my son feeds upon Christians?" But he said no and that he would not go, for he was so miserable that it was all one to him whether he died or not; that he had lost everything, and especially a splendid palace like none other in the whole world, for it had laths of gold and tiles of diamond and all the furniture was of silver and gold; and that he had sought it far and long, and in all the earth there was no man more unhappy. So the old woman's heart melted and she agreed to hide him.

When the sun arrived he declared that he smelled Christian flesh and he meant to have it for his dinner. But his mother told him such a pitiful story of the miserable wretch who had lost everything and had come from far to ask his help that at last he promised to see him.

So the young man came out from his hiding-place and begged the sun to tell him if in the course of his travels he had not seen somewhere a palace that had not its like in the whole world, for its laths were of gold and its tiles of diamond and all the furniture in silver and gold.

And the sun said no, but that perhaps the wind had seen it, for he entered everywhere and saw things that no one else ever saw, and if anyone knew where it was it was certainly the wind.

Then the poor young man again set forth as well as his horse could take him, begging his living as he went, and somehow or other he ended by reaching the home of the wind. He found there a little old woman busily occupied in filling great barrels with water. She asked him what had put it into his head to come there, for her son ate everything he saw, and that he would shortly arrive quite mad, and that the young man had better look out. But he answered that he was so unhappy that he had ceased to mind anything, even being eaten, and then he told her that he had been robbed of a palace that had not its equal in all the world, and of all that was in it, and that he had even left his wife and was wandering over the world until he found it. And that it was the sun who had sent him to consult the wind. So she hid him under the staircase, and soon they heard the south wind arrive, shaking the house to its foundations. Thirsty as he was, he did not wait to drink, but he told his mother that he smelled the blood of a Christian man, and that she had better bring him out at once and make him ready to be eaten. But she bade her son eat and drink what was before him, and said that the poor young man was much to be pitied, and that the sun had granted him his life in order that he might consult the Wind. Then she brought out the young man, who explained how he was seeking for his palace, and that no man had been able to tell him where it was, so he had come to the Wind. And he added that he had been shamefully robbed, and that the laths were of gold and the tiles of diamond, and all the furniture in silver and gold, and he inquired if the Wind had not seen such a palace during his wanderings.

And the Wind said yes, and that all that day he had been blowing backward and forward over it without being able to move one single tile.

"Oh, do tell me where it is," cried the young man." "It is a long way off," replied the Wind, "on the other side of the Red Sea." But our traveler was not discouraged—he had already journeyed too far.

So he set forth at once, and somehow or other he managed to reach that distant land. And he inquired if any one wanted a gardener. He was told that the head gardener at the castle had just left, and perhaps he might have a chance of getting the place. The young man lost no time, but walked up to the castle and asked if they were in want of a gardener; and how happy he was when they agreed to take him! Now he passed most of his day in gossiping with the servants about the wealth of their masters and the wonderful things in the house. He made friends with one of the maids, who told him the history of the snuffbox, and he coaxed her to let him see it. One evening she managed to get hold of it, and the young man watched carefully where she hid it away in a secret place in the bedchamber of her mistress.

The following night, when everyone was fast asleep, he crept in and took the snuffbox. Think of his joy as he opened the lid! When it asked him, as of yore, "What do you want?" he replied: "What do I want? What do I want? Why, I want to go with my palace to the old place, and for the king and the queen and all their servants to be drowned in the Red Sea."

He had hardly finished speaking when he found himself back again with his wife, while all the other inhabitants of the palace were lying at the bottom of the Red Sea.

THE GOLDEN BLACKBIRD

By Paul Sébillot

Once upon a time there was a great lord who had three sons. He fell very ill, sent for doctors of every kind, even bonesetters, but they none of them could find out what was the matter with him or even give him any relief. At last there came a foreign doctor, who declared that the golden blackbird alone could cure the sick man.

So the old lord dispatched his eldest son to look for the wonderful bird, and promised him great riches if he managed to find it and bring it back.

The young man began his journey and soon arrived at a place where four roads met. He did not know which to choose, and tossed his cap in the air, determining that the direction of its fall should decide him. After traveling for two or three days he grew tired of walking without knowing where or for how long, and he stopped at an inn which was filled with merrymakers and ordered something to eat and drink.

"My faith," said he, "it is sheer folly to waste more time hunting for this bird. My father is old, and if he dies I shall inherit his goods."

The old man, after waiting patiently for some time, sent his second son to seek the golden blackbird. The youth took the same direction as his brother, and when he came to the crossroads he too tossed up which road he should take. The cap fell in the same place as before, and he walked on till he came to the spot where his brother had halted. The latter, who was leaning out of the window of the inn, called to him to stay where he was and amuse himself.

"You are right," replied the youth. "Who knows if I should ever find the golden blackbird, even if I sought the whole world through for it? At the worst, if the old man dies we shall have his property."

He entered the inn and the two brothers made merry and feasted, till very soon their money was all spent. They even owed something to their landlord, who kept them as hostages till they could pay their debts.

The youngest son set forth in his turn, and he arrived at the place where his brothers where still prisoners. They called to him to stop and did all they could to prevent his going further.

"No," he replied, "my father trusted me, and I will go all over the world till I find the golden blackbird."

"Bah," said his brothers, "you will never succeed any better than we did. Let him die if he wants to. We will divide the property."

As he went his way he met a little hare, who stopped to looked at him and asked:

"Where are you going, my friend?"

"I really don't quite know," answered he. "My father is ill, and he cannot be cured unless I bring him back the golden blackbird. It is a long time since I set out, but no one can tell me where to find it."

"Ah," said the hare, "you have a long way to go yet. You will have to walk at least seven hundred miles before you get to it."

"And how am I to travel such a distance?"

"Mount on my back," said the little hare, "and I will conduct you."

The young man obeyed. At each bound the little hare went seven miles, and it was not long before they reached a castle that was as large and beautiful as a castle could be.

"The golden blackbird is in a little cabin near by," said the little hare, "and you will easily find it. It lives in a little cage, with another cage beside it made all of gold. But whatever you do, be sure not to put it in the beautiful cage, or everybody in the castle will know that you have stolen it."

The youth found the golden blackbird standing on a wooden perch, but as stiff and rigid as if he was dead. And beside, was the beautiful cage, the cage of gold.

"Perhaps he would revive if I were to put him in that lovely cage," thought the youth.

The moment the golden blackbird had touched the bars of the splendid cage he awoke and began to whistle, so that all the servants of the castle ran to see what was the matter, saying that he was a thief and must be put in prison.

"No," he answered, "I am not a thief. If I have taken the golden blackbird, it is only that it may cure my father, who is ill, and I have traveled more than seven hundred miles in order to find it."

"Well," they replied, "we will let you go, and will even give you the golden blackbird if you are able to bring us the porcelain maiden."

The youth departed, weeping, and met the little hare, who was munching wild thyme.

"What are you crying for, my friend?" asked the hare.

"It is because," he answered, "the castle people will not allow me to carry off the golden blackbird without giving them the porcelain maiden in exchange."

"You have not followed my advice," said the little hare. "And you have put the golden blackbird into the fine cage."

"Alas! yes!"

"Don't despair. The porcelain maiden is a young girl, beautiful as Venus, who dwells two hundred miles from here. Jump on my back and I will take you there."

The little hare, who took seven miles in a stride, was there in no time at all, and he stopped on the borders of a lake.

"The porcelain maiden," said the hare to the youth, "will come here to bathe with her friends. Keep yourself out of sight behind the thicket, while I just eat a mouthful of thyme to refresh me. When she is in the lake be sure you hide her clothes, which are of dazzling whiteness, and do not give them back to her unless she consents to follow you."

The little hare left him, and almost immediately the porcelain maiden arrived with her friends. She undressed herself and got into the water. Then the young man glided up noiselessly and laid hold of her clothes, which he hid under a rock at some distance.

When the porcelain maiden was tired of playing in the water she came out to dress herself, but though she hunted for her clothes high and low she could find them nowhere. Her friends helped her in the search, but, seeing at last that it was of no use, they left her alone on the bank, weeping bitterly.

"Why do you cry?" said the young man, approaching her.

"Alas!" answered she, "while I was bathing some one stole my clothes, and my friends have abandoned me."

"I will find your clothes if you will only come with me."

And the porcelain maiden agreed to follow him, and after having given up her clothes the young man bought a small horse for her which went like the wind. The little hare brought them both back to seek for the golden blackbird, and when they drew near the castle where it lived the little hare said to the young man:

"Now, do be a little sharper than you were before, and you will manage to carry off both the golden blackbird and the porcelain maiden. Take the golden cage in one hand and leave the bird in the old cage where he is, and bring that away too."

The little hare then vanished. The youth did as he was bid, and the castle servants never noticed that he was carrying off the golden blackbird. When he reached the inn where his brothers were detained he delivered them by paying their debt. They set out all together, but as the two elder brothers were jealous of the success of the youngest, they took the opportunity as they were passing by the shores of a lake to throw themselves upon him, seize the golden blackbird, and fling him in the water. Then they continued their journey, taking with them the porcelain maiden, in the firm belief that their brother was drowned. But happily he had snatched in falling at a tuft of rushes and called loudly for help. The little hare came running to him and said: "Take hold of my leg and pull yourself out of the water."

When he was safe on shore the little hare said to him:

"Now, this is what you have to do: dress yourself like a Breton seeking a place as stableboy, and go and offer your services to your father. Once there, you will easily be able to make him understand the truth."

The young man did as the little hare bade him, and he went to his father's castle and inquired if they were not in want of a stableboy.

"Yes," replied his father, "very much indeed. But it is not an easy place. There is a little horse in the stable which will not let anyone go near it, and it has already kicked to death several people who have tried to groom it."

"I will undertake to groom it," said the youth. "I never saw the horse I was afraid of yet."

The little horse allowed itself to be rubbed down without a toss of its head and without a kick.

"Good gracious!" exclaimed the master. "How is it that he lets you touch him when no one else can go near him?"

"Perhaps he knows me," answered the stableboy.

Two or three days later the master said to him: "The porcelain maiden is here; but though she is as lovely as the dawn, she is so wicked that she scratches every one that approaches her. Try if she will accept your services."

When the youth entered the room where she was the golden blackbird broke forth into a joyful song, and the porcelain maiden sang too and jumped for joy.

"Good gracious!" cried the master." The porcelain maiden and the golden blackbird know you too?"

"Yes," replied the youth, "and the porcelain maiden can tell you the whole truth if she only will."

Then she told all that had happened, and how she had consented to follow the young man who had captured the golden blackbird.

"Yes," added the youth, "I delivered my brothers, who were kept prisoners in an inn, and as a reward they threw me into a lake. So I disguised myself and came here in order to prove the truth to you.

So the old lord embraced his son and promised that he should inherit all his possessions, and he put to death the two elder ones, who had deceived him and had tried to slay their own brother.

The young man married the porcelain maiden and had a splendid wedding feast

THE HALF-CHICK

Retold by Andrew Lang

Once upon a time there was a handsome black Spanish hen who had a large brood of chickens. They were all fine, plump little birds except the youngest, who was quite unlike his brothers and sisters. Indeed, he was such a strange, queer-looking creature that when he first clipped his shell his mother could scarcely believe her eyes, he was so different from the twelve other fluffy, downy, soft little chicks who nestled under her wings. This one looked just as if he had been cut in two. He had only one leg, and one wing, and one eye, and he had half a head and half a beak. His mother shook her head sadly as she looked at him and said:

"My youngest born is only a half-chick. He can never grow up a tall, handsome cock like his brothers. They will go out into the world and rule over poultry yards of their own; but this poor little fellow will always have to stay at home with his mother." And she called him Medio Pollito, which is Spanish for half-chick.

Now, though Medio Pollito was such an odd, helpless-looking little thing, his mother soon found that he was not at all willing to remain under her wing and protection. Indeed, in character he was as unlike his brothers and sisters as he was in appearance. They were good, obedient chickens, and when the old hen chicked after them they chirped and ran back to her side. But Medio Pollito had a roving spirit in spite of his one leg, and when his mother called to him to return to the coop, he pretended that he could not hear, because he had only one ear.

When she took the whole family out for a walk in the fields, Medio Pollito would hop away by himself and hide among the corn. Many an anxious minute his brothers and sisters had looking for him, while his mother ran to and fro cackling in fear and dismay.

As he grew older he became more self-willed and disobedient, and his manner to his mother was often very rude and his temper to the other chickens very disagreeable.

One day he had been out for a longer expedition than usual in the fields. On his return he strutted up to his mother with the peculiar little hop and kick which was his way of walking, and cocking his one eye at her in a very bold way, he said:

"Mother, I am tired of this life in a dull f farmyard, with nothing but a dreary maize-field to look at. I'm off to Madrid to see the king."

"To Madrid, Medio Pollito!" exclaimed his mother. "Why, you silly chick, it would be a long Journey for a grown-up cock, and a poor little thing like you would be tired out before you had gone half the distance. No, no, stay at home with your mother, and some day, when you are bigger, we will go a little journey together."

But Medio Pollito had made up his mind, and he would not listen to his mother's advice nor to the prayers and entreaties of his brothers and sisters.

"What is the use of our all crowding each other up in this poky little place?" he said. "When I have a fine courtyard of my own at the king's palace, I shall perhaps ask some of you to come and pay me a short visit."

And scarcely waiting to say good-by to his family, away he stumped down the high road that led to Madrid.

"Be sure that you are kind and civil to every one you meet," called his mother, running after him; but he was in such a hurry to be off that he did not wait to answer her or even to look back.

A little later in the day, as he was taking a short cut through a field, he passed a stream. Now, the stream was all choked up and overgrown with weeds and water-plants, so that its waters could not flow freely.

"Oh! Medio Pollito," it cried as the half-chick hopped along its banks, "do come and help me by clearing away these weeds."

"Help you, indeed!" exclaimed Medio Pollito, tossing his head and shaking the few feathers in his tail. "Do you think I have nothing to do but to waste my time on such trifles? Help yourself and don't trouble busy travelers. I am off to Madrid to see the king," and hoppity-kick, hoppity-kick, away stumped Medio Pollito.

A little later he came to a fire that had been left by some gypsies in a wood. It was burning very low and would soon be out.

"Oh! Medio Pollito," cried the fire in a weak, wavering voice as the half-chick approached, "in a few minutes I shall go quite out unless you put some sticks and dry leaves upon me. Do help me or I shall die!"

"Help you, indeed!" answered Medio Pollito. "I have other things to do. Gather sticks for yourself and don't trouble me. I am off to Madrid to see the king," and hoppity-kick, hoppity-kick, away stumped Medio Pollito.

The next morning, as he was getting near Madrid, he passed a large chestnut tree, in whose branches the wind was caught and entangled.

"Oh! Medio Pollito," called the wind, "do hop up here and help me to get free of these branches. I cannot come away and it is so uncomfortable."

"It is your own fault for going there," answered Medio Pollito. "I can't waste all my morning stopping here to help you. Just shake yourself off, and don't hinder me, for I am off to Madrid to see the king," and hoppity-kick, hoppity-kick, away stumped Medio Pollito in great glee, for the towers and roofs of Madrid were now in sight. When he entered the town he saw before him a great, splendid house, with soldiers standing before the gates. This he knew must be the king's palace, and he determined to hop up to the front gate and wait there until the king came out. But as he was hopping past one of the back windows the king's cook saw him.

"Here is the very thing I want," he exclaimed, "for the king has just sent a message to say that he must have chicken broth for his dinner." Opening the window he stretched out his arm, caught Medio Pollito, and popped him into the broth pot that was standing near the fire. Oh! how wet and clammy the water felt as it went over Medio Pollito's head, making his feathers cling to him.

"Water! water!" he cried in his despair, "do have pity upon me and do not wet me like this."

"Ah! Medio Pollito," replied the water, "you would not help me when I was a little stream away on the fields. Now you must be punished."

Then the fire began to burn and scald Medio Pollito, and he danced and hopped from one side of the pot to the other, trying to get away from the heat and crying out in pain:

"Fire! fire! do not scorch me like this; you can't think how it hurts."

"Ah! Medio Pollito," answered the fire, "you would not help me when I was dying away in the wood. You are being punished."

At last, just when the pain was so great that Medio Pollito thought he must die, the cook lifted up the lid of the pot to see if the broth was ready for the king's dinner.

"Look here!" he cried in horror, "this chicken is quite useless. It is burned to a cinder. I can't send it up to the royal table." And opening the window he threw Medio Pollito out in the street. But the wind caught him up and whirled him through the air so quickly that Medio Pollito could scarcely breathe, and his heart beat against his side till he thought it would break.

"Oh, wind I" at last he gasped out, "if you hurry me along like this you will kill me. Do let me rest a moment, or — "

But he was so breathless that he could not finish his sentence.

"Ah! Medio Pollito," replied the wind, "when I was caught in the branches of the chestnut tree you would not help me. Now you are punished." And he swirled Medio Pollito over the roofs of the houses till they reached the highest church in the town, and there he left him fastened to the top of the steeple.

And there stands Medio Pollito to this day. And if you go to Madrid and walk through the streets till you come to the highest church, you will see Medio Pollito perched on his one leg on the steeple, with his one wing drooping at his side and gazing sadly out of his one eye over the town.

THE THREE BROTHERS

By Hermann R. Kletke

There was once upon a time a witch who in the shape of a hawk used every night to break the windows of a certain village church. In the same village there lived three brothers, who were all determined to kill the mischievous hawk. But in vain did the two eldest mount guard in the church with their guns; as soon as the bird appeared high above their heads sleep overpowered them, and they only awoke to hear the windows crashing in.

Then the younger brother took his turn of guarding the windows, and to prevent his being overcome by sleep he placed a lot of thorns under his chin, so that if he felt drowsy and nodded his head they would prick him and keep him awake.

The moon was already risen and it was as light as day, when suddenly he heard a fearful noise, and at the same time a terrible desire to sleep overpowered him.

His eyelids closed and his head sank on his shoulders, but the thorns ran into him and were so painful that he awoke at once. He saw the hawk swooping down upon the church, and in a moment he had seized his gun and shot at the bird. The hawk fell heavily under a big stone, severely wounded in its right wing. The youth ran to look at it and saw that a huge abyss had opened below the stone. He went at once to fetch his brothers, and with their help dragged a lot of pine wood and ropes to the spot. They fastened some of the burning pine wood to the end of the rope and let it slowly down to the bottom of the abyss. At first it was quite dark, and the flaming torch only lit up dirty gray stone walls. But the youngest brother determined to explore the abyss, and letting himself down by the rope he soon reached the bottom. Here he found a lovely meadow full of green trees and exquisite flowers.

In the middle of the meadow stood a huge stone castle, with an iron gate leading to it, which was wide open. Everything in the castle seemed to be made of copper, and the only inhabitant he could discover was a lovely girl, who was combing her golden hair; and he noticed that whenever one of her hairs fell on the ground it rang out like pure metal. The youth looked at her more closely, and saw that her skin was smooth and fair, her blue eyes bright and sparkling, and her hair as golden as the sun. He fell in love with her on the spot, and kneeling at her feet he implored her to become his wife.

The lovely girl accepted his proposal gladly; but at the same time she warned him that she could never come up to the world above till her mother, the old witch, was dead. And she went on to tell him that the only way in which the old creature could be killed was with the sword that hung up in the castle; but the sword was so heavy that no one could lift it.

Then the youth went into a room in the castle where everything was made of silver, and here he found another beautiful girl, the sister of his bride. She was combing her silver hair, and every hair that fell on the ground rang out like pure metal. The second girl handed him the sword, but though he tried with all his strength he could not lift it. At last a third sister came to him and gave him a drop of something to drink, which she said would give him the needful strength. He drank one drop, but still he could not lift the sword; then he drank a second and the sword began to move; but only after he had drunk a third drop was he able to swing the sword over his head.

Then he hid himself in the castle and awaited the old witch's arrival. At last as it was beginning to grow dark she appeared. She swooped down upon a big apple tree, and after shaking some golden apples from it she pounced down upon the earth. As soon as her feet touched the ground she became transformed from a hawk into a woman. This was the moment the youth was waiting for, and he swung his mighty sword in the air with all his strength and the witch's head fell off, and her blood spurted upon the walls.

Without fear of any further danger, he packed up all the treasures of the castle into great chests and gave his brothers a signal to pull them up out of the abyss. First the treasures were attached to the rope and then the three lovely girls. And now everything was up above and only he himself remained below. But as he was a little suspicious of his brothers, he fastened a heavy stone on to the rope and let them pull it up. At first they heaved with a will, but when the stone was halfway up they let it drop suddenly, and it fell to the bottom broken into a hundred pieces.

"So that's what would have happened to my bones had I trusted myself to them," said the youth sadly; and he cried bitterly, not because of the treasures, but because of the lovely girl with her swanlike neck and golden hair.

For a long time he wandered sadly all through the beautiful underworld, and one day he met a magician who asked him the cause of his tears. The youth told him all that had befallen him, and the magician said:

"Do not grieve, young man! If you will guard the children who are hidden in the golden apple tree I will bring you at once up to the earth. Another magician who lives in this land always eats my children up. It is in vain that I have hidden them under the earth and locked them into the castle. Now I have hidden them in the apple tree; hide yourself there, too, and at midnight you will see my enemy."

The youth climbed up the tree and picked some of the beautiful golden apples, which he ate for his supper. At midnight the wind began to rise and a rustling sound was heard at the foot of the tree. The youth looked down and beheld a long thick serpent beginning to crawl up the tree. It wound itself round the stem and gradually got higher and higher. It stretched its huge head, in which the eyes glittered fiercely, among the branches, searching for the nest in which the little children lay. They trembled with terror when they saw the hideous creature and hid themselves beneath the leaves.

Then the youth swung his mighty sword in the air, and with one blow cut off the serpent's head. He cut up the rest of the body into little bits and strewed them to the four winds.

The father of the rescued children was so delighted over the death of his enemy that he told the youth to get on his back, and thus he carried him up to the world above.

With what joy did he hurry now to his brothers' house! He burst into a room where they were all assembled, but no one knew who he was. Only his bride, who was serving as cook to her sisters, recognized her lover at once.

His brothers, who had quite believed he was dead, yielded him up his treasures at once and flew into the woods in terror. But the good youth forgave them all they had done and divided his treasures with them. Then he built himself a big castle with golden windows, and there he lived happily with his golden-haired wife till the end of their lives.

THE GLASS MOUNTAIN

By Hermann R. Kletke

Once upon a time there was a glass mountain at the top of which stood a castle made of pure gold, and in front of the castle there grew an apple tree on which there were golden apples.

Anyone who picked an apple gained admittance into the golden castle, and there in a silver room sat an enchanted princess of surpassing fairness and beauty. She was as rich, too, as she was beautiful, for the cellars of the castle were full of precious stones, and great chests of the finest gold stood round the walls of all the rooms.

Many knights had come from afar to try their luck, but it was in vain they attempted to climb the mountain. In spite of having their horses shod with sharp nails, no one managed to get more than halfway up, and then they all fell back right down to the bottom of the steep, slippery hill. Sometimes they broke an arm, sometimes a leg, and many a brave man had broken his neck even.

The beautiful princess sat at her window and watched the bold knights trying to reach her on their splendid horses. The sight of her always gave men fresh courage, and they flocked from the four quarters of the globe to attempt the work of rescuing her. But all in vain, and for seven years the princess had sat now and waited for some one to scale the glass mountain.

A heap of corpses both of riders and horses lay round the mountain, and many dying men lay groaning there unable to go any further with their wounded limbs. The whole neighborhood had the appearance of a vast churchyard. In three more days the seven years would be at an end, when a knight in golden armor and mounted on a spirited steed was seen making his way toward the fatal hill.

Sticking his spurs into his horse he made a rush at the mountain and got up halfway, then he calmly turned his horse's head and came down again without a slip or stumble. The following day he started in the same way; the horse trod on the glass as if it had been level earth, and sparks of fire flew from its hoofs. All the other knights gazed in astonishment, for he had almost gained the summit, and in another moment he would have reached the apple tree; but of a sudden a huge eagle rose up and spread its mighty wings, hitting as it did so the knight's horse in the eye. The beast shied, opened its wide nostrils, and tossed its mane, then rearing high up in the air, its hind feet slipped and it fell with its rider down the steep mountain side. Nothing was left of either of them except their bones, which rattled in the battered, golden armor like dry peas in a pod.

And now there was only one more day before the close of the seven years. Then there arrived on the scene a mere school boy—a merry, happy-hearted youth, but at the same time strong and well grown. He saw how many knights had broken their necks in vain, but undaunted he approached the steep mountain on foot and began the ascent.

For long he had heard his parents speak of the beautiful princess who sat in the golden castle at the top of the glass mountain. He listened to all he heard and determined that he too would try his luck. But first he went to the forest and caught a lynx, and cutting off the creature's sharp claws, he fastened them on to his own hands and feet.

Armed with these weapons he boldly started up the glass mountain. The sun was nearly going down, and the youth had not got more than halfway up. He could hardly draw breath he was so worn out, and his mouth was parched by thirst. A huge black cloud passed over his head, but in vain did he beg and beseech her to let a drop of water fall on him. He opened his mouth, but the black cloud sailed past and not as much as a drop of dew moistened his dry lips.

His feet were torn and bleeding, and he could only hold on now with his hands. Evening closed in, and he strained his eyes to see if he could behold the top of the mountain. Then he gazed beneath him, and what a sight met his eyes! A yawning abyss, with certain and terrible death at the bottom, reeking with half-decayed bodies of horses and riders! And this had been the end of all the other brave men who like himself had attempted the ascent.

It was almost pitch dark now, and only the stars lit up the glass mountain. The poor boy still clung on as if glued to the glass by his blood-stained hands. He made no struggle to get higher, for all his strength had left him, and seeing no hope he calmly awaited death. Then all of a sudden he fell into a deep sleep, and forgetful of his dangerous position he slumbered sweetly. But all the same, although he slept, he had stuck his sharp claws so firmly into the glass that he was quite safe not to fall.

Now, the golden apple tree was guarded by the eagle which had overthrown the golden knight and his horse. Every night it flew round the glass mountain keeping a careful lookout, and no sooner had the moon emerged from the clouds than the bird rose up from the apple tree, and circling round in the air caught sight of the sleeping youth.

Greedy for carrion, and sure that this must be a fresh corpse, the bird swooped down upon the boy. But he was awake now, and perceiving the eagle, he determined by its help to save himself.

The eagle dug its sharp claws into the tender flesh of the youth, but he bore the pain without a sound and seized the bird's two feet with his hands. The creature in terror lifted him high up into the air and began to circle round the tower of the castle. The youth held on bravely. He saw the glittering palace, which by the pale rays of the moon looked like a dim lamp; and he saw the high windows, and round one of them a balcony in which the beautiful princess sat lost in sad thoughts. Then the boy saw that he was close to the apple tree, and drawing a small knife from his belt he cut off both the eagle's feet. The bird rose up in the air in its agony and vanished into the clouds, and the youth fell on to the broad branches of the apple tree.

Then he drew out the claws of the eagle's feet that had remained in his flesh and put the peel of one of the golden apples on the wound, and in one moment it was healed and well again. He pulled several of the beautiful apples and put them in his pocket; then he entered the castle. The door was guarded by a great dragon, but as soon as he threw an apple at it the beast vanished.

At the same moment a gate opened, and the youth perceived a courtyard full of flowers and beautiful trees, and on a balcony sat the lovely enchanted princess with her retinue.

As soon as she saw the youth she ran toward him and greeted him as her husband and master. She gave him all her treasures, and the youth became a rich and mighty ruler. But he never returned to the earth, for only the mighty eagle, who had been the guardian of the princess and of the castle, could have carried on his wings the enormous treasure down to the world. But as the eagle had lost its feet, it died, and its body was found in a wood on the glass mountain.

One day when the youth was strolling about the palace garden with the princess, his wife, he looked down over the edge of the glass mountain and saw to his astonishment a great number of people gathered there. He blew his silver whistle, and the swallow who acted as messenger in the golden castle flew past.

"Fly down and ask what the matter is," he said to the little bird, who sped off like lightning and soon returned saying:

"The blood of the eagle has restored all the people below to life. All those who have perished on this mountain are awakening up to-day, as it were from a sleep, and are mounting their horses, and the whole population are gazing on this unheard-of wonder with joy and amazement."

HUNTSMAN THE UNLUCKY

By John T. Naaké

Once upon a time there lived a huntsman. He would go every day in search of game, but it often happened that he killed nothing, and so was obliged to return home with his bag empty. On that account he was nicknamed "Huntsman the Unlucky." At last he was reduced by his ill fortune to such extremities that he had not a piece of bread nor a kopek left. The wretched man wandered about the forest, cold and hungry; he had eaten nothing for three days, and was nearly dying of starvation. He lay down on the grass determined to put an end to his existence; happily better thoughts came into his mind; he crossed himself, and threw away the gun. Suddenly he heard a rustling noise near him. It seemed to issue from some thick grass close at hand. The hunter got up and approached the spot. He then observed that the grass partly hid a gloomy abyss, from the bottom of which there rose a stone, and on it lay a small jar. As he looked and listened the hunter heard a small voice crying—

"Dear, kind traveler, release me!"

The voice seemed to proceed from the little jar. The courageous hunter, walking carefully from one stone to another, approached the spot where the jar lay, took it up gently, and heard a voice crying from within like the chirping of a grasshopper—

"Release me, and I will be of service to you."

"Who are you, my little friend?" asked Huntsman the Unlucky.

"I have no name, and cannot be seen by human eyes," answered a soft voice. "If you want me, call 'Murza!' A wicked magician put me in this jar, sealed it with the seal of King Solomon, and then threw me into this fearful place, where I have lain for seventy years."

"Very good," said Huntsman the Unlucky; "I will give you your liberty, and then we shall see how you will keep your word." He broke the seal and opened the little jar—there was nothing in it!

"Halloa! where are you, my friend?" cried the hunter.

"By your side," a voice answered.

The hunter looked about him, but could see no one.

"Murza!"

"Ready! I await your orders. I am your servant for the next three days, and will do whatever you desire. You have only to say, 'Go there, I know not where; bring something, I know not what.'"

"Very well," said the hunter. "You will doubtless know best what is wanted: Go there, I know not where; bring something, I know not what."

As soon as the hunter had uttered these words there appeared before him a table covered with dishes, each filled with the most delicious viands, as if they had come direct from a banquet of the czar. The hunter sat down at the table, and ate and drank till he was satisfied. He then rose, crossed himself, and, bowing on all sides, exclaimed —

"Thank you! thank you!"

Instantly the table, and everything else with it, disappeared, and the hunter continued his journey.

After walking some distance he sat down by the roadside to rest. It so happened that while the hunter was resting himself, there passed through the forest a gypsy thief, leading a horse which he wanted to sell.

"I wish I had the money to buy the horse with," thought the hunter; "what a pity my pockets are empty! However, I will ask my invisible friend. Murza!"

"Ready!"

"Go there, I know not where; bring something, I know not what."

In less than a minute the hunter heard the money chinking in his pocket; gold poured into them, he knew not how nor whence.

"Thanks! you have kept your word," said the hunter.

He then began to bargain with the gypsy for the horse. Having agreed upon the price, he paid the man in gold, who, staring at the hunter with his mouth wide open, wondered where Huntsman the Unlucky had got so much money from. Parting from the hunter, the gypsy thief ran with all his speed to the farther end of the forest, and whistled. There was no answer. "They are asleep," thought the gypsy, and entered a cavern where some robbers, lying on the skins of animals, were resting themselves.

"Halloa, comrades! Are you asleep?" cried the gypsy. "Get up, quick! or you will lose a fine bird. He is alone in the forest, and his pockets are full of gold. Make haste!"

The robbers sprang up, mounted their horses, and galloped after the hunter.

The hunter heard the clatter, and seeing himself suddenly surrounded by robbers, cried out— "Murza!"

"Ready!" answered a voice near him. "Go there, I know not where; bring something, I know not what."

There was a rustling noise heard in the forest, and then something from behind the trees fell upon the robbers. They were knocked from their horses, and scattered on all sides; yet no hand was seen to touch them. The robbers, thrown upon the ground, could not raise themselves, and the hunter, thankful and rejoicing at his deliverance, rode on, and soon found his way out of the dark forest, and came upon a town.

Near this town there were pitched tents full of soldiers. Huntsman the Unlucky was told that an enormous army of Tartars had come, under the command of their khan, who, angry at being refused the hand of the beautiful Princess Milovzora, the daughter of the czar, had declared war against him. The hunter had seen the Princess Milovzora when she was out hunting in the forest. She used to ride a beautiful horse, and carry a golden lance in her hand; a magnificent quiver of arrows hung from her shoulder. When her veil was lifted up she appeared like the spring sunlight, to give light to the eyes and warmth to the heart.

The hunter reflected for a little while, and then cried, "Murza!"

In an instant he found himself dressed in splendid attire; his jacket was embroidered with gold, he wore a beautiful mantle on his shoulders, and ostrich feathers hung gracefully down from the top of his helmet, fastened by a brooch of a ruby surrounded by pearls. The hunter went into the castle, presented himself before the czar, and offered to drive away the forces of the enemy on condition that the czar gave him the beautiful Princess Milovzora for his wife.

The czar was greatly surprised, but did not like to refuse such an offer at once; he first asked the hunter his name, his birth and his possessions.

"I am called Huntsman the Unlucky, Master of Murza the Invisible."

The czar thought the young stranger was mad; the courtiers, however, who had seen him before, assured the czar that the stranger exactly resembled Huntsman the Unlucky, whom they knew; but how he had got that splendid dress they could not tell.

Then the czar demanded:

"Do you hear what they say? If you are telling lies, you will lose your head. Let us see, then, how you will overcome the enemy with the forces of your invisible Murza?"

"Be of good hope, czar," answered the hunter; "as soon as I say the word, everything will be completed."

"Good," said the czar. "If you have spoken the truth you shall have my daughter for your wife; if not, your head will be the forfeit."

The hunter said to himself, "I shall either become a prince, or I am a lost man."

He then whispered, "Murza, go there, I know not where; do this, I know not what."

A few minutes passed, and there was nothing to be heard or seen. Huntsman the Unlucky turned pale; the czar, enraged, ordered him to be seized and put in irons, when suddenly the firing of guns was heard in the distance. The czar and his courtiers ran out on the steps leading to the castle, and saw bodies of men approaching from both right and left, their standards waving gracefully in the air; the soldiers were splendidly equipped. The czar could hardly believe his eyes, for he himself had no troops so fine as these.

"This is no delusion!" cried Huntsman the Unlucky. "These are the forces of my invisible friend."

"Let them drive away the enemy then, if they can," said the czar.

The hunter waved his handkerchief. The army wheeled into position; music burst forth in a martial strain, and then a great cloud of dust arose. When the dust had cleared away, the army was gone.

The czar invited Huntsman the Unlucky to dinner, and asked him numerous questions about Murza the Invisible. At the second course the news came that the enemy was flying in every direction, completely routed. The terrified Tartars had left all their tents and baggage behind them. The czar thanked the hunter for his assistance, and informed his daughter that he had found a husband for her. Princess Milovzora blushed upon receiving this intelligence, then turned pale, and began to shed tears. The hunter whispered something to Murza, and the princess's tears changed into precious stones as they fell. The courtiers hastened to pick them up—they were pearls and diamonds. The princess smiled at this, and overcome with pleasure gave her hand to Huntsman the Unlucky—unlucky no longer. Then began the feast. But here the story must end.

STORY OF LITTLE SIMPLETON

By John T. Naaké

Once there lived a peasant and his wife who had three daughters. The two elder girls were cunning and selfish; the youngest was simple and open-hearted, and on that account came to be called, first by her sisters and afterward by her father and mother, "Little Simpleton." Little Simpleton was pushed about, had to fetch everything that was wanted, and was always kept at work; but she was ever ready to do what she was told, and never uttered a word of complaint. She would water the garden, prepare pine splinters, milk the cows, and feed the ducks; she had to wait upon everybody — in a word, she was the drudge of the family.

One day, as the peasant was going with the hay to market, he asked his daughters what they would like him to buy for them.

"Buy me some kumach (Red wool stuff from Bucharest) for a sarafan (A long dress worn by the Russian peasant women) father," answered the eldest daughter.

"And me some nankeen," said the second. The youngest daughter alone did not ask for a present. The peasant was moved with compassion for the girl; although a simpleton she was still his daughter.

Turning to her he asked "Well, Little Simpleton, what shall I buy for you?"

Little Simpleton smiled and replied —

"Buy me, dearest father, a little silver plate and a little apple."

"What do you want them for?" asked her sisters.

"I will make the little apple roll round the plate, and will say some words to it which an old woman taught me because I gave her a cake."

The peasant promised to buy his daughters what they asked of him, and then started for market. He sold his hay, and bought the presents: some nankeen for one of his daughters, for another some kumach, and for Little Simpleton a little silver plate and a little apple. Then he returned home and gave these things to his daughters.

The girls were delighted; the two elder ones made themselves sarafans, and laughed at Little Simpleton, wondering what she would do with the silver plate and the apple.

Little Simpleton did not eat the apple, but sat down in a corner and cried—

"Roll, roll, little apple on the silver plate, and show me towns and fields, forests and seas, lofty mountains and beautiful skies."

And the apple began to roll on the plate, and there appeared on it town after town; ships sailing on the seas, and people in the fields; mountains and beautiful skies; suns and stars. All these things looked so beautiful, and were so wonderful, that it would be impossible to tell of them in a story, or describe them with the pen.

At first the elder sisters looked at the little plate with delight; soon, however, their hearts were filled with envy, and they began to try to get it from their younger sister. But the girl would not part with it on any account. Then the wicked girls said— "Dearest sister, let us go into the forest to gather blackberries."

Little Simpleton got up, gave the plate and apple to her father, and went with them into the forest. They walked about and gathered blackberries. All at once they saw a spade lying upon the ground. The wicked sisters killed Little Simpleton with it, and buried her under a birch tree.

They returned home late, and told their father, "The Simpleton is lost; she ran away from us in the forest; we searched, but could not find her anywhere. The wolves must have eaten her."

The peasant regretted the loss of his daughter bitterly; for although so simple she was still his child. The wicked sisters also shed tears. Her father put the little silver plate and the little apple into a box, and locked them up.

Next morning a shepherd was tending his sheep near the place, playing on his pipe, and searching in the forest for one of his flock that was missing. He observed the little grave under the birch tree; it was covered by the most lovely flowers, and out of the middle of the grave there grew a reed. The shepherd cut off the reed, and made a pipe of it. As soon as the pipe was prepared, oh, wonderful! It began to play of itself, and say—

"Play, oh pipe, play! and comfort my poor parents and sisters. I was killed for the sake of my little silver plate and my little apple."

When the people heard of this they ran out of their huts, and all came round the shepherd and began to ask him who was killed.

"Good people," answered the shepherd, "I don't know who it is. While searching for one of my sheep in the forest, I came upon a grave covered with flowers. Above them all stood a reed. I cut off the reed and made this pipe of it. It plays of itself, and you have heard what it says."

The father of Little Simpleton happened to be present. He took the pipe into his own hand, and it began to play:

"Play, oh pipe, play! Comfort my poor father and mother. I was killed for the sake of my little silver plate and my little apple." The peasant asked the shepherd to take him to the place where he had cut the reed. They all went into the forest, saw the grave, and were astonished at the sight of the lovely flowers which grew there. They opened the grave, and there discovered the body of a girl, which the poor man recognized as that of his youngest daughter. There she lay, murdered—but by whom no one could tell. The people asked one another who it was that had killed the poor girl. Suddenly the pipe began to play—

"Oh, my dearest father; my sisters brought me to this forest, and here killed me for the sake of my little plate and my little apple. You will not bring me to life until you fetch some of the water from the czar's well."

Then the wicked sisters confessed it all. They were seized and cast into a dark prison, to await the pleasure of the czar. The peasant set out for the capital. As soon as he arrived at the city, he went to the palace, saw the czar, told his story, and begged permission to take some water from the well. The czar said, "You may take some water of life from my well, and as soon as you have restored your daughter to life, bring her here with her little plate and the little apple; bring your other two daughters also."

The peasant bowed to the ground, and returned home with a bottle full of the water of life. He hastened to the grave in the forest, lifted up the body of his daughter, and as soon as he had sprinkled it with the water the girl came to life again, and threw herself into his arms. All who were present were moved to tears.

Then the peasant started again for the capital, and arriving there went at once to the czar's palace. The czar came out, and saw the peasant with his three daughters, two of them with their arms bound, the third, as beautiful as the spring flowers, stood near, the tears like diamonds falling down her cheeks. The czar was very angry with the two wicked sisters; then he asked the youngest for her little plate and apple. The girl took the box from her father's hands, and said—

"Sire, what would you like to see? Your towns or your armies; the ships at sea, or the beautiful stars in the sky?"

Then she made the little apple roll round the plate, and there appeared on it many towns, one after the other, with bodies of soldiers near them, with their standards and artillery. Then the soldiers made ready for the fight, and the officers stood in their places. The firing commenced, the smoke arose, and hid it all from view. The little apple began again to roll on the plate, and there appeared the sea covered with ships, their flags streaming in the wind. The guns began to fire, the smoke arose, and again all disappeared from their sight. The apple again began to roll on the plate, and there appeared on it the beautiful sky with suns and stars.

The czar was astonished. The girl fell down on her knees before him, and cried —

"Oh, Sire, take my little plate and my little apple, and forgive my sisters!"

The czar was moved by her tears and entreaties and forgave the wicked sisters; the delighted girl sprang up and began to embrace and kiss them. The czar smiled, took her by the hand and said, "I honor the goodness of your heart, and admire your beauty. Would you like to become my wife?"

"Sire," answered the beautiful girl, "I obey your royal command; but allow me first to ask my parents' permission."

The delighted peasant at once gave his consent; they sent for the mother, and she, too, gladly bestowed her blessing.

"One favor more," said the beautiful girl to the czar. "Permit my parents and sisters to remain with me."

On hearing this the sisters fell down on their knees before her, and cried —

"We are not worthy of so much favor!"

"Dearest sisters," said the beautiful girl, "all is forgotten and forgiven. They who remember the past with malice deserve to lose their sight."

She then tried to lift them up from the ground, but they, shedding bitter tears, would not rise. Then the czar, looking at them with a frown, bade them get up; he allowed them, however, to stay in the palace.

A magnificent entertainment then began: the palace was splendidly lighted up, and looked like the sun among the clouds. The czar and czarina rode out in an open chariot and showed themselves to the people, who cried joyfully —

"Long live czar and czarina! May they shine upon us like the glorious sun for years and years to come!"

THE GOLDEN FISH

By L. M. Gask

Upon a certain island in the middle of the sea dwelt an old man and his wife. They were so poor that they often went short of bread, for the fish he caught were their only means of livelihood.

One day when the man had been fishing for many hours without success, he hooked a small Gold Fish, whose eyes were bright as diamonds.

"Let me go, kind man," the little creature cried. "I should not make a mouthful either for yourself or your wife, and my own mate waits for me down in the waters."

The old man was so moved by his pleadings that he took him off the hook and threw him back into the sea. Before he swam off to rejoin his mate, the Gold Fish promised that in return for his kindness he would come to the fisherman's help if ever he wanted him. Laughing merrily at this, for he did not believe that a fish could help him except by providing him with food, the old man went home and told his wife.

"What!" she cried, "you actually let him go when you had caught him? It was just like your stupidity. We have not a scrap of bread in the house, and now, I suppose, we must starve!"

Her reproaches continued for so long that though he scarcely believed what the fish had said, the poor old man thought that at least it would do no harm to put him to the test. He therefore hastened back to the shore, and stood at the very edge of the waves.

"Golden Fish, Golden Fish!" he called. "Come to me, I pray, with your tail in the water, and your head lifted up toward me!"

As the last word was uttered the Gold Fish popped up his head.

"You see I have kept my promise," he said. "What can I do for you, my good friend?"

"There is not a scrap of bread in the house," quavered the old man, "and my wife is very angry with me for letting you go.

"Don't trouble about that!" said the Gold Fish in an off-hand manner; "you will find bread, and to spare, when you go home." And the old man hurried away to see if his little friend had spoken truly.

Surely enough, he found that the pan was full of fine white loaves.

"I did not do so badly for you after all, good wife!" he said, as they ate their supper; but his wife was anything but satisfied. The more she had, the more she wanted, and she lay awake planning what they should demand from the Gold Fish next.

"Wake up, you lazy man!" she cried to her husband, early next morning. "Go down to the sea and tell your fish that I must have a new washtub."

The old man did as his wife bade him, and the moment he called the Gold Fish reappeared. He seemed quite willing to grant the new request, and on his return home the old man found a beautiful new washtub in the small yard at the back of their cabin.

"Why didn't you ask for a new cabin too?" his wife said angrily. "If you had had a grain of sense you would have done this without being told. Go back at once, and say that we must have one.

The old man was rather ashamed to trouble his friend again so soon; but the Gold Fish was as obliging as ever.

"Very well," he said, "a new cabin you shall have." And the old mart found one so spick-and-span that he hardly dare cross the floor for fear of soiling it. It would have pleased him greatly had his wife been contented, but she, good woman, did nothing but grumble still.

"Tell your Gold Fish," she said next day, "that I want to be a duchess, with many servants at my beck and call, and a splendid carriage to drive in.

Once more her wish was granted, but now her husband's plight was hard indeed. She would not let him share her palace, but ordered him off to the stables, where he was forced to keep company with her grooms. In a few days, however, he grew reconciled to his lot, for here he could live in peace, while he learned that she was leading those around her a terrible life, it was not long before she sent for him again.

"Summon the Gold Fish," she commanded haughtily, "and tell him I wish to be Queen of the Waters, and to rule over all the fish."

The poor old man felt sorry for the fish if they had to be under her rule, for prosperity had quite spoiled her. However, he dared not disobey, and once more summoned his powerful friend.

"Make your wife the Queen of the Waters?" exclaimed the Gold Fish. "That is the last thing I should do. She is unfit to reign, for she cannot rule herself or her desires. I shall make her once more a poor old woman. Adieu! You will see me no more."

The old man returned sorrowfully with this unpleasant message, to find the palace transformed into a humble cabin, and his wife in a skirt of threadbare stuff in place of the rich brocade which she had worn of late. She was sad and humble, and much more easy to live with than she had been before. Her husband therefore had occasion many times to think gratefully of the Gold Fish, and sometimes when drawing up his net the glint of the sun upon the scales of his captives would give him a moment's hope—which, alas! was as often disappointed—that once again he was to see his benefactor.

THE WONDERFUL HAIR

By W. S. Karajich

There once lived a man who was very poor, and who had many children; so many that he was unable to support them. As he could not endure the idea of their perishing of hunger, he was often tempted to destroy them; his wife alone prevented him. One night, as he lay asleep, there appeared to him a lovely child in a vision. The child said—

"Oh, man! I see your soul is in danger, in the thought of killing your helpless children. But I know you are poor, and am come here to help you. You will find under your pillow in the morning a looking-glass, a red handkerchief, and an embroidered scarf. Take these three things, but show them to no one, and go to the forest. In that forest you will find a rivulet. Walk by the side of this rivulet until you come to its source; there you will see a girl, as bright as the sun, with long hair streaming down her shoulders. Take care that she does you no harm. Say not a word to her; for if you utter a single syllable, she will change you into a fish or some other creature, and eat you. Should she ask you to comb her hair, obey her. As you comb it, you will find one hair as red as blood; pull it out, and run away with it. Be swift, for she will follow you. Then throw on the ground, first the embroidered scarf, then the red handkerchief, and last of all the looking-glass; they will delay her pursuit of you. Sell the hair to some rich man; but see that you do not allow yourself to be cheated, for it is of boundless worth. Its produce will make you rich and thus you will be able to feed your children."

Next morning, when the poor man awoke, he found under his pillow exactly the things the child mad told him of in his dream. He went immediately into the forest, and when he had discovered the rivulet he walked by the side of it, on and on, until he reached its source. There he saw a girl sitting on the bank, threading a needle with the rays of the sun. She was embroidering a net made of the hair of heroes, spread on a frame before her. He approached and bowed to her. The girl got up and demanded—

"Where did you come from, strange knight?"

The man remained silent. Again she asked him—

"Who are you, and why do you come here?" And many other questions. But he remained silent as a stone, indicating with his hands only that he was dumb and in need of help. She told him to sit at her feet, and when he had gladly done so, she inclined her head toward him, that he might comb her hair. He began to arrange her hair as if to comb it, but as soon as he had found the red one, he separated it from the rest, plucked it out, leaped up, and ran from her with his utmost speed.

The girl sprang after him, and was soon at his heels. The man, turning round as he ran, and seeing that his pursuer would soon overtake him, threw the embroidered scarf on the ground, as he had been told. When the girl saw it, she stopped and began to examine it; turning it over on both sides, and admiring the embroidery. Meanwhile the man gained a considerable distance in advance. The girl tied the scarf round her bosom and recommenced the pursuit. When the man saw that she was again about to overtake him, he threw down the red handkerchief. At the sight of it, the girl again stopped, examined, and wondered at it; the peasant, in the meantime, was again enabled to increase the distance between them. When the girl perceived this, she became furious, and throwing away both scarf and handkerchief began to run with increased speed after him. She was just upon the point of catching the poor peasant, when he threw the looking-glass at her feet. At the sight of the looking-glass, the like of which she had never seen before, the girl checked herself, picked it up, and looked in it. Seeing her own face, she fancied there was another girl looking at her. While she was thus occupied the man ran so far that she could not possibly overtake him. When the girl saw that further pursuit was useless, she turned back, and the peasant, joyful and unhurt, reached his home. Once within doors he showed the hair to his wife and children, and told them all that had happened to him; but his wife only laughed at the story. The peasant, however, took no heed of her ridicule, but went to a neighboring town to sell the hair. He was soon surrounded by a crowd of people, and some merchants began to bid for his prize. One merchant offered him one gold piece, another two, for the single hair, and so on, until the price rose to a hundred gold pieces. Meanwhile the king, hearing of the wonderful red hair, ordered the peasant to be called in, and offered him a thousand gold pieces for it. The man joyfully sold it for that sum.

What wonderful kind of hair was this after all? The king split it carefully open from end to end, and in it was found the story of many marvelous secrets of nature, and of things that had happened since the creation of the world.

Thus the peasant became rich, and henceforth lived happily with his wife and children. The child he had seen in his dream, was an angel sent down from heaven to succor him, and to reveal to mankind the knowledge of many wonderful things which had hitherto remained unexplained.

THE LANGUAGE OF ANIMALS

By W. S. Karajich

A certain man had a shepherd who had served him faithfully and honestly for many years. One day, as the Shepherd was tending his sheep, he heard a hissing noise in the forest, and wondered what it could he. He went, therefore, into the wood in the direction of the sound, to learn what it was. There he saw that the dry grass and leaves had caught fire, and in the middle of a burning circle a Snake was hissing. The Shepherd stopped to see what the Snake would do, for the fire was burning all around it, and the flames approached it nearer and nearer every moment. Then the Snake cried from amid the fire—

"Oh, Shepherd! for heaven's sake save me from this fire!"

The Shepherd stretched out his crook over the flames to the Snake, and the Snake passed along it on to his hand, and from his hand it crawled to his neck, where it twisted itself round.

When the Shepherd perceived this, he was greatly alarmed, and said to the Snake—

"What have I done in an evil hour? Have I saved you to my own destruction?"

The Snake answered him, "Fear not, but carry me to my father's house. My father is the King of the snakes."

The Shepherd, however, began to beg the Snake to excuse him, saying that he could not leave the sheep; but the Snake answered—

"Be not troubled about the sheep; no harm shall happen to them; only go as fast as you can."

The Shepherd then walked through the forest with the Snake until he came to a gate which was entirely made of snakes knotted together. There the Snake on the Shepherd's neck gave a whistle, and all the other snakes untwisted themselves. Then the Snake said to the Shepherd—

"When we come to my father's palace he will give you whatever you ask for: silver, gold, and precious stones. Do you, however, take nothing of these, but beg to know the language of the brutes and other creatures. He will refuse you this for a long time, but at last he will grant your request."

Meanwhile they came to the palace, to the father, who, shedding many tears, cried—

"For heaven's sake! my dearest daughter, where have you been?"

And she told him in due order how she had been surrounded by the forest fire, and how the Shepherd had rescued her. Then the King of the snakes turned to the Shepherd and said to him—

"What would you have me give you for the deliverance of my daughter?"

The Shepherd answered, "Only let me understand the language of animals; I want nothing else."

Then the King said, "That is not good for you; for if I were to bestow upon you the gift of the knowledge of the tongue of animals, and you were to tell anyone of it, you would instantly die. Ask, therefore, for something else; whatever you desire to possess, I will give to you."

To which the Shepherd replied—

"If you wish to give me anything, then grant me the knowledge of the language of brute creatures; but if you do not care to give me that—farewell, and God protect you! I want nothing else." And the Shepherd turned to leave the place.

Then the King called him back, saying—

"Stay! come here to me, since you will have it at all hazards. Open your mouth."

The Shepherd opened his mouth, and the King of the snakes breathed into it, and said—

"Do you now breathe into my mouth."

The Shepherd breathed into his mouth, and the Snake King breathed again into that of the Shepherd. After they had breathed each three times into the other's mouth, the King said—

"Now you understand the language of animals, and of all created things. Go in peace, and God be with you! but for the life of you, tell no one of this; if you do, you will die on the instant!"

The Shepherd returned home through the forest. As he walked he heard and understood all that the birds said, and the grass and all the other things that are upon the earth. When he came to his sheep and found them all together and quite safe, he laid himself down to rest. Scarcely had he lain down when there flew two ravens toward him, who took their perch upon a tree, and began to talk together in their own language.

"What if that Shepherd only knew that underneath the place where the black lamb lies there is a cellar full of silver and gold!'

When the Shepherd heard this, he went to his master, and told him of it. The master took a cart with him, and they dug down to a door leading to the cave, and removed the treasure to his house. But the master was an honest man, and gave all the treasure to the Shepherd, saying—

"My son, all this treasure is yours, for heaven has given it to you. Buy yourself a house with it, marry, and live happily in it."

The Shepherd took the treasure, built himself a house, and, having married, lived a happy life. Soon he became known as the richest man, not only in his own village, but so rich that there was not his equal in the whole neighborhood. He had his own shepherd, cow keeper, hostler, and swineherd; plenty of goods and chattels, and great riches.

One day, just before Christmas, he said to his wife, "Get some wine, and some brandy, and all things necessary; to-morrow we will go to the farmyard and take the good things to the shepherds that they may also enjoy themselves."

The wife followed his directions and prepared all that he had told her. When they arrived on the following day at the farmhouse, the master said to the shepherds in the evening—

"Come here, all of you; eat, drink, and be merry. I will watch over the flocks for you to-night." And he went, in very deed, and remained with the flocks.

About midnight the wolves began to howl and the dogs to bark, and the wolves said in their language—

"May we come in and do what mischief we like? Then you, too, shall have your share."

And the dogs answered in their language, "Come in; and we will eat our fill with you."

But among the dogs there was an old one, who had but two teeth in his head, and he said to the wolves—

"That will not do. So long as I have my two teeth in my head you shall do no harm to my master nor his."

The master heard it all, and understood what was said. On the following morning he ordered all the dogs to be killed save only the old one. The hinds said, "Heaven forbid, sir; that would be a great pity!" But the master answered, "Do what I have told you."

Then he prepared to return home with his wife, and they both mounted their horses. And as they rode on, the husband got a little ahead, while the wife fell behind. At last the husband's horse neighed, and called to the mare—

"Come on! make haste! Why do you lag behind!"

And the mare answered him, "Ah yes, it is all very easy for you: you have only one to carry, the master; while I have to carry two, the mistress and her baby."

The husband turned round and laughed, and his wife seeing this, urged the mare forward, overtook her husband, and asked him what he had been laughing at.

"Nothing; I do not know; just something that came into my mind," answered the husband.

But the wife was not satisfied with this answer, and she pressed him again and again to tell her why he had laughed.

But he excused himself, and said—

"Let me alone, wife! What is the matter with you? I do not know myself why I laughed."

But the more he denied her the more she insisted upon his telling her what he had been laughing at. At last the husband said to her—

"Know then, that if I tell you the reason, I shall instantly die."

The woman, however, did not care for that, but urged him to tell her notwithstanding.

Meanwhile they had reached home. The husband ordered a coffin to be made immediately, and when it was ready he had it placed before the house, and said to his wife—

"See now, I now lay me down in this coffin, and then tell you why I laughed; but as soon as I have told you I shall die."

The husband lay down in the coffin, and looked around him for the last time. And there came the old Dog from the farmyard, and sat down at his head and whined. The husband seeing this, said to his wife—

"Bring a piece of bread and give it to this Dog."

The wife brought out a piece of bread, and threw it down to the Dog; but the Dog would not even look at it. Then the House Cock ran up, and began to pick at the bread; and the Dog said to it—

"You miserable greedy thing, you! You can eat, and yet you see that the master is going to die!"

The Cock answered the Dog, "And let him die since he is such a fool. I have a hundred wives, and I call them all together whenever I find a grain of corn, and as soon as they have come round me, I swallow it myself. And if any one of them got angry, I should be at her directly with my beak. The master has only one wife, and he cannot even manage her."

When the husband heard this he quickly sprang out of the coffin, took up a stick, and called his wife into the room.

"Come, wife," he said, "I will tell you what you so much want to hear."

Then as he beat her with the stick he cried, "This is it, wife! This is it."

In this way he quieted his wife, and she never asked him again what he had been laughing at.

THE EMPEROR TROJAN'S GOAT'S EARS

By W. S. Karajich

There once lived an emperor whose name was Trojan. This emperor had goat's ears, and he used to call in barber after barber to shave him. But whoever went in never came out again; for while the barber was shaving him, the emperor would ask what he observed uncommon in him, and when the barber would answer that he observed his goat's ears, the Emperor would immediately cut him into pieces.

At last it came to the turn of a certain barber to go who feigned illness, and sent his apprentice instead. When the apprentice appeared before the emperor he was asked why his master did not come, and he answered, "Because he is ill." Then the emperor sat down, and allowed the youth to shave him.

As he shaved him the apprentice noticed the emperor's goat's ears, but when Trojan asked him what he had observed, he answered, "I have observed nothing."

Then the emperor gave him twelve ducats, and said to him—

"From this time forth you shall always come and shave me.

When the apprentice came home, his master asked him how he got on at the emperor's, and the youth answered—

"All well; and the emperor has told me that I am to shave him in future."

Then he showed the twelve ducats he had received; but as to the emperor's goat's ears, of that he said nothing.

From this time forth the apprentice went regularly to Trojan to shave him, and for each shaving he received twelve ducats; but he told no one that the emperor had goat's ears.

At last it began to worry and torment him that he dare tell no one his secret; and he became sick and began to pine away. His master, who could not fail to observe this, asked him what ailed him, and after much pressing the apprentice confessed that he had something on his heart which he dared not confide to anyone, and he added, "If I could only tell it to somebody, I should feel better at once."

Then said the master —

"Tell it to me, and I will faithfully keep it from everybody else; or if you fear to trust me with it, then go to the confessor and confide it to him; but if you will not do even that, then go into the fields outside the town, there dig a hole, thrust your head into it, and tell the earth three times what you know, then throw the mold in again and fill up the hole."

The apprentice chose the last course; went into the field outside the city, dug a hole, into which he thrust his head, and called out three times —

"The Emperor Trojan has goat's ears."

Then he filled up the hole again, and with his mind quite relieved went home.

When some time had passed by, there sprang an elder tree out of this very hole, and three slender sterns grew up, beautiful and straight as tapers. Some shepherds found this elder, cut off one of the stems, and made a pipe of it. But as soon as they began to blow into the new pipe, out burst the words:

"The Emperor Trojan has goat's ears!"

The news of this strange occurrence spread immediately through the whole city, and at last the Emperor Trojan himself heard the children blowing on a pipe:

"The Emperor Trojan has goat's ears!"

He sent instantly for the barber's apprentice, and shouted to him —

"Heh! what is this you have been telling the people about me."

The poor youth began at once to explain that he had indeed noticed the emperor's ears, but had never told a soul of it. The emperor tore his saber out of its sheath to hew the apprentice down, at which the youth was so frightened that he told the whole story in its order: how he had confessed himself to the earth; how an elder tree had sprang up on the very spot; and how, when a pipe was made of one of its sterns, the tale was sounded in every direction.

Then the emperor took the apprentice with him in a carriage to the place, to convince himself of the truth of the story; and when they arrived there they found there was only a single stem left. The Emperor Trojan ordered a pipe to be made out of this stem, that he might hear how it sounded. As soon as the pipe was ready, and one of them blew into it, out poured the words:

"The Emperor Trojan has goat's ears!"

Then the emperor was convinced that nothing on this earth could be hidden, spared the barber apprentices life, and henceforth allowed any barber, without exception, to come and shave him.

THE MAIDEN WHO WAS WISER THAN THE KING

By W. S. Karajich

There once lived a poor man in a miserable hovel, who had no one with him save an only daughter. But she was very wise, and went about everywhere seeking alms, and taught her father also to speak in a becoming manner when he begged. It happened once that the poor man came to the king and asked for a gift. The king demanded whence he came, and who had taught him to speak so well. The man said whence he came, and that it was his daughter who had taught him.

"And who taught your daughter?" asked the king.

The poor man answered: "God, and our great poverty."

Then the king gave him thirty eggs, saying—

"Take these eggs to your daughter, and tell her to hatch chickens out of them, and I will reward her handsomely; but if she cannot hatch them, it will go ill with you."

The poor man went crying back to his hovel, and related to his daughter what had passed. The maiden saw at once that the eggs had been boiled, but she told her father to go to rest, and assured him that she would see that all went well. The father followed her advice, and went to sleep; the maiden took a pot, filled it with water and beans, and set it on the fire. On the following morning, the beans being quite boiled, she told her father to take a plow and oxen, and to plow along the road where the king would pass.

"And," she added, "when you see the king, take the beans, sow them, and cry, 'Hi! go on, oxen mine! Heaven be with me, and make my boiled beans take root and grow!' And when the king asks you how it is possible for boiled beans to grow, answer him, that it is quite as possible as for boiled eggs to yield chickens."

The poor man hearkened to his daughter, went away, and began to plow. When he saw the king coming he began to cry— "Hi, go on, oxen mine! God help me, and make my boiled beans take root and grow!"

The king, hearing these words, stopped on the road, and said to the poor man—

"Here, fellow! how is it possible for boiled beans to grow?"

And the poor man answered him—

"Heaven prosper you, king! just as possible as for boiled eggs to yield chickens."

The king guessed at once that it was the poor man's daughter who had taught him this answer. He ordered his servants to seize him and bring him into his presence. Then he gave him a bundle of flax, and said to him—

"Take this flax and make out of it ropes and sails and all that is wanted on shipboard; if you do not, you shall lose your head."

The poor man took the bundle in great fear, and went crying home to his daughter, to whom he related all that had passed. But the maiden sent him again to rest with the promise that all should go well. On the following day she took a small piece of wood, awoke her father, and said to him—

"Take this wood, and carry it to the king; let him cut a spinning wheel, a spindle, and a loom out of it, and I will do all that he demands of me."

The poor man again followed the directions of his daughter; he went to the king and delivered the maiden's message. The king was astonished at hearing this, and began to think what he should do next. At last he took up a small cup, and said as he gave it to the father—

"Take this cup to your daughter, and let her empty the sea with it, so that it shall become like a dry field."

The poor man obeyed with tears in his eyes, and took the cup to his daughter with the king's message. But the maiden told him he need only leave the matter till the morning, when she would see to it.

In the morning she called her father, and gave him a pound of tow to take to the king, and bade him say:

"Let the king stop up all the springs and river mouths of the earth with this tow, and then will I dry up the sea for him."

And the poor man went and told this to the king.

Now the king saw that this maiden was wiser that he was himself, and he ordered her to be brought before him. And when the father and daughter stood in his presence and bowed before him, he said to the daughter—

"Tell me, girl, what is it that man hears the farthest?"

And the maiden answered— "Great king! that which man hears the farthest is the thunder, and a lie."

Upon this the king took hold of his beard, and turning to his councilors, demanded of them:

"Tell me what my beard is worth?"

And when one valued it at so much, and another at so much more, the maiden told them outright that they could not guess it. "The king's beard," she said, "is of as much worth as three rainy days in summer time."

The king was astonished and exclaimed, "The maiden has made the best answer!"

Then he asked her if she would be his wife, nor would he desist from pressing his suit, until she agreed to it. The maiden bent before him and said—

"Glorious king! let it be as you will; but I beg of you to write on a piece of paper with your own hand, that, should you ever be angry with me, and should drive me forth from your palace, I shall be at liberty to take whatever I love dearest away with me."

And the king agreed and wrote out the paper. After some time had passed away, it came, in fact, to pass, that the king became one day so angry with his wife, that he said to her—

"I will have you no longer for my wife; leave my palace, and go where you will."

"Illustrious king!" answered the queen, "I will obey you. Permit me, however, to stay here over the night, then in the morning I will go forth."

The king granted her prayer; and the queen before supper mixed some brandy and some sweet herbs in the king's wine, and pressed him to partake of it, saying—

"Drink, O king, and be merry. To-morrow we part; and believe me, I shall then be happier than when I married you."

The king drank too much, and when he was fast asleep, the queen had him laid in a wagon ready prepared, and drove with him into a rocky cavern. And when the king awoke in the cavern, and saw where he was, he cried out—

"Who has brought me here?"

"I have brought you here," answered the queen.

The king demanded of her:

"Why have you done this? Have I not told you that you are no longer my wife?"

Then said she, as she drew forth a sheet of paper —

"It is true what you say; but see what you yourself have laid down on this sheet: that when I should leave you, I might take with me, from your palace, that which I loved best."

When the king heard this, he kissed her, and went back with her to the palace.

THE THREE SONS

By Lady Gregory

I'll tell you a story, says the old man who was bringing fish from the sea; and after that I'll be going on to Ballinrobe, to one that has a shop there and that was reared by my grandmother. It is likely he'll give me a tasty suit of clothes.

Working all my life I am, working with the flail in the barn, working with the spade at the potato tilling and the potato digging, breaking stones on the road. And four years ago the wife died, and it's lonesome to be housekeeping alone.

There was a King long ago in Ireland, and he had three sons, and one of them was something silly. There came a sickness on the King, and he called his three sons, and he said to them that he had knowledge the only thing would cure him was the apples from Burnett's orchard, and he bade them to go look for them, for that orchard was in some far-away place, and no one could tell where it was.

The three sons went then, and they caught their horses, and put on their bridles, and they set out, and went on till they came to three crossroads. There they stopped, and they settled among themselves that each one of them would take one of the roads and go searching for the apples, and they would meet at the same place at the end of a year and a day.

The youngest son, that was a bit silly, took the crossest of the roads, and he went on till he came to a cottage by the roadside. He went in, and there was a withered old man in the house, and he said: "There is a great welcome before the King of Ireland's son!" The son was astonished at that because he thought no one could know him. He was well received there, and in the course of the evening he asked the old man did he know where was Burnett's garden. "I am a hundred years old," said the man, "and I never heard of such a place. But I have a brother," he said, "that is a hundred years older than I am, and it may be he would know," he said.

So in the morning he gave a canoe to the King's son, and it went on of itself without him turning or guiding it, till it brought him to the old man's brother, and he got a welcome there and good treatment, and in the course of the night he asked that old man did he know where was Burnett's orchard.

"I do not," said he: "though I am two hundred years old I never heard of it. But go on," he said, "to a brother I have that has a hundred years more than myself."

So in the morning, he went into the canoe, and it went on of itself till it came to where the third old man was, that was older again than the other two, and the King's son asked did he know where was Burnett's garden. "I do not," he said, "although I am three hundred years old; but I will tell you how you will know it," he said. "Go on till you come to shore, where you will see a Swan-Gander standing by the water, and he is the one that can tell you and can bring you to it," he said. "And ask him to bring you to that garden in the name of the Almighty God."

So the King's son went on in the canoe till he came where the Swan-Gander was standing on the shore. "Can you tell me," says he, "where can I get the apples that are in Burnett's orchard? And can you bring me there?" he said.

"Indeed," said the Swan-Gander, "I am in no way obliged to your leader, or to whoever it was sent you to me and gave you that teaching. And those apples are well minded," he said, "by wolves; and the only time they sleep is for three hours once in every seven years. And it chances they are asleep for those three hours at this time; and so I will bring you there," he said.

With that he stretched out his wings, and he bade the King's son to get on his back. And it was long before he could start flying with the weight that was on him; but at last he flew away, and he brought the King's son to Burnett's garden, and there was a high wall around it, but he flew over the wall, and put him down in the garden. The King's son filled his bag with the apples, and when he had done that he went looking around, and he came to a large cottage in the garden, and he went in, and there was no one in the house but a beautiful young girl, and she was asleep. So he went away; but he brought with him the gold rings and the gold garters that he saw there in the window.

He got up again on the back of the Swan-Gander, but it was hard for it to rise with the weight of the bag of apples. But it did rise at last, and it brought him to where the old man was that was three hundred years old. The King's son gave one of the apples to the old man, and no sooner did he eat it than his age left him, and he was like a boy of fifteen years.

He went on then to the two other old men, and gave an apple to both of them, and no sooner did they eat it than they were like young boys again.

Then the King's son went back to the crossroads, for it was the end of the year and a day, and he was the first to come there, and he fell asleep. The two brothers came and saw him there, and they stole the bag of apples from under his head and put in the place of it a bag of apples that were no use at all. Then they went on to their father's house, and they gave him the apples they had stolen, and he was cured on the moment; but they told him that what the youngest son was bringing to him was poison apples, that would bring him to his death.

The King was very angry when he heard that, and he went to his butler and said, "Go out to the wood where my son is, and shoot him, and bring his heart here with you on the top of a gun and throw it to the dogs at the door; for I will never have him, or anything belonging to him, brought into the house," he said.

So the butler got the gun, and went out to the wood; and when he saw the young man he was going to shoot him. "Why would you do that?" said he. So the butler told him all the father ordered him; and the young man said, "Do not shoot me, but save me. And this is what you will do. Go into the wood until you meet with a woodcock, and shoot it, and take the heart out of it, for that is most like the heart of a man. Bring the woodcock's heart to my father's house," he said, "and throw it to the dogs at the door."

So the butler did that, and spared him, and took the woodcock's heart and threw it to the dogs at the door.

It was a good while after that, a beautiful young lady came to the King's doorway in a coach and four, and stopped at the door. "Send out my husband to me here," she said. So the eldest son came out to her. "Was it you came to the garden for the apples?" says she. "It was," says he. "What things did you take notice of in the cottage where I was?" says she.

So he began telling of this thing and that thing that never was in it at all.

And when she heard that she gave him a clout that knocked his head as solid as any stone in the wall.

Then the second son came out, and she asked him the same question, and he told the same lies, and she gave him another clout that left his head as solid as any stone in the wall.

When the King heard all that, he knew they had deceived him, and that it was the youngest son who got the apples for his cure, and he began to cry after him and to lament that he was not living to come back again. "Would you like to know he is living yet?" says the butler. "I would sooner hear it than any word ever I heard," says the King.

"Well he is living yet, and is in the wood," says the butler.

When the young lady heard that, she bade the butler bring her to where he was, and they went together to the wood, and there they found him, where he had been living on the fruits of trees through the most of the year. When the young lady saw him, she said: "Was it you came to the house where I was in the garden?" "It was," says he.

"What things did you take notice of in it?"

"Here they are," says he. And he put his hand in his pocket, and brought out the gold rings and the golden garters, and the other signs he had brought away.

So she knew that he was the right one, and she married him, and they lived happy ever after, and there was great rejoicing in the King of Ireland's house.

HOK LEE AND THE DWARFS

Retold by Andrew Lang

There once lived in a small town in China a man named Hok Lee. He was a steady, industrious man, who not only worked hard at his trade, but did all his own housework as well, for he had no wife to do it for him. "What an excellent, industrious man is this Hok Lee!" said his neighbors. "How hard he works! He never leaves his house to amuse himself or to take a holiday as others do!"

But Hok Lee was by no means the virtuous person his neighbors thought him. True, he worked hard enough by day, but at night, when all respectable folk were fast asleep, he used to steal out and join a dangerous band of robbers, who broke into rich people's houses and carried off all they could lay hands on.

This state of things went on for some time, and though a thief was caught now and then and punished, no suspicion ever fell on Hok Lee, he was such a very respectable, hard-working man.

Hok Lee had already amassed a good store of money as his share of the proceeds of these robberies, when it happened one morning on going to market that a neighbor said to him:

"Why, Hok Lee, what is the matter with your face? One side of it is all swelled up."

True enough, Hok Lee's right cheek was twice the size of his left, and it soon began to feel very uncomfortable.

"I will bind up my face," said Hok Lee. "Doubtless the warmth will cure the swelling." But no such thing. Next day it was worse, and day by day it grew bigger and bigger till it was nearly as large as his head and became very painful.

Hok Lee was at his wits' end what to do. Not only was his cheek unsightly and painful, but his neighbors began to jeer and make fun of him, which hurt his feelings very much indeed.

One day, as luck would have it, a traveling doctor came to the town. He sold not only all kinds of medicine, but also dealt in many strange charms against witches and evil spirits.

Hok Lee determined to consult him and asked him into his house. After the doctor had examined him carefully he spoke thus:

"This, Hok Lee, is no ordinary swelled face. I strongly suspect you have been doing some wrong deed which has called down the anger of the spirits on you. None of my drugs will avail to cure you, but if you are willing to pay me handsomely I can tell you how you may be cured."

Then Hok Lee and the doctor began to bargain together, and it was a long time before they could come to terms. However, the doctor got the better of it in the end, for he was determined not to part with his secret under a certain price, and Hok Lee had no mind to carry his huge cheek about with him to the end of his days. So he was obliged to part with the greater portion of his ill-gotten gains.

When the doctor had pocketed the money he told Hok Lee to go on the first night of the full moon to a certain wood and there to watch by a particular tree. After a time he would see the dwarfs and little sprites who live underground come out to dance. When they saw him they would be sure to make him dance too. "And mind you dance your very best," added the doctor. "If you dance well and please them they will grant you a petition and you can then beg to be cured; but if you dance badly they will most likely do you some mischief out of spite." With that he took leave and departed.

Happily the first night of the full moon was near, and at the proper time Hok Lee set out for the wood. With a little trouble he found the tree the doctor had described, and feeling nervous he climbed up into it.

He had hardly settled himself on a branch when he saw the little dwarfs assembling in the moonlight. They came from all sides, till at length there appeared to be hundreds of them. They seemed in high glee and danced and skipped and capered about, while Hok Lee grew so eager watching them that he crept farther and farther along his branch till at length it gave a loud crack. All the dwarfs stood still, and Hok Lee felt as if his heart stood still also.

Then one of the dwarfs called out: "Some one is up in that tree. Come down at once, whoever you are, or we must come and fetch you."

In great terror Hok Lee proceeded to come down; but he was so nervous that he tripped near the ground and came rolling down in the most absurd manner. When he had picked himself up he came forward with a low bow, and the dwarf who had first spoken and who appeared to be the leader said: "Now, then, who art thou and what brings thee here?"

So Hok Lee told him the sad story of his swelled cheek, and how he had been advised to come to the forest and beg the dwarfs to cure him.

"It is well," replied the dwarf. "We will see about that. First, however, thou must dance before us. Should thy dancing please us, perhaps we may be able to do something; but shouldst thou dance badly we shall assuredly punish thee, so now take warning and dance away."

With that, he and all the other dwarfs sat down in a large ring, leaving Hok Lee to dance alone in the middle. He felt half-frightened to death, and besides was a good deal shaken by his fall from the tree and did not feel at all inclined to dance. But the dwarfs were not to be trifled with.

"Begin!" cried their leader, and "Begin!" shouted the rest in chorus.

So in despair Hok Lee began. First he hopped on one foot and then on the other, but he was so stiff and so nervous that he made but a poor attempt, and after a time sank down on the ground and vowed he could dance no more.

The dwarfs were very angry. They crowded round Hok Lee and abused him. "Thou to come here to be cured, indeed!" they cried. "Thou hast brought one big cheek with thee, but thou shalt take away two." And with that they ran off and disappeared, leaving Hok Lee to find his way home as best he might.

He hobbled away, weary and depressed, and not a little anxious on account of the dwarfs' threat.

Nor were his fears unfounded, for when he rose next morning his left cheek was swelled up as big as his right, and he could hardly see out of his eyes. Hok Lee felt in despair, and his neighbors jeered at him more than ever. The doctor, too, had disappeared, so there was nothing for it but to try the dwarfs once more.

He waited a month till the first night of the full moon came round again, and then he trudged back to the forest and sat down under the tree from which he had fallen. He had not long to wait. Ere long the dwarfs came trooping out till all were assembled.

"I don't feel quite easy," said one. "I feel as if some horrid human being were near us."

When Hok Lee heard this he came forward and bent down to the ground before the dwarfs, who came crowding round and laughed heartily at his comical appearance with his two big cheeks.

"What dost thou want?" they asked; and Hok Lee proceeded to tell them of his fresh misfortunes and begged so hard to be allowed one more trial at dancing that the dwarfs consented, for there is nothing they love so much as being amused.

Now, Hok Lee knew how much depended on his dancing well, so he plucked up a good spirit and began, first quite slowly and faster by degrees, and he danced so well and gracefully, and made such new and wonderful steps, that the dwarfs were quite delighted with him.

They clapped their tiny hands and shouted:

"Well done, Hok Lee, well done. Go on — dance more, for we are pleased."

And Hok Lee danced on and on, till he really could dance no more and was obliged to stop.

Then the leader of the dwarfs said: "We are well pleased, Hok Lee, and as a recompense for thy dancing thy face shall he cured. Farewell."

With these words he and the other dwarfs vanished, and Hok Lee, putting his hands to his face, found to his great joy that his cheeks were reduced to their natural size. The way home seemed short and easy to him, and he went to bed happy and resolved never to go out robbing again.

Next day the whole town was full of the news of Hok's sudden cure. His neighbors questioned him, but could get nothing from him, except the fact that he had discovered a wonderful cure for all kinds of diseases.

After a time a rich neighbor, who had been ill for some years, came and offered to give Hok Lee a large sum of money if he would tell him how he might get cured. Hok Lee consented on condition that he swore to keep the secret. He did so, and Hok Lee told him of the dwarfs and their dances.

The neighbor went off, carefully obeyed Hok Lee's directions, and was duly cured by the dwarfs. Then another and another came to Hok Lee to beg his secret, and from each he extracted a vow of secrecy and a large sum of money. This went on for some years, so that at length Hok Lee became a very wealthy man and ended his days in peace and prosperity.

A DREADFUL BOAR

By Adele M. Fielde

A poor Old Woman, who lived with her one little granddaughter in a wood, was out gathering sticks for fuel and found a green stalk of sugar-cane which she added to her bundle. She presently met an elf in the form of a Wild Boar, that asked her for the cane. She declined giving it to him, saying that at her age to stoop and to rise again was to earn what she picked up, and she was going to take the cane home and let her little granddaughter suck its sap.

The Boar, angry at her refusal, said that during the coming night he would come and eat her granddaughter instead of the cane, and went off into the wood.

When the Old Woman reached her cabin she sat down by the door and wailed, for she knew that she had no means of defending herself against the Boar. While she sat crying a vender of needles came along and asked her what was the matter. She told him, but all that he could do for her was to give her a box of needles. The Old Woman stuck the needles thickly over the lower half of the door, on its outer side, and then went on crying.

Just then a Man came along with a basket of crabs, heard her lamentations, and stopped to inquire what was the matter. She told him, but he said he knew no help for her, but he would do the best he could for her by giving her half his crabs. The woman put the crabs in her water jar, behind her door, and again sat down and cried.

A Farmer, who was coming along from the fields, leading his ox, also asked the cause of her distress and heard her story. He said he was sorry he could not think of any way of preventing the evil she expected, but that he would leave his ox to stay all night with her, as it might be a sort of company for her in her loneliness. She led the ox into her cabin, tied it to the head of her bedstead, gave it some straw, and then sat down to cry again.

A courier returning on horseback from a neighboring town was the next to pass her door, and he dismounted to inquire what troubled her. Having heard her tale, he said he would leave his horse to stay with her, and make the ox more contented. So she tied the horse to the foot of the bed, and, thinking how surely evil was coming upon her, she burst out crying anew.

A boy just then came along with a snapping turtle that he had caught and stopped to ask what had happened to her. On learning the cause of her weeping he said it was no use to contend against sprites, but that he would give her his snapping turtle as a proof of his sympathy. She took the turtle, tied it in front of her bedstead, and continued to cry.

Some men who were carrying millstones then came along, inquired into her trouble, and expressed their compassion by giving her a millstone, which they rolled into her back yard. While they were doing this a Man went by carrying hoes and a pickaxe, and he stopped and asked her why she was crying so hard. She told him her grief, and he said he would gladly help her if he could, but he was only a well digger and could do nothing for her except to dig a well. She pointed out a place in the backyard, and he went to work and quickly dug a well.

On his departure the old woman cried again, until a Paper Seller came and inquired what was the matter. When she told him he gave her a large sheet of white paper, as a token of pity, and she laid it smoothly over the mouth of the well.

Nightfall came. The old woman shut and barred her door, put her granddaughter snugly on the wall side of the bed, and then lay down beside her to await the foe.

At midnight the Boar came and threw himself against the door to break it in. The needles wounded him sorely, so that when he had gained an entrance he was heated and thirsty, and went to the water jar to drink.

When he thrust in his snout the crabs attacked him, clung to his bristles, and pinched his ears, till he rolled over and over to free himself.

Then in a rage he approached the front of the bed; but the snapping turtle nipped his tail and made him retreat under the feet of the horse, who kicked him over to the ox, and the ox tossed him back to the horse. Thus beset, he was glad to escape to the back yard to take a rest and to consider the situation.

Seeing a clean paper spread on the ground, he went to lie upon it, and fell into the well. The Old Woman, hearing the fall, rushed out and rolled the millstone down on him and crushed him.

THE FIVE QUEER BROTHERS

By Adele M. Fielde

An old woman had five grown-up sons that looked just alike. The eldest could gulp up the ocean at a mouthful; the second was hard enough to nick steel; the third had extensible legs; the fourth was unaffected by fire; the fifth lived without breathing. They all concealed their peculiar traits, and their neighbors did not know they were queer.

The eldest supported the family by fishing, going alone to the sea, and bringing back loads of spoil. The neighbors often besought him to teach their sons how to fish, and he at last let all their boys go with him, one day, to learn his art. On reaching the shore he sucked the sea into his mouth, and sent the boys to the dry bottom to collect the fish. When he was tired of holding the water, he beckoned to the boys to return, but they were playing among strange objects and paid no heed to him. When he could contain the sea no longer, he had to let it flow back into its former basin, and all the boys were drowned.

As he went homeward, he passed the doom of the parents, who inquired how many fish their sons had caught and how long they would be in coming back. He told them the facts, but they would not excuse him. They dragged him before the magistrate to account for the loss of their children. He defended himself by saying he had not invited the boys to go with him, and had consented to their going only when the parents had repeatedly urged him; that after the boys were on the ocean bed, he had done his utmost to induce them to come ashore; that he had held the water as long as he could, and had then put it in the sea basin solely because nothing else would contain it.

Notwithstanding this defense the judges decided that since he took the boys away and did not bring them back, he was guilty of murder and sentenced him to be beheaded.

He entreated leave to pay, before his execution, one visit to his aged mother, and this was granted.

He went alone and told his brothers of his doom, and the second brother returned in his stead to the judge, thanked him for having given him permission to perform a duty required by filial piety, and said he was then ready to die.

He knelt with bowed head and the headsman brought the knife down across the back of his neck, but the knife was nicked and the neck was left unharmed.

A second knife and a third of finer steel were brought and tried by headsmen who were accustomed to sever heads clean off at one stroke. Having spoiled their best blades without so much as scratching his neck, they took him back to prison and informed the judge that the sentence could not be executed.

The judge accordingly decreed that he should be dropped into the sea which covered his victims.

When the old woman's son heard this decision he said that he took leave of his mother supposing that his head was to be cut off, and that if he was to be drowned he must go to her and make known his fate and get her blessing anew.

Permission being given, he went and told his brothers what had happened. The third brother took the place of the second and presented himself before the judge as the criminal that was to be sunk in the sea. He was carried far from shore and thrown overboard, but he stretched his legs till his feet touched bottom, and he stood with his head in the air. They hauled him aboard and took him farther from land, but still his extensible legs supported him above the waters. Then they sailed to mid-ocean and cast him into its greatest depths, but his legs still lengthened so that he was not drowned. They brought him back to the judge, reported what had been done, and said that some other method of destroying him must be followed.

On hearing this the judge condemned him to death by being boiled in oil. While the caldron was being heated he begged and obtained permission to go and tell his mother of the way he had survived from the attempt to drown him, and of the manner in which he was soon to be taken off.

His brothers having heard the latest judgment, the fourth one went to bear the penalty of the law and was lowered into the kettle of boiling oil. In this he disported himself as if in a tepid bath, and he even asked his executioners to stir up the fire a little to increase the warmth. Finding that he could not be fried, he was remanded to prison.

At this the populace, the bereaved parents, and the magistrate joined in an effort to invent a sure method of putting him to death. Water, fire, and sword all having failed, they finally fixed upon smothering him in a vast cream cake.

The whole country round made contributions of flour for the pastry, of sugar for the filling, and of bricks for a huge oven; and it was made and baked on a plain outside the city walls.

Meanwhile the prisoner was allowed to go and bid his mother farewell, and the fifth brother secretly became his substitute.

When the cake was done, a multitude of people with oxen, horses, and ropes dragged it to the execution ground, and within it the culprit was interred.

As he was able to exist without air he rested peacefully till the next midnight, and then safely crawled forth, returned to his home, and dwelt there happily for many years with his remarkable brothers.

THE ACCOMPLISHED AND LUCKY TEAKETTLE

By A. B. Mitford

A long time ago, at a temple called Morinji, there was an old teakettle. One day, when the priest of the temple was about to hang it over the hearth to boil the water for his tea, to his amazement the kettle all of a sudden put forth the head and tail of a badger. What a wonderful kettle, to come out all over fur!

The priest, thunderstruck, called in the novices or assistants of the temple to see the sight; and while they were stupidly staring, one suggesting one thing and another another, the kettle, jumping up into the air, began flying about the room. More astonished than ever, the priest and his pupils tried to pursue it; but no thief or cat was ever half so sharp as the wonderful badger kettle. At last, however, they managed to knock it down and secure it; and, holding it in with their united efforts, they forced it into a box, intending to carry it off and throw it away in some distant place, so that they might no more be plagued with the goblin.

For this day their troubles were over, but as luck would have it, the tinker who was in the habit of working for the temple called in, and the priest suddenly bethought him that it was a pity to throw the kettle away for nothing, and that he might as well get a trifle for it, no matter how small. So he brought out the kettle, which had resumed its former shape and had got rid of its head and tail, and showed it to the tinker. When the tinker saw the kettle, he offered twenty copper coins for it, and the priest was only too glad to close the bargain and be rid of his troublesome piece of furniture. And the tinker trudged off home with his pack and his new purchase.

That night, as he lay asleep, he heard a strange noise near his pillow; so he peeped out from under the bedclothes and there he saw the kettle that he had bought in the temple covered with fur and walking about on four legs. The tinker started up in a fright to see what it could all mean, when all of a sudden the kettle resumed its former shape. This happened over and over again, until at last the tinker showed the teakettle to a friend of his, who said,

"This is certainly an accomplished and lucky teakettle—you should take it about as a show, with songs and accompaniments of musical instruments, and make it dance and walk on the tight rope."

The tinker, thinking this good advice, made arrangements with a showman, and set up an exhibition. The noise of the kettle's performances soon spread abroad, until even the princes of the land sent to order the tinker to come to them; and he grew rich beyond all expectations. Even the princesses, too, and the great ladies of the court, took great delight in the dancing kettle, so that no sooner had it shown its tricks in one place than it was time for them to keep some other engagement.

At last the tinker grew so rich that he took the kettle back to the temple, where it was laid up as a precious treasure and worshiped as a saint.

THE ADVENTURES OF LITTLE PEACHLING

By A. B. Mitford

Many hundred years ago there lived an honest old woodcutter and his wife. One fine morning the old man went off to the hills with his bill hook to gather a faggot of sticks, while his wife went down to the river to wash the dirty clothes. When she came to the river, she saw a peach floating down the stream; so she picked it up and carried it homeward with her, thinking to give it to her husband to eat when he should come in. The old man soon came down from the hills, and the good wife set the peach before him, when, just as she was inviting him to eat it, the fruit split in two and a little baby was born into the world. So the old couple took the babe and brought it up as their own; and because it had been born in a peach, they called it Momotaro, or Little Peachhing!

By degrees Little Peachling grew up to be strong and brave, and at last one day he said to his old foster parents—

"I am going to the ogres' island, to carry off the riches they have stored up there. Pray, then, make me some millet dumplings for my journey."

So the old folks ground the millet and made the dumplings for him; and Little Peachling, after taking an affectionate leave of them, cheerfully set out on his travels.

As he was journeying on, he fell in with an Ape, who gibbered at him, and said,

"Kia! kia! kia! where are you off to, Little Peachling?"

"I'm going to the ogres' island, to carry off their treasure," answered Little Peachling.

"What are you carrying at your girdle?"

"I'm carrying the very best millet dumplings in all Japan.

"If you'll give me one, I will go with you," said the Ape.

So Little Peachhing gave one of his dumplings to the Ape, who received it and followed him. When he had gone a little farther, he heard a Pheasant calling—

"Ken! ken! ken! where are you off to, Master Peachling?"

Little Peachling answered as before; and the Pheasant, having begged and obtained a millet dumpling, entered his service and followed him. A little while after this they met a Dog, who cried —

Bow! wow! wow! whither away, Master Peachling?"

"I'm going off to the ogres' island, to carry off their treasure.

"If you will give me one of those nice millet dumplings of yours, I will go with you," said the Dog.

"With all my heart," said Little Peachling. So he went on his way, with the Ape, the Pheasant, and the Dog following after him.

When they got to the ogres' island, the Pheasant flew over the castle gate and the Ape clambered over the castle wall, while Little Peachling, leading the Dog, forced in the gate and got into the castle. Then they did battle with the ogres and put them to flight, and took their King prisoner. So all the ogres did homage to Little Peachling, and brought out the treasures which they had laid up. There were caps and coats that made their wearers invisible, jewels which governed the ebb and the flow of the tide, coral, musk, emeralds, amber, and tortoise shells, besides gold and silver. All these were laid before Little Peachling by the conquered ogres.

So Little Peachling went home laden with riches, and maintained his foster parents in peace and plenty for the remainder of their lives.

THE TWO LIZARDS

By Annie Ker

In the old days there lived two lizards, Webubu and Nagari. Webubu was plain of speech, and moreover was unable to cry aloud, but Nagari, by stretching his long neck, could produce a sweet low sound, somewhat after the manner of a whistle.

Nagari longed for companions, so he stretched his neck and cried "U-u-u-u-u." Then many women, hearing the sweet sound, flocked to where Nagari sat, and listened to his music. This pleased Nagari, and he continued to sound his long note. "U-u-u-u-u," he sang, and the women sat so still, one might have thought them dead or weeping.

Webubu, on the contrary, had no one to cheer him in his loneliness. "What can I do," he said, "to draw women to me as Nagari has done? I have not a sweet voice as he has. What can I do?"

As he was speaking a thought grew up in his heart, and he began to act. He cut a slim piece of hollow bamboo, and pierced small holes in it. Thus was the first flute (duraio) born. Webubu then built himself a platform high in a corkwood tree, which we call "troba" on the beach, and seating himself there he began to play his flute.

The women sat patiently around Nagari, while he sounded his one note, "U-u-u!" But on a sudden, upon the still air, broke the sweet voice of Webubu's flute. High and sweet were the notes which Webubu sent forth from his flute.

"M! m!" said the listening women.

"U-u-u-u," sang Nagari.

"Ah, ss-ss-ss!" cried the women. "Deafen us not with thy 'U,' when we would hear this strange music!"

Nagari was much troubled at this saying, and marveled greatly. Then one woman made bold to rise up, and saying, "I shall return," she went to seek the sweet music. Now this woman lied, for she never returned. After a time, another woman arose and said, "Stay here, my friends; I shall return."

Then she went in like manner to look for the music. And she also lied, for she returned not. And so with each woman, until Nagari was left sitting alone as he had been at the beginning.

Now Webubu was still playing his flute on the platform he had built in the corkwood tree, when the women came in sight. He was alarmed for the safety of his frail platform, when he saw these many people advancing, and he cried, "Come not up into the tree. Remain below, I beseech you, O women!"

But the women were consumed with eagerness to be close to the music which had taken their hearts, and they climbed, all of them, until they were upon the platform of Webubu.

Then straightway what he had feared came to pass, and Webubu, and his flute, and the multitude of women fell crashing through the branches of the corkwood tree to the ground beneath.

And from that hour until now, all corkwood trees lean toward the earth, as I will show thee, if thou wilt go with me to the beach where they grow.

DE KING AND DE PEAFOWL

By Mary Pamela Milne-Horne

One day once 'pon a time de King hab a party of ladies an' genelmen. An' arter de party, de band was ter come an' play. But de fiddler was took sick, so dey could not dance. So de King said, "I am gwine ter sen' ober ter my frien's an' ask dem ter come an' sing." So he sen', an' de genelman say he was very glad an' his family was Dog, Peafowl, and Tiger. So he sen' Missis Duck fus, an' dey said, "Can you sing? let me har you voice."

Dey put her in a rocking-chair 'pon de platform, an' de Duck say, "Hahh! hahh!" an' den he say, "Dat will not do. Sen' for Dog." An' dey took her an' put her in a coop, an' all de ducks come round an' ask to have her let out, an' say, "Hahh! hahh! hahh!"

Den dey sen' for Dog an' tole him dat if he fin' a salt beef bone in de road, he mus' not pick it up, 'cos it mek him rough in his troat. So Dog did not pick it up, but pass it; but arter, when he go, his voice did not suit either. Dey tole Dog to sing, an' he said, "How! how! how!" An' de King say, "Don't wan' a man ter ask me how—he will not do." Dey saw a Fowl coming. "Can you sing?" An' de Fowl say "Ka! ka! ka!" an' dey said, "Dat will not do," an' dribe de Fowl 'way. De Cock came in arter, an' de Cock said, "Coquericou," an' dey said, "De King don' wan' ter know when de daylight, sah!" De King came in an' said, "All dese people cannot sing; dey will not do."

Dey sen' Tiger, an' dey said, "You must not pick up a big salt beef bone in de road." An' de Tiger did pick it up, an' Tiger could not sing, an' said, "Grum! grum! grum!"

"Dat voice is wuss dan all, dat voice will not do."

Den dey sen' off for Peafowl, but Peafowl would not go. Dey went back ter dinner, all de people went back ter dinner, an' when dey were at dinner in a large house, de Peafowl came in an' sing—

Mi - kale an' iv'ry, Mi - kale an' iv'rv. Mi -

kale an' iv'ry, Mi - kale an' iv'ry, Why - ou, Why - ou

Why - ou Why - ou Why-ou Wife gwine ter die.

Den de genelmen jump up an' say, "Hullo! What dat?" De King say, "Sing again, my pritty lil' bird," an' den de Peafowl sang, "Mikale an' iv'ry, Mikale an' iv'ry, Mikale an' iv'ry, Whyou, Whyou, Whyou, Whyou, Whyou wife gwine ter die." "What dat? What dat? What dat?" dey say, an' de bird den settin' on de tree sing, "Mikale an' iv'ry," etc.

De King say, "Sing again, you pritty lil' bird. You dress shall be tipped with blue, an' you shall hab a beautiful field of corn as a present." An' de bird sang again better, when he har dat, "Mikale an' iv'ry, Mikale an' iv'ry, Mikale an' iv'ry, Mikale an' iv'ry, whyou, whyou, whyou, whyou, whyou wife gwine ter die." De King jump up an' call de buggy, an' jump in an' tek de Peafowl in, an' all de horses was richly decked, an' all de company very fine, dey dribe de Peafowl home, an' dat why de Peafowl hav such a beautiful dress.

HANSEL AND GRETHEL

By William and Jacob Grimm

Once upon a time there dwelt near a large wood a poor woodcutter with his wife and two children by his former marriage, a little boy called Hansel and a girl named Grethel. He had little enough to break or bite, and once, when there was a great famine in the land, he could not procure even his daily bread; and as he lay thinking in his bed one evening, rolling about for trouble, he sighed, and said to his wife, "What will become of us? How can we feed our children when we have no more than we can eat ourselves?"

"Know, then, my husband," answered she, "we will lead them away quite early in the morning into the thickest part of the wood, and there make them a fire, and give them each a little piece of bread; then we will go to our work and leave them alone, so they will not find the way home again and we shall be freed from them." "No, wife," replied he, "that I can never do; how can you bring your heart to leave my children all alone in the wood, for the wild beasts will soon come and tear them to pieces?"

"Oh, you simpleton!" said she, "then we must all four die of hunger; you had better plane the coffins for us." But she left him no peace till he consented saying, "Ah, but I shall regret the poor children."

The two children, however, had not gone to sleep for very hunger, and so they overheard what the stepmother said to their father. Grethel wept bitterly, and said to Hansel, "What will become of us?" "Be quiet, Grethel," said he; "do not cry, I will soon help you." And as soon as their parents had fallen asleep, he got up, put on his coat, and, unbarring the back door, slipped out. The moon shone brightly, and the white pebbles which lay before the door seemed like silver pieces, they glittered so brightly. Hansel stooped down, and put as many into his pocket as it would hold, and then going back he said to Grethel, "Be comforted, dear sister, and sleep in peace; God will not forsake us;" and so saying he went to bed again.

The next morning, before the sun arose, the wife went and awoke the two children. "Get up, you lazy things; we are going into the forest to chop wood." Then she gave them each a piece of bread, saying, "There is something for your dinner; do not eat it before the time, for you will get nothing else." Grethel took the bread in her apron, for Hansel's pocket was full of pebbles; and so they all set out upon their way. When they had gone a little distance Hansel stood still, and peeped back at the house; and this he repeated several times, till his father said, "Hansel, what are you peeping at, and why do you lag behind? Take care, and remember your legs."

"Ah! father," said Hansel, "I am looking at my white cat sitting upon the roof of the house, and trying to say good-by." "You simpleton!" said the wife, "that is not a cat; it is only the sun shining on the white chimney." But in reality Hansel was not looking at a cat; but every time he stopped he dropped a pebble out of his pocket upon the path.

When they came to the middle of the wood the father told the children to collect wood, and he would make them a fire, so that they should not be cold; so Hansel and Grethel gathered together quite a little mountain of twigs. Then they set fire to them, and as the flame burned up high the wife said, "Now, you children, lie down near the fire and rest yourself, while we go into the forest and chop Wood; when we are ready, I will come and call you."

Hansel and Grethel sat down by the fire, and when it was noon each ate the piece of bread, and, because they could hear the blows of an ax, they thought their father was near; but it was not an ax, but a branch which he had bound to a withered tree, so as to be blown to and fro by the wind. They waited so long that at last their eyes closed from weariness, and they fell fast asleep. When they awoke it was quite dark, and Grethel began to cry; "How shall we get out of the wood?" But Hansel tried to comfort her by saying, "Wait a little while till the moon rises, and then we will quickly find the way." The moon soon shone forth, and Hansel, taking his sister's hand, followed the pebbles, which glittered like new-coined silver pieces, and showed them the path. All night long they walked on, and as day broke they came to their father's house. They knocked at the door, and when the wife opened it, and saw Hansel and Grethel, she exclaimed, "You wicked children! why did you sleep so long in the wood? We thought you were never coming home again." But their father was very glad, for it had grieved his heart to leave them all alone.

Not long afterward there was again great scarcity in every corner of the land; and one night the children overheard their mother saying to their father, "Everything is again consumed; we have only half a loaf left, and then the song is ended: the children must be sent away. We will take them deeper into the wood, so that they may not find the way out again; it is the only means of escape for us."

But her husband felt heavy at heart, and thought, "It were better to share the last crust with the children." His wife, however, would listen to nothing that he said and scolded and, reproached him without end. He who says A must say B too; and he who consents the first time must also the second.

The children, however, had heard the conversation as they lay awake, and as soon as the old people went to sleep Hansel got up intending' to pick up some pebbles as before; but the wife had locked the door, so that he could not get out. Nevertheless he comforted Grethel, saying, "Do not cry; sleep in quiet; the good God will not forsake us."

Early in the morning the stepmother came and pulled them out of bed, and gave them each a slice of bread, which was still smaller than the former piece. On the way Hansel broke his in his pocket, and, stopping every now and then, dropped a crumb upon the path. "Hansel, why do you stop and look about?" said the father. "Keep in the path." — "I am looking at my little dove," answered Hansel, "nodding a good-by to me."

"Simpleton!" said the wife, "that is no dove, but only the sun shining on the chimney."

So Hansel kept still dropping crumbs as he went along.

The mother led the children deep into the wood, where they had never been before, and there making an immense fire, she said to them, "Sit down here and rest, and when you feel tired you can sleep for a little while. We are going into the forest to hew wood, and in the evening, when we are ready, we will come and fetch you."

When noon came Grethel shared her bread with Hansel, who had strewn his on the path. Then they went to sleep; but the evening arrived, and no one came to visit the poor children, and in the dark night they awoke, and Hansel comforted his sister by saying, "Only wait, Grethel, till the moon comes out, then we shall see the crumbs of bread which I have dropped, and they will show us the way home." The moon shone and they got up, but they could not see any crumbs, for the thousands of birds which had been flying about in the woods and fields had picked them all up. Hansel kept saying to Grethel, "We will soon find the way"; but they did not, and they walked the whole night long and the next day, but still they did not come out of the wood; and they got so hungry, for they had nothing to eat but the berries which they found upon the bushes.

Soon they got so tired that they could not drag themselves along, so they laid down under a tree and went to sleep.

It was now the third morning since they had left their father's house, and they still walked on; but they only got deeper and deeper into the wood, and Hansel saw that if help did not come very soon they would die of hunger.

As soon as it was noon they saw a beautiful snow-white bird sitting upon a bough which sang so sweetly that they stood still and listened to it. It soon left off, and spreading its wings, flew off; and they followed it until it arrived at a cottage, upon the roof of which it perched; and when they went close up to it they saw that the cottage was made of bread and cakes, and the windowpanes were of clear sugar.

"We will go in there," said Hansel, "and have a glorious feast. I will eat a piece of the roof, and you can eat the window. Will they not be sweet?" So Hansel reached up and broke a piece off the roof, in order to see how it tasted; while Grethel stepped up to the window and began to bite it. Then a sweet voice called out in the room, "Tip-tap, tip-tap, who raps at my door?" and the children answered, "The wind, the wind, the child of heaven"; and they went on eating without interruption. Hansel thought the roof tasted very nice, and so he tore off a great piece; while Grethel broke a large round pane out of the window, and sat down quite contentedly. Just then the door opened, and a very old woman, walking upon crutches, came out. Hansel and Grethel were so frightened that they let fall what they had in their hands; but the old woman, nodding her head, said, "Ah, you dear children, what has brought you here? Come in and stop with me, and no harm shall befall you;" and so saying she took them both by the hand, and led them into her cottage. A good meal of milk and pancakes, with sugar, apples, and nuts, was spread on the table, and in the back room were two nice little beds, covered with white, where Hansel and Grethel laid themselves down, and thought themselves in heaven. The old woman had behaved very kindly to them, but in reality she was a wicked witch who waylaid children, and built the bread house in order to entice them in; but as soon as they were in her power she killed them, cooked and ate them, and made a great festival of the day. Witches have red eyes, and cannot see very far; but they have a fine sense of smelling, like wild beasts, so that they know when children approach them. When Hansel and Grethel came near the witch's house she laughed wickedly, saying, "Here come two who shall not escape me." And early in the morning, before they awoke, she went up to them, and saw how lovingly they lay sleeping, with their chubby red cheeks; and she mumbled to herself, "That will be a good bite." Then she took up Hansel with her rough hand, and shut him up in a little cage with a lattice door; and although he screamed loudly, it was of no use. Grethel came next, and, shaking her till she awoke, she said, "Get up, you lazy thing, and fetch some water to cook something good for your brother, who must remain in that stall and get fat; when he is fat enough I shall, eat him." Grethel began to cry, but it was all useless, for the old witch made her do as she wished. So a nice meal was cooked for Hansel, but Grethel got nothing else but a crab's claw.

Every morning the old witch came to the cage and said, "Hansel, stretch your finger that I may feel whether you are getting fat." But Hansel used to stretch out a bone, and the old woman, having very bad sight, thought it was his finger, and wondered very much that it did not get fat. When four weeks had passed, and Hansel still kept quite lean, she lost all her patience and would not wait any longer. "Grethel." she called out in a passion, "get some water quickly; be Hansel fat or lean, this morning I will kill and cook him." Oh, how the poor little sister grieved, as she was forced to fetch the water, and how fast the tears ran down her cheeks! "Dear good God, help us now!" she exclaimed. "Had we only been eaten by the wild beasts in the wood then we should have died together." But the old witch called out, "Leave off that noise; it will not help you a bit."

So early in the morning Grethel was forced to go out and fill the kettle, and make a fire. "First we will bake, however," said the old woman; "I have already heated the oven and kneaded the dough"; and so saying she pushed poor Grethel up to the oven, out of which the flames were burning fiercely. "Creep in," said the witch, "and see if it is hot enough, and then we will put in the bread"; but she intended when Grethel got in to shut up the oven and let her bake, so that she might eat her as well as Hansel. Grethel perceived what her thoughts were, and said, "I do not know how to do it; how shall I get in?" "You stupid goose," said she, "the opening is big enough. See, I could even get in myself!" and she got up and put her head into the oven. Then Grethel gave her a push, so that she fell right in, and then shutting the iron door, she bolted it. Oh! how horribly she howled; but Grethel ran away, and left the ungodly witch to burn to ashes.

Now she ran to Hansel, and, opening his door, called out, "Hansel, we are saved; the old witch is dead!" So he sprang out, like a bird out of his cage when the door is opened; and they were so glad that they fell upon each other's neck, and kissed each other over and over again. And now, as there was nothing to fear, they went into the witch's house, where in every corner were caskets full of pearls and precious stones. "These are better than pebbles," said Hansel, putting as many into his pocket as it would hold; while Grethel thought, "I will take some home, too," and filled her apron full. "We must be off now," said Hansel, "and get out of this bewitched forest"; but when they had walked for two hours they came to a large piece of water. "We cannot get over," said Hansel. "I can see no bridge at all." "And there is no boat either," said Grethel; "but there swims a white duck, I will ask her to help us over;" and she sang,

"Little duck, good little duck,
   Grethel and Hansel, here we stand,
There is neither stile nor bridge,
   Take us on your back to land."

So the duck came to them, and Hansel sat himself on, and bade his sister sit behind him. "No," answered Grethel, "that will be too much for the duck, she shall take us over one at a time." This the good little bird did, and when both were happily arrived on the other side, and had gone a little way, they came to a well-known wood, which they knew the better every step they went, and at last they perceived their father's house. Then they began to run, and, bursting into the house, they fell on their father's neck. He had not had one happy hour since he had left the children in the forest; and his wife was dead. Grethel shook her apron, and the pearls and precious stones rolled out upon the floor, and Hansel threw down one handful after the other out of his pocket. Then all their sorrows were ended, and they lived together in great happiness.

My tale is done. There runs a mouse; whoever catches her may make a great, great cap out of her fur.

THUMBLING

By William and Jacob Grimm

Once upon a time there lived a poor peasant, who used to sit every evening by the hearth, poking the fire, while his wife spun. One night he said, "How sad it is that we have no children; everything is so quiet here, while in other houses it is so noisy and merry."

"Ah!" sighed his wife, "if we had but only one, and were he no bigger than my thumb, I should still be content, and love him with all my heart." A little while after the wife fell ill; and after seven months a child was born, who, although he was perfectly formed in all his limbs, was not actually bigger than one's thumb. So they said to one another that it had happened just as they wished; and they called the child "Thumbling." Every day they gave him all the food he could eat; still he did not grow a bit, but remained exactly the height he was when first born; he looked about him, however, very knowingly, and showed himself to be a bold and clever fellow, who prospered in everything he undertook.

One morning the peasant was making ready to go into the forest to fell wood, and said, "Now I wish I had some one who could follow me with the cart."

"Oh! father," exclaimed Thumbling, "I will bring the cart; don't you trouble yourself; it shall be there at the right time."

The father laughed at this speech, and said, "How shall that be? You are much too small to lead the horse by the bridle."

"That matters not, father. If mother will harness the horse, I can sit in his car, and tell him which way to take."

"Well, we will try for once," said the father; and so, when the hour came, the mother harnessed the horse, and placed Thumbling in its ear, and told him how to guide it. Then he set out quite like a man, and the cart went on the right road to the forest; and just as it turned a corner, and Thumbling called out "Steady, steady," two strange men met it; and one said to the other, "My goodness, what is this? Here comes a cart, and the driver keeps calling to the horse; but I can see no one." "That cannot be all right," said the other: "let us follow and see where the cart stops."

The cart went on safely deep into the forest, and straight to the place where the wood was cut. As soon as Thumbling saw his father, he called to him, "Here, father; here I am, you see, with the cart; just take me down." The peasant caught the bridle of the horse with his left hand, and with his right took his little son out of its ear; and he sat himself down merrily on a straw. When the two strangers saw the little fellow, they knew not what to say for astonishment; and one of them took his companion aside, and said, "This little fellow might make our fortune if we could exhibit him in the towns. Let us buy him." They went up to the peasant, and asked, "Will you sell your son? We will treat him well." "No," replied the man; "he is my heart's delight, and not to be bought for all the money in the world!" But Thumbling, when he heard what was said, climbed up by his father's skirt, and set himself on his shoulder, and whispered in his ear, "Let me go now, and I will soon come back again." So his father gave him to the two men for a fine piece of gold; and they asked him where he would sit. "Oh," replied he, "put me on the rim of your hat; and then I can walk round and survey the country. I will not fall off." They did as he wished; and when he had taken leave of his father, they set out. Just as it was getting dark he asked to be lifted down; and, after some demur, the man on whose hat he was, took him off and placed him on the ground. In an instant Thumbling ran off, and crept into a mousehole, where they could not see him. "Good evening, masters," said he, "you can go home without me"; and with a quiet laugh he crept into his hole still further. The two men poked their sticks into the hole, but all in vain; for Thumbling only went down further; and when it had grown quite dark they were obliged to return home full of vexation and with empty pockets.

As soon as Thumbling perceived that they were off, he crawled out of his hiding place, and said, "How dangerous it is to walk in this field in the dark: one might soon break one's head or legs;" and so saying he looked around, and by great good luck saw an empty snail shell. "God be praised," he exclaimed, "here I can sleep securely; and in he went. Just as he was about to fall asleep he heard two men coming by, one of whom said to the other, "How shall we manage to get at the parson's gold and silver?"

"That I can tell you," interrupted Thumbling.

"What was that?" exclaimed the thief, frightened. "I heard some one speak." They stood still and listened; and then Thumbling said, "Take me with you, and I will help you."

"Where are you?" asked the thieves.

"Search on the ground, and mark where my voice comes from," replied he. The thief looked about, and at last found him; and lifted him up in the air.

"What, will you help us, you little wight?" said they.

"Do you not see I can creep between the iron bars into the chamber of the parson, and reach out to you whatever you require?"

"Very well; we will see what you can do," said the thief.

When they came to the house, Thumbling crept into the chamber, and cried out with all his might, "Will you have all that is here?" The thieves were terrified, and said, "Speak gently, or some one will awake."

But Thumbling feigned not to understand, and exclaimed, louder still, "Will you have all that is here?"

This awoke the cook, who slept in the room, and sitting up in her bed she listened. The thieves, however, had run back a little way, quite frightened; but taking courage again, and thinking the little fellow wished to tease them, they came and whispered to him to make haste and hand them out something. At this, Thumbling cried out still more loudly, "I will give you it all, only put your hands in." The listening maid heard this clearly, and springing out of bed, hurried out at the door. The thieves ran off as if they were pursued by the wild huntsman, but the maid, as she could see nothing, went to strike a light. When she returned, Thumbling escaped without being seen into the barn, and the maid, after she had looked round and searched in every corner, without finding anything, went to bed again, believing she had been dreaming with her eyes open. Meanwhile Thumbling had crept in amongst the hay, and found a beautiful place to sleep, where he intended to rest till daybreak, and then to go home to his parents.

Other things however, was he to experience, for there is much tribulation and trouble going on in this world.

The maid got up at dawn of day to feed the cow. Her first walk was to the barn, where she took an armful of hay, and just the bundle where poor Thumbling lay asleep. He slept so soundly, however, that he was not conscious, and only awoke when he was in the cow's mouth. "Ah, goodness!" exclaimed he, "however came I into this mill?" but soon he saw where he really was. Then he took care not to come between the teeth, but presently slipped quite down the cow's throat. "There are no windows in this room," said he to himself, "and no sunshine, and I brought no light with me." Overhead his quarters seemed still worse, and more than all, he felt his room growing narrower, as the cow swallowed more hay. So he began to call out in terror as loudly as he could, "Bring me no more food. I do not want any more food!" Just then the maid was milking the cow, and when she heard the voice without seeing anything, and knew it was the same she had listened to in the night, she was so frightened that she slipped off her stool and overturned the milk. In great haste she ran to her master, saying, "Oh, Mr. Parson, the cow has been speaking."

"You are crazy," he replied; but still he went himself into The stable to see what was the matter, and scarcely had he stepped in when Thumbling began to shout out again, "Bring me no more food, bring me no more food." This terrified the parson himself, and he thought an evil spirit had entered into his cow, and so ordered her to be killed. As soon as that was done, and they were dividing the carcass, a fresh accident befell Thumbling, for a wolf, who was passing at the time, made a snatch at the cow, and tore away the part where he was stuck fast. However, he did not lose courage, but as soon as the wolf had swallowed him, he called out from inside, "Oh, Mr. Wolf, I know of a capital meal for you." "Where is it to be found?" asked the wolf

"In the house by the meadow; you must creep through the gutter, and there you will find cakes, and bacon, and sausages, as many as you can eat," replied Thumbling, describing exactly his father's house.

The wolf did not wait to be told twice, but in the night crept in, and ate away in the larder, to his heart's content. When he had finished, he tried to escape by the way he entered, but the hole was not large enough. Thereupon Thumbling, who had reckoned on this, began to make a tremendous noise inside the poor wolf, screaming and shouting as loud as he could. "Will you be quiet?" said the wolf; "you will awake the people." "Eh, what!" cried the little man, "since you have satisfied yourself, it is my turn now to make merry;" and he set up a louder howling than before. At last his father and mother awoke, and came to the room and looked through the chinks of the door; and as soon as they perceived the ravages the wolf had committed, they ran and brought the man his ax and the woman the scythe. "Stop you behind," said the man, as they entered the room; "if my blow does not kill him, you must give him a cut with your weapon, and chop off his head if you can."

When Thumbling heard his father's voice, he called out, "Father dear, I am here, in the wolf's body!" "Heaven be praised," said the man, full of joy, "our dear child is found again;" and he bade his wife take away the scythe, lest it should do any harm to his son. Then he raised his ax, and gave the wolf such a blow on its head that it fell dead, and, taking a knife, he cut it open and released the little fellow, his son. "Ah," said his father, "what trouble we have had about you." "Yes, father," replied Thumbling, "I have been traveling a great deal about the world. Heaven be praised! I breathe fresh air again."

"Where have you been, my son?" he inquired.

"Once I was in a mouse's hole, once inside a cow, and lastly inside that wolf; and now I will stop here with you," said Thumbling.

"Yes," said the old people, "we will not sell you again for all the riches of the world;" and they embraced and kissed him with great affection. Then they gave him plenty to eat and drink, and had new clothes made for him, for his old ones were worn out with traveling.

THE SIX SWANS

By William and Jacob Grimm

A king was once hunting in a large wood, and pursued his game so hotly, that none of his courtiers could follow him. But when evening approached he stopped, and looking around him perceived that he had lost himself. He sought a path out of the forest, but could not find one, and presently he saw an old woman with a nodding head, who came up to him. "My good woman," said he to her, "can you not show me the way out of the forest?" "Oh, yes, my lord King," she replied, "I can do that very well, but upon one condition, which if you do not fulfill you will never again get out of the wood, but will die of hunger."

"What, then, is this condition?" asked the King.

"I have a daughter," said the old woman, "who is as beautiful as anyone you can find in the whole world, and well deserves to be your bride. Now, if you will make her your Queen, I will show you your way out of the wood." In the anxiety of his heart the King consented, and the old woman led him to her cottage, where the daughter was sitting by a fire. She received the King as if she had expected him, and he saw at once that she was very beautiful, but yet she did not quite please him, for he could not look at her without a secret shuddering. However, after all, he took the maiden up on his horse, and the old woman showed him the way, and the King arrived safely at his palace, where the wedding was to be celebrated.

The King had been married once before, and had seven children by his first wife, six boys and a girl, whom he loved above everything else in the world. He became afraid, soon, that the stepmother might not treat them very well, and might even do them some great injury, so he took them away to a lonely castle which stood in the midst of a forest. This castle was so hidden, and the way to it so difficult to discover, that he himself could not have found it if a wise woman had not given him a ball of cotton which had the wonderful property, when he threw it before him, of unrolling itself and showing him the right path. The King went, however, so often to see his dear children, that the Queen noticed his absence, became inquisitive, and wished to know what he went to fetch out of the forest. So she gave his servants a great quantity of money, and they disclosed to her the secret, and also told her of the ball of cotton which alone could show the way. She had now no peace until she discovered where this ball was concealed, and then she made some fine silken shirts, and, as she had learned of her mother, she sewed within each one a charm. One day soon after, when the King was gone out hunting, she took the little shirts and went into the forest, and the cotton showed her the path. The children, seeing some one coming in the distance, thought it was their dear father, and ran out toward her full of joy. Then she threw over each of them a shirt, which as it touched their bodies changed them into Swans, which flew away over the forest. The Queen then went home quite contented, and thought she was free of her stepchildren; but the little girl had not met her with the brothers, and the Queen did not know of her.

The following day the King went to visit his children, but he found only the maiden. "Where are your brothers?" asked he. "Ah, dear father," she replied, "they are gone away and have left me alone;" and she told him how she had looked out of the window and seen them changed into Swans, which had flown over the forest; and then she showed him the feathers which they had dropped in the courtyard, and which she had collected together. The King was much grieved, but he did not think that his wife could have done this wicked deed, and, as he feared the girl might also be stolen away, he took her with him. She was, however, so much afraid of the stepmother, that she begged him not to stop more than one night in the castle.

The poor maiden thought to herself: "This is no longer my place, I will go and seek my brothers;" and when night came she escaped and went quite deep into the wood. She walked all night long and great part of the next day, until she could go no further from weariness. Just then she saw a rude hut, and walking in she found a room with six little beds, but she dared not get into one, but crept under, and, laying herself upon the hard earth, prepared to pass the night there. Just as the sun was setting, she heard a rustling, and saw six white Swans come flying in at the window. They settled on the ground and began blowing one another until they had blown all their feathers off, and their swan's down stripped off like a shirt. Then the maiden knew them at once for her brothers, and gladly crept out from under the bed, and the brothers were not less glad to see their sister, but their joy was of short duration. "Here you must not stay," said they to her; "this is a robber's hiding-place; if they should return and find you here, they will murder you." "Can you not protect me, then?" inquired the sister.

"No," they replied, "for we can only lay aside our swan's feathers for a quarter of an hour each evening, and for that time we retain our human form, but afterward we resume our usual appearance."

Their sister then asked them with tears, "Can you not be restored again?"

"Oh, no," replied they, "the conditions are too difficult. For six long years you must neither speak nor laugh, and during that time you must sew together for us six little shirts of star flowers, and should there fall a single word from your lips, then all your labor will be vain." Just as the brother finished speaking, the quarter of an hour elapsed, and they all flew out of the window again like Swans.

The little sister, however, made a solemn resolution to rescue her brothers or die in the attempt; and she left the cottage, and, penetrating deep into the forest, passed the night amid the branches of a tree. The next morning she went out and collected the star flowers to sew together. She had no one to converse with, and as for laughing she had no spirits, so there up in the tree she sat, intent only upon her work. After she had passed some time there, it happened that the King of that country was hunting in the forest, and his huntsmen came beneath the tree on which the maiden sat. They called to her and asked, "Who art thou?" But she gave no answer. "Come down to us," continued they, "we will do thee no harm." She simply shook her head, and, when they pressed her further with questions, she threw down to them her gold necklace, hoping therewith to satisfy them. They did not, however, leave her, and she threw down her girdle, but in vain; and even her rich dress did not make them desist. At last the hunter himself climbed the tree and brought down the maiden and took her before the King. The King asked her, "Who art thou? What dost thou upon that tree? But she did not answer, and then he asked her, in all the languages that he knew, but she remained dumb to all, as a fish. Since, however, she was so beautiful, the King's heart was touched, and he conceived for her a strong affection. Then he put around her his cloak, and, placing her before him on his horse, took her to his castle. There he ordered rich clothing to be made for her, and, although her beauty shone as the sunbeams, not a word escaped her. The King placed her by his side at table, and there her dignified mien and manners so won upon him, that he said, "This maiden will I to marry, and no other in the world," and after some days he was united to her.

Now, the King had a wicked stepmother who was discontented with his marriage, and spoke evil of the young Queen. "Who knows whence the wench comes?" said she. "She who cannot speak is not worthy of a King." A year after, when the Queen brought her first-born son into the world, the old woman took him away. Then she went to the King and complained that the Queen was a murderess. The King, however, would not believe it, and suffered no one to do any injury to his wife, who sat composedly sewing at her shirts and paying attention to nothing else. When a second child was born, the false stepmother used the same deceit, but the King again would not listen to her words, but said, "She is too pious and good to act so: could she but speak and defend herself, her innocence would come to light." But when again the third time the old woman stole away the child, and then accused the Queen, who answered her not a word to the accusation, the King was obliged to give her up to be tried, and she was condemned to suffer death by fire.

When the time had elapsed, and the sentence was to be carried out, during which she had neither spoken nor laughed, it was the very day when her dear brothers should be made free; the six shirts were also ready, all but the last, which yet wanted the left sleeve. As she was led to the scaffold she placed the shirts upon her arm, and just as she had mounted it, and the fire was about to be kindled, she looked round, and saw six Swans come flying through the air. Her heart leaped for joy as she perceived her deliverers approaching, and soon the Swans, flying toward her, alighted so near that she was enabled to throw over them the shirts, and as soon as she had so done their feathers fell off and the brothers stood up alive and well; but the youngest wanted his left arm, instead of which he had a swan's wing. They embraced and kissed each other, and the Queen going to the King, who was thunderstruck, began to say, "Now may I speak, my dear husband, and prove to you that I am innocent and falsely accused;" and then she told him how the wicked old woman had stolen away and hidden her three children. When she had concluded, the King was overcome with joy, and the wicked stepmother was led to the scaffold and bound to the stake and burned to ashes.

The King and the Queen forever after lived in peace and prosperity with their six brothers.

SNOW-WHITE AND ROSE-RED

By William and Jacob Grimm

There was once a poor Widow who lived alone in her hut with her two children, who were called Snow-White and Rose-Red, because they were like the flowers which bloomed on two rosebushes which grew before the cottage. But they were two as pious, good, industrious, and amiable children as any that were in the world, only Snow-White was more quiet and gentle than Rose-Red. For Rose-Red would run and jump about the meadows, seeking flowers and catching butterflies, while Snow-White sat at home helping her Mother to keep house, or reading to her if there were nothing else to do. The two children loved one another dearly, and always walked hand in hand when they went out together; and ever when they talked of it they agreed that they would never separate from each other, and that whatever one had the other should share. Often they ran deep into the forest and gathered wild berries; but no beast ever harmed them. For the hare would eat cauliflowers out of their hands, the fawn would graze at their side, the goats would frisk about them in play, and the birds remained perched on the boughs singing as if nobody were near. No accident ever befell them; and if they stayed late in the forest, and night came upon them, they used to lie down on the moss and sleep till morning; and because their Mother knew they would do so, she felt no concern about them. One time when they had thus passed the night in the forest, and the dawn of morning awoke them, they saw a beautiful Child dressed in shining white sitting near their couch. She got up and looked at them kindly, but without saying anything went into the forest; and when the children looked round they saw that where they had slept was close to the edge of a pit, into which they would have certainly fallen had they walked a couple of steps further in the dark. Their Mother told them the figure they had seen was doubtless the good angel who watches over children.

Snow-White and Rose-Red kept their Mother's cottage so clean that it was a pleasure to enter it. Every morning in the summer time Rose-Red would first put the house in order, and then gather a nosegay for her Mother, in which she always placed a bud from each rose tree. Every winter's morning Snow-White would light the fire and put the kettle on to boil, and although the kettle was made of copper it yet shone like gold, because it was scoured so well. In the evenings, when the flakes of snow were falling, the Mother would say: "Go, Snow-White, and bolt the door;" and then they used to sit down on the hearth, and the Mother would put on her spectacles and read out of a great book while her children sat spinning. By their side, too, laid a little lamb, and on a perch behind them a little white dove reposed with her head under her wing.

One evening, when they were thus sitting comfortably together, there came a knock at the door as if somebody wished to come in. "Make haste, Rose-Red," cried her Mother; "make haste and open the door; perhaps there is some traveler outside who needs shelter." So Rose-Red went and drew the bolt and opened the door, expecting to see some poor man outside, but instead, a great fat Bear poked his black head in. Rose-Red shrieked out and ran back, the little lamb bleated, the dove fluttered on her perch, and Snow-White hid herself behind her Mother's bed. The Bear, however, began to speak, and said: "Be not afraid, I will do you no harm; but I am half frozen, and wish to come in and warm myself."

"Poor Bear!" cried the Mother; "come in and lie down before the fire; but take care you do not burn your skin;" and then she continued: "Come here, Rose-Red and Snow-White, the Bear will not harm you, he means honorably." So they both came back, and by degrees the lamb too and the dove overcame their fears and welcomed the rough visitor.

"You children!" said the Bear, before he entered, "come and knock the snow off my coat." And they fetched their brooms and swept him clean. Then he stretched himself before the fire and grumbled out his satisfaction; and in a little while the children became familiar enough to play tricks with the unwieldy animal. They pulled his long, shaggy skin, set their feet upon his back and rolled him to and fro, and even ventured to beat him with a hazel stick, laughing when he grumbled. The Bear bore all their tricks good temperedly, and if they hit him too hard he cried out:

"Leave me my life, you children,
Snow-White and Rose-Red,
Or you'll never wed."

When bedtime came and the others were gone, the Mother said to the Bear: "You may sleep here on the hearth if you like, and then you will be safely protected from the cold and bad weather."

As soon as day broke the two children let the Bear out again, and he trotted away over the snow, and ever afterward he came every evening at a certain hour. He would lie down on the hearth and allow the children to play with him as much as they liked, till by degrees they became so accustomed to him that the door was left unbolted till their black friend arrived.

But as soon as spring returned, and everything out of doors was green again, the Bear one morning told Snow-White that he must leave her, and could not return during the whole summer. "Where are you going, then, dear Bear?" asked Snow-White, "I am obliged to go into the forest and guard my treasures from the evil Dwarfs; for in winter, when the ground is hard, they are obliged to keep in their holes, and cannot work through; but now, since the sun has thawed the earth and warmed it, the Dwarf's pierce through, and steal all they can find; and what has once passed into their hands, and gets concealed by them in their caves, is not easily brought to light." Snow-White, however, was very sad at the departure of the Bear, and opened the door so hesitatingly that when he pressed through it he left behind on the sneck a piece of his hairy coat; and through the hole which was made in his coat Snow-White fancied she saw the glittering of gold; but she was not quite certain of it. The Bear, however, ran hastily away, and was soon hidden behind the trees.

Some time afterward the Mother sent the children into the wood to gather sticks; and while doing so, they came to a tree which was lying across the path, on the trunk of which something kept bobbing up and down from the grass, and they could not imagine what it was. When they came nearer they saw a Dwarf, with an old wrinkled face and a snow-white beard a yard long. The end of this beard was fixed in a split of the tree, and the little man kept jumping about like a dog tied by a chain, for he did not know how to free himself. He glared at the Maidens with his red fiery eyes, and exclaimed, "Why do you stand there? are you going to pass without offering me any assistance?" "What have you done, little man?" asked Rose-Red. "You stupid, gaping goose!" exclaimed he. "I wanted to have split the tree, in order to get a little wood for my kitchen, for the little wood which we use is soon burned up with great fagots, not like what you rough, greedy people devour! I had driven the wedge in properly, and everything was going on well, when the smooth wood flew upward, and the tree closed so suddenly together that I could not draw my beautiful beard out, and here it sticks and I cannot get away. There, don't laugh, you milk-faced things! are you dumfounded?"

The children took all the pains they could to pull the Dwarf's beard out; but without success. "I will run and fetch some help," cried Rose-Red at length.

"Crack-brained sheep's head that you are!" snarled the Dwarf; "what are you going to call other people for? You are two too many now for me; can you think of nothing else?"

"Don't be impatient," replied Snow-White; "I have thought of something;" and pulling her scissors out of her pocket she cut off the end of the beard. As soon as the Dwarf found himself at liberty, he snatched up his sack, which lay between the roots of the tree, filled with gold, and throwing it over his shoulder marched off, grumbling and groaning and crying: "Stupid people! to cut off a piece of my beautiful beard. Plague take you!" and away he went without once looking at the children.

Some time afterward Snow-White and Rose-Red went a-fishing, and as they neared the pond they saw something like a great locust hopping about on the bank, as if going to jump into the water. They ran up and recognized the Dwarf. "What are you after?" asked Rose-Red; "you will fall into the water." "I am not quite such a simpleton as that," replied the Dwarf: "but do you not see this fish will pull me in?" The little man had been sitting there angling, and unfortunately the wind had entangled his beard with the fishing line; and so, when a great fish bit at the bait, the strength of the weak little fellow was not able to draw it out, and the fish had the best of the struggle. The Dwarf held on by the reeds and rushes which grew near; but to no purpose, for the fish pulled him where it liked, and he must soon have been drawn into the pond. Luckily just then the two Maidens arrived, and tried to release the beard of the Dwarf from the fishing line; but both were too closely entangled for it to be done. So the Maiden pulled out her scissors again and cut off another piece of the beard. When the Dwarf saw this done he was in a great rage, and exclaimed: "You donkey! that is the way to disfigure my face. Was it not enough to cut it once, but you must now take away the best part of my fine beard? I dare not show myself again now to my own people. I wish you had run the soles off your boots before you had come here!" So saying, he took up a bag of pearls which lay among the rushes, and without speaking another word, slipped off and disappeared behind a stone.

Not many days after this adventure, it chanced that the Mother sent the two Maidens to the next town to buy thread, needles and pins, laces and ribbons. Their road passed over a common, on which here and there great pieces of rock were lying about. Just over their heads they saw a great bird flying round and round, and every now and then, dropping lower and lower, till at last it flew down behind a rock. Immediately afterward they heard a piercing shriek, and running up they saw with affright that the eagle had caught their old acquaintance. the Dwarf, and was trying to carry him off. The compassionate children thereupon laid hold of the little man, and held him fast till the bird gave up the struggle and flew off. As soon then as the Dwarf had recovered from his fright, he exclaimed in his squeaking voice: "Could you not hold me more gently? You have seized my fine brown coat in such a manner that it is all torn and full of holes, meddling and interfering rubbish that you are!" With these words he shouldered a bag filled with precious stones, and slipped away to his cave among the rocks.

The maidens were now accustomed to his ingratitude, and so they walked on to the town and transacted their business there. Coming home, they returned over the same common, and unawares walked up to a certain clean spot on which the Dwarf had shaken out his bag of precious stones, thinking nobody was near. The sun was shining, and the bright stones glittered in its beams and displayed such a variety of colors that the two Maidens stopped to admire them.

"What are you standing there gaping for?" asked the Dwarf, while his face grew as red as copper with rage; he was continuing to abuse the poor Maidens, when a loud roaring noise was heard, and presently a great black Bear came rolling out of the forest. The Dwarf jumped up terrified, but he could not gain his retreat before the Bear overtook him. Thereupon, he cried out: "Spare me, my dear Lord Bear! I will give you all my treasures. See these beautiful precious stones which lie here; only give me my life; for what have you to fear from a little weak fellow like me? you could not touch me with your big teeth. There are two wicked girls, take them; they would make nice morsels, as fat as young quails; eat them for heaven's sake."

The Bear, however, without troubling himself to speak, gave the bad-hearted Dwarf a single blow with his paw, and he never stirred after.

The Maidens were then going to run away, but the Bear called after them: "Snow-White and Rose-Red, fear not! wait a bit and I will accompany you." They recognized his voice and stopped; and when the Bear came, his rough coat suddenly fell off, and he stood up a tall man, dressed entirely in gold. "I am a king's son," he said, "and was condemned by the wicked Dwarf, who stole all my treasures, to wander about in this forest, in the form of a bear, till his death released me. Now he has received his well-deserved punishment."

Then they went home, and Snow-White was married to the prince, and Rose-Red to his brother, with whom they shared the immense treasure which the Dwarf had collected. The old Mother also lived for many years happily with her two children, and the rose trees which had stood before the cottage were planted now before the palace, and produced every year beautiful red and white roses.

THE UGLY DUCKLING

By Hans Christian Andersen

It was so glorious out in the country; it was summer; the cornfields were yellow, the oats were green, the hay had been put up in stacks in the green meadows, and the stork went about on his long red legs, and chattered Egyptian, for this was the language he had learned from his good mother. All around the fields and meadows were great forests, and in the midst of these forests lay deep lakes. Yes, it was right glorious out in the country. In the midst of the sunshine there lay an old farm, with deep canals about it, and from the wall down to the water grew great burdocks, so high that little children could stand upright under the loftiest of them. It was just as wild there as in the deepest wood, and here sat a Duck upon her nest; she had to hatch her ducklings; but she was almost tired out before the little ones came; and then she so seldom had visitors. The other ducks liked better to swim about in the canals than to run up to sit down under a burdock, and cackle with her.

At last one egg-shell after another burst open. "Piep! piep!" it cried, and in all the eggs there were little creatures that stuck out their heads.

"Quack! quack!" they said; and they all came quacking out as fast as they could, looking all round them under the green leaves; and the mother let them look as much as they chose, for green is good for the eye.

"How wide the world is!" said all the young ones, for they certainly had much more room now than when they were in the eggs.

"D'ye think this is all the world?" said the mother. "That stretches far across the other side of the garden, quite into the parson's field; but I have never been there yet. I hope you are all together," and she stood up. "No, I have not all. The largest egg still lies there. How long is that to last? I am really tired of it." And she sat down again.

"Well, how goes it?" asked an old Duck who had come to pay her a visit.

"It lasts a long time with that one egg," said the Duck who sat there. "It will not burst. Now, only look at the others; are they not the prettiest little ducks one could possibly see? They are all like their father: the rogue, he never comes to see me."

"Let me see the egg which will not burst," said the old visitor. "You may be sure it is a turkey's egg. I was once cheated in that way, and had much anxiety and trouble with the young ones, for they are afraid of the water. Must I say it to you, I could not get them to venture in. I quacked and I clacked, but it was no use. Let me see the egg. Yes, that's a turkey's egg. Let it lie there, and teach the other children to swim."

"I think I will sit on it a little longer," said the Duck. "I've sat so long now that I can sit a few days more."

"Just as you please," said the old Duck; and she went away.

At last the great egg burst. "Piep! piep!" said the little one, and crept forth, it was very large and very ugly. The Duck looked at it.

"It's a very large duckling," said she; "none of the others look like that: can it really be a turkey chick? Well, we shall soon find out. It must go into the water, even if I have to thrust it in myself."

The next day, it was bright, beautiful weather; the sun shone on all the green trees. The Mother Duck went down to the canal with all her family. Splash! she jumped into the water. "Quack! quack!" she said, and one duckling after another plunged in. The water closed over their heads, but they came up in an instant, and swam capitally; their legs went of themselves, and they were all in the water. The ugly gray Duckling swam with them.

"No, it's not a turkey," said she; "look how well it can use its legs, and how straight it holds itself. It is my own child! On the whole it's quite pretty, if one looks at it rightly. Quack! quack! come with me, and I'll lead you out into the great world, and present you in the duckyard; but keep close to me, so that no one may tread on you, and take care of the cats!"

And so they came into the duckyard. There was a terrible riot, going on in there, for two families were quarreling about an eel's head, and the cat got it after all.

"See, that's how it goes in the world!" said the Mother Duck; and she whetted her beak, for she too wanted the eel's head. "Only use your legs," she said. "See that you can bustle about, and bow your heads before the old Duck yonder. She's the grandest of all here; she's of Spanish blood—that's why she's so fat; and d'ye see she has a red rag round her leg; that's something particularly fine, and the greatest distinction a duck can enjoy; it signifies that one does not want to lose her, and that she's to be known by the animals and by men too. Shake yourselves—don't turn in your toes; a well-brought-up duck turns its toes quite out, just like father and mother—so! Now bend your necks and say 'Quack!'"

And they did so: but the other ducks round about looked at them, and said quite boldly:

"Look there! now we're to have these hanging on, as if there were not enough of us already! And — fie! — how that Duckling yonder looks; we won't stand that!" And one duck flew up at it, and bit it in the neck.

"Let it alone," said the mother: "it does no harm to anyone."

"Yes, but it's too large and peculiar," said the Duck who had bitten it; "and therefore it must be put down."

"Those are pretty children that the mother has there," said the old Duck with the rag round her leg. They're all pretty but that one; that was rather unlucky. I wish she could bear it over again."

"That cannot be done, my lady," replied the Mother Duck. "It is not pretty, but it has a really good disposition, and swims as well as any other; yes, I may even say it, swims better. I think it will grow up pretty, and become smaller in time; it has lain too long in the egg, and therefore is not properly shaped." And then she pinched it in the neck, and smoothed its feathers. Moreover it is a drake," she said, "and therefore it is not so much consequence. I think he will be very strong: he makes his way already."

"The other duckling's are graceful enough," said the old Duck. "Make yourself at home; and if you find an eel's head, you may bring it to me."

And now they were at home. But the poor Duckling which had crept last out of the egg, and looked so ugly, was bitten and pushed and jeered, as much by the ducks as by the chickens.

"It is too big!" they all said. And the turkey cock, who had been born with spurs, and therefore thought himself an emperor, blew himself up like a ship in full sail, and bore straight down upon it; then he gobbled and grew quite red in the face. The poor Duckling did not know where it should stand or walk; it was quite melancholy because it looked ugly, and was the butt of the whole duckyard.

So it went on the first day; and afterward it became worse and worse. The poor Duckling was hunted about by everyone: even its brothers and sisters were quite angry with it, and said: "If the cat would only catch you, you ugly creature!" And the mother said: "If you were only far away!" And the ducks hit it, and the chickens beat it, and the girl who had to feed the poultry kicked at it with her foot.

Then it ran and flew over the fence, and the little birds in the bushes flew up in fear.

"That is because I am so ugly!" thought the Duckling; and it shut its eyes, but flew on further; and so it came out into the great moor, where the wild ducks lived. Here it lay the whole night long; and it was weary and downcast.

Toward morning the wild chicks flew up, and looked at their new companion.

"What sort of a one are you?" they asked; and the Duckling turned in every direction, and bowed as well as it could. You are remarkably ugly!" said the Wild Ducks. "But that is nothing to us, so long as you do not marry into our family."

Poor thing! it certainly did not think of marrying, and only hoped to obtain leave to lie among the reeds and drink some of the swamp water.

Thus it lay two whole days; then came thither two wild geese, or, properly speaking, two wild ganders. It was not long since each had crept out of an egg, and that's why they were so saucy.

"Listen, comrade," said one of them. "You're so ugly that I like you. Will you go with us, and become a bird of passage? Near here, in another moor, there are a few sweet lovely geese, all unmarried, and all able to say 'Rap?' You've a chance of' making your fortune, ugly as you are."

"Piff! paff!" resounded through the air; and the two ganders fell down dead in the swamp, and the water became blood red. "Piff paff!" it sounded again, and the whole flock of wild geese rose up from the reeds. And then there was another report. A great hunt was going on. The sportsmen were lying in wait all round the moor, and some were even sitting up in the branches of the trees, which spread far over the reeds. The blue smoke rose up like clouds among the dark trees, and was wafted far away across the water; and the hunting dogs came—splash, splash!—into the swamp, and the rushes and the reeds bent down on every side. That was a fright for the poor Duckling! It turned its head, and put it under its wing; but at that moment a frightful great dog stood close by the Duckling. His tongue hung far out of his mouth, and his eyes gleamed horrible and ugly; he thrust out his nose close against the Duckling, showed his Sharp teeth, and—splash, splash!—on he went, without seizing it.

"O, Heaven be thanked!" sighed the Duckling. "I am so ugly, that even the dog does not like to bite me!"

And so it lay quite quiet, while the shots rattled through the reeds and gun after gun was fired. At last, late in the day, all was still; but the poor Duckling did not dare to rise up; it waited several hours before it looked round, and then hastened away out of the moor as fast it could. It ran on over field and meadow; there was such a storm raging that it was difficult to get from one place to another.

Toward evening the Duck came to a little miserable peasant's hut. This hut was so dilapidated that it did not itself know on which side it should fall; and that's why it remained standing. The storm whistled round the Duckling in such a way that the poor creature was obliged to sit down, to stand against it; and the wind blew worse and worse. Then the Duckling noticed that one of the hinges of the door had given way, and the door hung so slanting that the Duckling could slip through the crack into the room; and that is what it did.

Here lived a woman, with her Cat and her Hen. And the Cat, whom she called Sonnie, could arch his back and purr, he could even give out sparks; but for that one had to stroke his fur the wrong way. The Hen had quite little short legs, and therefore she was called Chickabiddy Shortshanks; she laid good eggs, and the woman loved her as her own child.

In the morning the strange Duckling was at once noticed, and the Cat began to purr and the Hen to cluck.

"What's this?" said the woman, and looked all round; but she could not see well, and therefore she thought the Duckling was a fat duck that had strayed. "This is a rare prize!" she said, "Now I shall have ducks' eggs. I hope it is not a drake. We must try that."

And so the Duckling was admitted on trial for three weeks; but no eggs came. And the Cat was master of the house, and the Hen was the lady, and always said "We and the world!" for she thought they were half the world, and by far the better half. The Duckling thought one might have a different opinion, but the Hen would not allow it.

"Can you lay eggs?" she asked.

"No."

"Then will you hold your tongue!"

And the Cat said, "Can you curve your back, and purr, and give out sparks?"

"No."

"Then you will please have no opinion of your own when sensible folks are speaking.

And the Duckling sat in a corner and was melancholy; then the fresh air and the sunshine streamed in; and it was seized with such a strange longing to swim on the water, that it could not help telling the Hen of it.

"What are you thinking of?" cried the Hen. "You have nothing to do, that's why you have these fancies. Lay eggs, or purr, and they will pass over."

"But it is so charming to swim on the water!" said the Duckling, "so refreshing to let it close over one's head, and to dive down to the bottom."

"Yes, that must be a mighty pleasure, truly," quoth the Hen. "I fancy you must have gone crazy. Ask the Cat about it—he's the cleverest animal I know—ask him if he likes to swim on the water, or to dive down: I won't speak about myself. Ask our mistress, the old woman; no one in the world is cleverer than she. Do you think she has any desire to swim, and to let the water close above her head?"

"You don't understand me," said the Duckling.

"We don't understand you? Then pray who is to understand you? You surely don't pretend to be cleverer than the Cat and the woman—I won't say anything of myself. Don't be conceited, child, and thank your Maker for all the kindness you have received. Did you not get into a warm room, and have you not fallen into company from which you may learn something? But you are a chatterer, and it is not pleasant to associate with you. You may believe me, I speak for your good. I tell you disagreeable things, and by that one may always know one's true friends! Only take care that you learn to lay eggs, or to purr, and give out sparks!"

"I think I will go out into the wide world," said the Duckling.

"Yes, do go," replied the Hen.

And so the Duckling went away. It swam on the water, and dived, but it was slighted by every creature because of its ugliness.

Now came the autumn. The leaves in the forest turned yellow and brown; the wind caught them so that they danced about, and up in the air it was very cold. The clouds hung low, heavy with hail and snowflakes, and on the fence stood the raven, crying, "Croak! croak!" for mere cold; yes, it was enough to make one feel cold to think of this. The poor little Duckling certainly had not a good time. One evening—the sun was just setting in his beauty—there came a whole flock of great, handsome birds out of the bushes; they were dazzlingly white, with long, flexible necks; they were swans. They uttered a very peculiar cry, spread forth their glorious great wings, and flew away from that cold region to warmer lands, to fair open lakes. They mounted so high, so high! and the ugly Duckling felt quite strangely as it watched them. It turned round and round in the water like a wheel, stretched out its neck toward them, and uttered such a strange, loud cry as frightened itself. Oh! it could not forget those beautiful, happy birds; and so soon as it could see them no longer, it dived down to the very bottom, and when it came up again, it was quite beside itself. It knew not the name of those birds, and knew not whither they were flying; but it loved them more than it had ever loved anyone. It was not at all envious of them. How could it think of wishing to possess such loveliness as they had? It would have been glad if only the ducks would have endured its company the poor, ugly creature!

And the winter grew cold, very cold! The Duckling was forced to swim about in the water, to prevent the surface from freezing entirely; but every night the hole in which it swam about became smaller and smaller. It froze so hard that the icy covering crackled again; and the Duckling was obliged to use its legs continually to prevent the hole from freezing up. At last it became exhausted, and lay quite still, and thus froze fast into the ice. Early in the morning a peasant came by, and when he saw what had happened, he took his wooden shoe, broke the ice crust to pieces, and carried the Duckling home to his wife. Then it came to itself again. The children wanted to play with it; but the Duckling thought they wanted to hurt it, and in its terror fluttered up into the milk pan, so that the milk spurted down into the room. The woman clasped her hands, at which the Duckling flew down into the butter tub, and then into the meal barrel and out again. How it looked then! The woman screamed, and struck at it with the fire tongs; the children tumbled over one another in their efforts to catch the Duckling; and they laughed and they screamed!—well it was that the door stood open, and the poor creature was able to slip out between the shrubs into the newly fallen snow—there it lay quite exhausted.

But it would be too melancholy if I were to tell all the misery and care which the Duckling had to endure in the hard winter. It lay out on the moor among the reeds, when the sun began to shine again and the larks to sing: it was a beautiful spring.

Then all at once the Duckling could flap its wings: they beat the air more strongly than before, and bore it strongly away; and before it well knew how all this happened, it found itself in a great garden, where the elder trees smelled sweet, and bent their long green branches down to the canal that wound through the region. Oh, here it was so beautiful, such a gladness of spring! and from the thicket came three glorious white swans; they rustled their wings, and swam lightly on the water. The Duckling knew the splendid creatures, and felt oppressed by a peculiar sadness.

"I will fly away to them, to the royal birds! and they will beat me, because I, that am so ugly, dare to come near them. But it is all the same. Better to be killed by them than to be pursued by ducks, and beaten by fowls, and pushed about by the girl who takes care of the poultry yard, and to suffer hunger in winter!" And it flew out into the water, and swam toward the beautiful swans: these looked at it, and came sailing down upon it with outspread wings. "Kill me!" said the poor creature, and bent its head down upon the water, expecting nothing but death. But what was this that it saw in the clear water? It beheld its own image; and, lo! it was no longer a clumsy, dark-gray bird, ugly and hateful to look at, but a—swan!

It matters nothing if one is born in a duck yard, if one has only lain in a swan's egg.

It felt quite glad at all the need and misfortune it had suffered, now it realized its happiness in all the splendor that surrounded it. And the great swans swam round it, and stroked it with their beaks.

Into the garden came little children, who threw bread and corn into the water; and the youngest cried, "There is a new one!" and the other children shouted joyously, "Yes, a new one has arrived!" And they clapped their hands and danced about, and ran to their father and mother; and bread and cake were thrown into the water; and they all said, "The new one is the most beautiful of all so young and handsome!" and the old swans bowed their heads before him.

Then he felt quite ashamed, and hid his head under his wings, for he did not know what to do; he was so happy, and yet not at all proud. He thought how he had been persecuted and despised; and now he heard them saying that he was the most beautiful of all birds. Even the elder tree bent its branches straight down into the water before him, and the sun shone warm and mild. Then his wings rustled, he lifted his slender neck, and cried rejoicingly from the depths of his heart:

"I never dreamed of so much happiness when I was the Ugly Duckling!"

THE TINDER-BOX

By Hans Christian Andersen

There came a soldier marching along the high road—one, two! one, two! He had his knapsack on his back and a saber by his side, for he had been in the wars, and now he wanted to go home. And on the way he met with an old Witch: she was very hideous and her under lip hung down upon her breast. She said: "Good evening, Soldier. What a fine sword you have, and what a big knapsack! You're a proper soldier! Now you shall have as much money as you like to have."

"I thank you, you old Witch" said the Soldier.

"Do you see that great tree?" quoth the Witch; and she pointed to a tree which stood beside them.

"It's quite hollow inside. You must climb to the top, and then you'll see a hole, through which you can let yourself down and get deep into the tree. I'll tie a rope round your body, so that I can pull you up again when you call me."

"What am I to do down in the tree?" asked the Soldier.

"Get money," replied the Witch. "Listen to me. When you come down to the earth under the tree, you will find yourself in a great hall: it is quite light, for above three hundred lamps are burning there. Then you will see three doors; these you can open, for the keys are hanging there. If you go into the first chamber, you'll see a great chest in the middle of the floor; on this chest sits a dog, and he's got a pair of eyes as big as two teacups. But you need not care for that. I'll give you my blue-checked apron, and you can spread it out upon the floor; then go up quickly and take the dog, and set him on my apron; then open the chest, and take as many shillings as you like. They are of copper; if you prefer silver, you must go into the second chamber. But there sits a dog with a pair of eyes as big as mill wheels. But do not you care for that. Set him upon my apron, and take some of the money. And if you want gold, you can have that too—in fact, as much as you can carry—if you go into the third chamber. But the dog that sits on the money chest there has two eyes as big as round towers. He is a fierce dog, you may be sure; but you needn't be afraid, for all that. Only set him on my apron, and he won't hurt you; and take out of the chest as much gold as you like."

"That's not so bad," said the Soldier. "But what am I to give you, you old Witch? for you will not do it for nothing, I fancy."

"No," replied the Witch, "not a single shilling will I have. You shall only bring me an old Tinder-box which my grandmother forgot when she was down there last."

"Then tie the rope round my body," cried the Soldier.

"Here it is," said the Witch, "and here's my blue-checked apron."

Then the Soldier climbed up into the tree, let himself slip down into the hole, and stood, as the Witch had said, in the great hall where the three hundred lamps were burning.

Now he opened the first door. Ugh! there sat the dog with eyes as big as teacups, staring at him.

"You're a nice fellow!" exclaimed the Soldier; and he set him on the Witch's apron, and took as many shillings as his pockets would hold, and then locked the chest, set the dog on it again, and went into the second chamber, Aha! there sat the dog with eyes as big as mill wheels.

"You should not stare so hard at me," said the Soldier; "you might strain your eyes." And he set the dog upon the Witch's apron. And when he saw the silver money in the chest, he threw away all the copper money he had and filled his pockets and his knapsack with silver only. Then he went into the third chamber. Oh, but that was horrid! The dog there really had eyes as big as towers, and they turned round and round in his head like wheels.

"Good evening!" said the Soldier; and he touched his cap, for he had never seen such a dog as that before. When he had looked at him a little more closely, he thought: "That will do," and lifted him down to the floor, and opened the chest. Mercy! What a quantity of gold was there! He could buy with it the whole town, and the sugar sucking pigs of the cake woman, and all the tin soldiers, whips, and rocking-horses in the whole world. Yes, that was a quantity of money! Now the Soldier threw away all the silver coin with which he had filled his pockets and his knapsack, and took gold instead; yes, all his pockets, his knapsack, his boots, and his cap were filled, so that he could scarcely walk. Now indeed he had plenty of money. He put the dog on the chest shut the door, and then called up through the tree: "Now pull me up, you old Witch!"

"Have you the Tinder-box?" asked the Witch.

"Plague on it!" exclaimed the Soldier, "I had clean forgotten that." And he went and brought it.

The Witch drew him up, and he stood on the high road again, with pockets, boots, knapsack, and cap full of gold.

"What are you going to do with the Tinder-box?" asked the Soldier.

"That's nothing to you," retorted the Witch. "You've had your money; just give me the Tinder-box."

"Nonsense!" said the Soldier. "Tell me directly what you're going to do with it or I'll draw my sword and cut off your head."

"No!" cried the Witch.

So the Soldier cut off her head. There she lay! But he tied up all his money in her apron, took it on his back like a bundle, put the Tinder-box in his pocket, and went straight off toward the town.

That was a splendid town! And he put up at the very best inn, and asked for the finest rooms, and ordered his favorite dishes, for now he was rich, as he had so much money. The servant who had to clean his boots certainly thought them a remarkably old pair for such a rich gentleman; but he had not bought any new ones yet. The next day he procured proper boots and handsome clothes. Now our Soldier had become a fine gentleman; and the people told him of all the splendid things which were in their city, and about the King, and what a pretty Princess the King's daughter was.

"Where can one get to see her?" asked the Soldier.

"She is not to be seen at all," said they all together; "she lives in a great copper castle, with a great many walls and towers round about it: no one but the King may go in and out there, for it has been prophesied that she shall marry a common soldier, and the King can't bear that."

"I should like to see her," thought the Soldier; but he could not get leave to do so. Now he lived merrily, went to the theater, drove in the King's garden, and gave much money to the poor; and this was very kind of him, for he knew from old times how hard it is when one has not a shilling.

Now he was rich, had new clothes, and gained many friends, who all said he was a rare one, a true cavalier; and that pleased the Soldier well. But as he spent money every day and never carried any, he had at last only two shillings left; and he was obliged to turn out of the fine rooms in which he had dwelt, and had to live in a little garret under the roof, and clean his boots for himself, and mend them with a darning-needle. None of his friends came to see him, for there were too many stairs to climb.

It was quite dark one evening, and he could not even buy himself a candle, when it occurred to him that there was a candle end in the Tinder-box which he had taken out of the hollow tree into which the Witch had helped him. He brought out the Tinder-box and the candle end; but as soon as he struck fire and the sparks rose up from the flint, the door flew open, and the dog who had eyes as big as a couple of teacups, and whom he had seen in the tree, stood before him, and said:

"What are my lord's commands?"

"What is this?" said the Soldier. "That's a famous Tinder-box, if I can get everything with it that I want! Bring me some money," said he to the dog; and whisk! the dog was gone, and whisk! he was back again, with a great bag full of shillings in his mouth.

Now the Soldier knew what a capital Tinder-box this was. If he struck it once, the dog came who sat upon the chest of copper money; if he struck it twice, the dog came who had the silver; and if he struck it three times, then appeared the dog who had the gold. Now the Soldier moved back into the fine rooms, and appeared again in handsome clothes; and all his friends knew him again, and cared very much for him indeed.

Once he thought to himself: "It is a very strange thing that one cannot get to see the Princess. They all say she is very beautiful; but what is the use of that, if she has always to sit in the great copper castle with the many towers? Can I not get to see her at all? Where is my Tinder-box?" And so he struck a light, and whisk! came the dog with eyes as big as teacups.

"It is midnight, certainly," said the Soldier, "but I should very much like to see the Princess, only for one little moment."

And the dog was outside the door directly, and, before the Soldier thought it, came back with the Princess. She sat upon the dogs back and slept; and everyone could see she was a real Princess, for she was so lovely. The Soldier could not refrain from kissing her, for he was a thorough soldier. Then the dog ran back again with the Princess. But when morning came, and the King and Queen were drinking tea, the Princess said she had had a strange dream the night before about a dog and a soldier — that she had ridden upon the dog, and the soldier had kissed her.

"That would be a fine history!" said the Queen.

So one of the old court ladies had to watch the next night by the Princess's bed, to see if this was really a dream, or what it might be.

The Soldier had a great longing to see the lovely Princess again; so the dog came in the night, took her away, and ran as fast as he could. But the old lady put on water boots, and ran just as fast after him. When she saw that they both entered a great house, she thought: "Now I know where it is; and with a bit of chalk she drew a great cross on the door. Then she went home and lay down, and the dog came up with the Princess; but when he saw that there was a cross drawn on the door where the Soldier lived, he took a piece of chalk too, and drew crosses on all the doors in the town. And that was cleverly done, for now the lady could not find the right door, because all the doors had crosses upon them.

In the morning early came the King and Queen, the old court lady and all the officers, to see where it was the Princess had been. "Here it is!" said the King, when he saw the first door with a cross upon it. "No, my dear husband, it is there!" said the Queen, who descried another door which also showed a cross. "But there is one, and there is one!" said all, for wherever they looked there were crosses on the doors. So they saw that it would avail them nothing if they searched on.

But the Queen was an exceedingly clever woman, who could do more than ride in a coach. She took her great gold scissors, cut a piece of silk into pieces, and made a neat little bag; this bag she filled with fine wheat flour, and tied it on the Princess's back, and when that was done, she cut a little hole in the bag, so that the flour would be scattered along all the way which the Princess should take.

In the night the dog came again, took the Princess on his back, and ran with her to the Soldier, who loved her very much, and would gladly have been a prince, so that he might have her for his wife. The dog did not notice at all how the flour ran out in a stream from the castle to the windows of the Soldier's house, where he ran up the wall with the Princess. In the morning the King and Queen saw well enough where their daughter had been, and they took the Soldier and put him in prison.

There he sat. Oh, but it was dark and disagreeable there! And they said to him: "To-morrow you shall be hanged." That was not amusing to hear, and he had left his Tinder-box at the inn. In the morning he could see, through the iron grating of the little window, how the people were hurrying out of the town to see him hanged. He heard the drums beat and saw the soldiers marching. All the people were running out, and among them was the shoemaker's boy with leather apron and slippers, and he galloped so fast that one of his slippers flew off, and came right against the wall where the Soldier sat looking through the iron grating.

"Halloo, you shoemaker's boy! you needn't be in such a hurry," cried the Soldier to him: "it will not begin till I come. But if you will run to where I lived and bring me my Tinder-box, you shall have four shillings: but you must put your best leg foremost."

The shoemaker's boy wanted to get the four shillings, so he went and brought the Tinder-box, and—well, we shall hear now what happened.

Outside the town a great gallows had been built, and round it stood the soldiers and many hundred thousand people. The King and Queen sat on a splendid throne, opposite to the judges and the whole council. The soldiers already stood upon the ladder; but as they were about to put the rope round his neck, he said that before a poor criminal suffered his punishment an innocent request was always granted to him. He wanted very much to smoke a pipe of tobacco, and it would be the last pipe he should smoke in the world. The King would not say "No" to this; so the Soldier took his Tinder-box and struck fire. One — two — three! — and there suddenly stood all the dogs — the one with eyes as big as teacups, the one with eyes as large as mill wheels, and the one whose eyes were as big as round towers.

"Help me now, so that I may not be hanged," said the Soldier.

And the dogs fell upon the judges and all the council, seized one by the leg and another by the nose, and tossed them many feet into the air, so that they fell down and were all broken to pieces.

"I won't!" cried the King; but the biggest dog took him and the Queen, and threw them after the others. Then the soldiers were afraid, and the people cried: "Little Soldier, you shall be our king, and marry the beautiful Princess."

So they put the Soldier into the King's coach, and all the three dogs darted on in front and cried "Hurrah!" and the boys whistled through their fingers, and the soldiers presented arms. The Princess came out of the copper castle, and became Queen, and she liked that well enough. The wedding lasted a week, and the three dogs sat at the table too, and opened their eyes wider than ever at all they saw.

THE CONSTANT TIN SOLDIER

By Hans Christian Andersen

There were once five-and-twenty tin soldiers; they were all brothers, for they had all been born of one old tin spoon. They shouldered their muskets, and looked straight before them; their uniform was red and blue, and very splendid. The first thing they had heard in the world, when the lid was taken off the box, had been the words "Tin soldiers!" These words were tittered by a little boy, clapping his hands; the soldiers had been given to him, for it was his birthday; and now he put them upon the table. Each soldier was exactly like the rest; but one of them had been cast last of all, and there had not been enough tin to finish him; but he stood as firmly upon his one leg as the others on their two; and it was just this soldier who became remarkable.

On the table on which they had been placed stood many other playthings, but the toy that attracted most attention was a neat castle of cardboard. Through the little windows one could see straight into the hall. Before the castle some little trees were placed round a little looking-glass, which was to represent a clear lake. Waxen swans swam on this lake, and were mirrored in it. This was all very pretty; but the prettiest of all was a little Lady, who stood at the open door of the castle; she was also cut out in paper, but she had a dress of the clearest gauze, and a little narrow blue ribbon over her shoulders that looked like a scarf; and in the middle of this ribbon was a shining tinsel rose, as big as her whole face. The little Lady stretched out both her arms, for she was a dancer, and then she lifted one leg so high that the Tin Soldier could not see it at all, and thought that, like himself, she had but one leg.

"That would be the wife for me," thought he; "but she is very grand. She lives in a castle, and I have only a box, and there are five-and-twenty of us in that. It is no place for her. But I must try to make acquaintance with her."

And then he lay down at full length behind a snuffbox which was on the table; there he could easily watch the little dainty lady, who continued to stand on one leg without losing her balance.

When the evening came, all the other tin soldiers were put into their box, and the people in the house went to bed. Now the toys began to play at "visiting," and at "war," and "giving balls." The tin soldiers rattled in their box, for they wanted to join, but could not lift the lid. The Nutcracker threw somersaults, and the Pencil amused itself on the table; there was so much noise that the Canary woke up, and began to speak too, and even in verse. The only two who did not stir from their places were the Tin Soldier and the Dancing Lady; she stood straight up on the point of one of her toes, and stretched out both her arms: and he was just as enduring on his one leg; and he never turned his eyes away from her.

Now the clock struck twelve — and, bounce! — the lid flew off the snuffbox; but there was not snuff in it, but a little black goblin; you see, it was a trick.

"Tin Soldier," said the Goblin, "don't stare at things that don't concern you."

But the Tin Soldier pretended not to hear him. "Just you wait till to-morrow!" said the Goblin. But when the morning came, and the children got up, the Tin Soldier was placed in the window; and whether it was the Goblin or the draft that did it, all at once the window flew open, and the Soldier fell, head over heels, out of the third story. That was a terrible passage! He put his leg straight up, and struck with his helmet downward, and his bayonet between the paving stones.

The servant maid and the little boy came down directly to look for him, but though they almost trod upon him they could not see him. If the Soldier had cried out, "Here I am!" they would have found him; but he did not think it fitting to call out loudly, because he was in uniform.

Now it began to rain; the drops soon fell thicker, and at last it came down in a complete stream. When the rain was past, two street boys came by.

"Just look!" said one of them, "there lies a tin soldier. He must come out and ride in the boat."

And they made a boat out of a newspaper, and put the Tin Soldier in the middle of it; and so he sailed down the gutter, and the two boys ran beside him and clapped their hands. Goodness preserve us! how the waves rose in that gutter, and how fast the stream ran! But then it had been a heavy rain. The paper boat rocked up and down, and sometimes turned round so rapidly that the Tin Soldier trembled; but he remained firm and never changed countenance, and looked straight before him, and shouldered his musket.

All at once the boat went into a long drain, and it became as dark as if he had been in his box.

"Where am I going now?" he thought. "Yes, yes, that's the Goblin's fault. Ah! if the little Lady only sat here with me in the boat, it might be twice as dark for what I should care."

Suddenly there came a great water rat, which lived under the drain.

"Have you a passport?" said the Rat. "Give me your passport."

But the Tin Soldier kept silence, and only held his musket tighter than ever.

The boat went on, but the Rat came after it. Hu! how he gnashed his teeth, and called out to the bits of straw and wood:

"Hold him! hold him! he hasn't paid toll — he hasn't showed his passport!"

But the stream became stronger and stronger. The Tin Soldier could see the bright daylight where the arch ended; but he heard a roaring noise, which might well frighten a bolder man. Only think — just where the tunnel ended the drain ran into a great canal; and for him that would have been as dangerous as for us to be carried down a great waterfall.

Now he was already so near it that he could not stop. The boat was carried out, the poor Tin Soldier stiffening himself as much as he could, and no one could say that he moved an eyelid. The boat whirled round three or four times, and was full of water to the very edge — it must sink. The Tin Soldier stood up to his neck in water, and the boat sank deeper and deeper, and the paper was loosened more and more, and now the water closed over the Soldier's head. Then he thought of the pretty little dancer, and how he should never see her again; and it sounded in the Soldier's ears:

"Farewell, farewell, thou warrior brave,
Die shalt thou this day."

And now the paper parted, and the Tin Soldier fell out; but at that moment he was snapped up by a great fish.

Oh, how dark it was in that fish's body! It was darker yet than in the drain tunnel; and then it was very narrow, too. But the Tin Soldier remained unmoved, and lay at full length, shouldering his musket.

The fish swam to and fro; he made the most wonderful movements, and then became quite still. At last something flashed through him like lightning. The daylight shone quite clear, and a voice said aloud, "The Tin Soldier!" The fish had been caught, carried to market, bought, and taken into the kitchen, where the cook cut him open with a large knife. She seized the Soldier round the body with both her hands, and carried him into the room, where all were anxious to see the remarkable man who had traveled about in the inside of a fish; but the Tin Soldier was not at all proud. They placed him on the table, and there — no! What curious things may happen in the world! The Tin Soldier was in the very room in which he had been before! he saw the same children, and the same toys stood upon the table; and there was the pretty castle with the graceful little Dancer. She was still balancing herself on one leg and held the other extended in the air. She was faithful, too. That moved the Tin Soldier: he was very near weeping tin tears, but that would not have been proper. He looked at her, but they said nothing to each other.

Then one of the little boys took the Tin Soldier and flung him into the stove. He gave no reason for doing this. It must have been the fault of the Goblin in the snuffbox.

The Tin Soldier stood there quite illuminated, and felt a heat that was terrible; but whether this heat proceeded from the real fire or from love he did not know. The colors had quite gone off from him; but whether that had happened on the journey, or had been caused by grief, no one could say. He looked at the little Lady, she looked at him, and he felt that he was melting; but he stood firm, shouldering his musket. Then suddenly the door flew open, and the draft of air caught the Dancer, and she flew like a sylph just into the stove to the Tin Soldier, and flashed up in a flame, and then was gone! Then the Tin Soldier melted down into a lump, and when the servant maid took the ashes out next day, she found him in the shape of a little tin heart. But of the Dancer nothing remained but the tinsel rose, and that was burned as black as coal.

THE FIR TREE

By Hans Christian Andersen

Out in the woods stood a nice little Fir tree. The place he had was a very good one; the sun shone on him; as to fresh air, there was enough of that, and round him grew many large-sized comrades, pines as well as firs. But the little Fir wanted so very much to be a grown-up tree.

He did not think of the warm sun and of the fresh air; he did not care for the little cottage children that ran about and prattled when they were in the wood looking for wild strawberries. The children often came with a whole pitcher full of berries, or a long row of them threaded on a straw, and sat down near the young Tree and said, "Oh, how pretty he is! what a nice little fir!" But this was what the Tree could not bear to hear.

At the end of a year he had shot up a good deal, and after another year he was another long bit taller; for with fir trees one can always tell by the shoots how many years old they are.

"Oh, were I but such a high tree as the others are," sighed he. "Then I should be able to spread out my branches, and with the tops to look into the wide world! Then would the birds build nests among my branches; and when there was a breeze, I could bend with as much stateliness as the others!"

Neither the sunbeams, nor the birds, nor the red clouds which morning and evening sailed above him, gave the little Tree any pleasure.

In winter, when the snow lay glittering on the ground, a hare would often come leaping along, and jump right over the little Tree. Oh, that made him so angry! But two winters were past, and in the third the Tree was so large that the hare was obliged to go round it. "To grow and grow, to get older and be tall," thought the Tree—"that, after all, is the most delightful thing in the world!"

In autumn the woodcutters always came and felled some of the largest trees. This happened every year; and the young Fir tree, that had now grown to a very comely size, trembled at the sight; for the magnificent great trees fell to the earth with noise and cracking, the branches were lopped off, and the trees looked long and bare: they were hardly to be recognized; and then they were laid in carts, and the horses dragged them out of the wood.

Where did they go to? What became of them? In spring, when the Swallows and the Storks came, the Tree asked them: "Don't you know where they have been taken? Have you not met them anywhere?"

The Swallows did not know anything about it; but the Stork looked musing, nodded his head, and said: "Yes; I think I know; I met many ships as I was flying hither from Egypt; on the ships were magnificent masts, and I venture to assert that it was they that smelled so of fir. I may congratulate you, for they lifted themselves on high most majestically!"

"Oh, were I but old enough to fly across the sea! But how does the sea look in reality? What is it like?"

"That would take a long time to explain," said the Stork, and with these words off he went.

"Rejoice in thy growth!" said the Sunbeams, "rejoice in thy vigorous growth, and in the fresh life that groweth within thee!"

And the Wind kissed the Tree, and the Dew wept tears over him; but the Fir understood it not.

When Christmas came, quite young trees were cut down; trees which often were not even as large or of the same age as this Fir tree, who could never rest, but always wanted to be off. These young trees, and they were always the finest looking, retained their branches; they were laid on carts, and the horses drew them out of the wood.

"Where are they going to?" asked the Fir.

"They are not taller than I; there was one indeed that was considerably shorter; — and why do they retain all their branches? Whither are they taken?"

"We know! we know!" chirped the Sparrows. "We have peeped in at the windows in the town below! We know whither they are taken! The greatest splendor and the greatest magnificence one can imagine await them. We peeped through the windows, and saw them planted in the middle of the warm room, and ornamented with the most splendid things—with gilded apples, with gingerbread, with toys, and many hundred lights!"

"And then?" asked the Fir tree, trembling in every bough. "And then? What happens then?"

"We did not see anything more: it was incomparably beautiful."

"I would fain know if I am destined for so glorious a career," cried the Tree, rejoicing. "That is still better than to cross the sea! What a longing do I suffer! Were Christmas but come! I am now tall, and my branches spread like the others that were carried off last year! Oh, were I but already on the cart! Were I in the warm room with all the splendor and magnificence! Yes; then something better, something still grander, will surely follow, or wherefore should they thus ornament me? Something better, something still grander, must follow—but what? Oh, how I long, how I suffer! I do not know myself what is the matter with me!"

"Rejoice in our presence!" said the Air and the Sunlight; "rejoice in thy own fresh youth!"

But the Tree did not rejoice at all; he grew and grew, and was green both winter and summer. People that saw him said, "What a fine tree!" and toward Christmas he was one of the first that was cut down. The ax struck deep into the very pith; the tree fell to the earth with a sigh: he felt a pang—it was like a swoon; he could not think of happiness, for he was sorrowful at being separated from his home, from the place where he had sprung up. He well knew that he should never see his dear old comrades, the little bushes and flowers around him, any more; perhaps not even the birds! The departure was not at all agreeable.

The Tree only came to himself when he was unloaded in a courtyard with the other trees, and heard a man say, "That one is splendid! we don't want the others." Then two servants came in rich livery and carried the Fir tree into a large and splendid drawing-room. Portraits were hanging on the walls, and near the white porcelain stove stood two large Chinese vases with lions on the covers. There, too, were large easy-chairs, silken sofas, large tables full of picture books, and full of toys worth hundreds and hundreds of crowns—at least the children said so. And the Fir tree was stuck upright in a cask that was filled with sand: but no one could see that it was a cask, for green cloth was hung all round it, and it stood on a large gayly colored carpet. Oh, how the Tree quivered! What was to happen? The servants, as well as the young ladies, decorated it. On one branch there hung little nets cut out of colored paper, and each net was filled with sugarplums; and among the other boughs gilded apples and walnuts were suspended, looking as though they had grown there, and little blue and white tapers were placed among the leaves. Dolls that looked for all the world like men—the Tree had never beheld such before—were seen among the foliage, and at the very top a large star of gold tinsel was fixed. It was really splendid—beyond description splendid.

"This evening!" said they all; "how it will shine this evening!"

"Oh," thought the Tree, "if the evening were but come! If the tapers were but lighted! And then I wonder what will happen! Perhaps the other trees from the forest will come to look at me! Perhaps the sparrows will beat against the windowpanes! I wonder if I shall take root here, and winter and summer stand covered with ornaments!"

He knew very much about the matter! but he was so impatient that for sheer longing he got a pain in his back, and this with trees is the same thing as a headache with us.

The candles were now lighted. What brightness! What splendor! The Tree trembled so in every bough that one of the tapers set fire to the foliage. It blazed up splendidly.

"Help! help!" cried the young ladies, and they quickly put out the fire.

Now the Tree did not even dare tremble. What a state he was in! He was so uneasy lest he should lose something of his splendor, that he was quite bewildered amid the glare and brightness; when suddenly both folding doors opened, and a troop of children rushed in as if they would upset the Tree. The older persons followed quietly; the little ones stood quite still. But it was only for a moment; then they shouted so that the whole place reechoed with their rejoicing; they danced round the Tree, and one present after the other was pulled off.

"What are they about?" thought the Tree. "What is to happen now!" And the lights burned down to the very branches, and as they burned down they were put out one after the other, and then the children had permission to plunder the Tree. So they fell upon it with such violence that all its branches cracked; if it had not been fixed firmly in the cask, it would certainly have tumbled down.

The children danced about with their beautiful playthings; no one looked at the Tree except the old nurse, who peeped between the branches; but it was only to see if there was a fig or an apple left that had been forgotten.

"A story! a story!" cried the children, drawing a little fat man toward the Tree. He seated himself under it, and said: "Now we are in the shade, and the Tree can listen too. But I shall tell only one story. Now which will you have; that about IvedyAvedy, or about Klumpy-Dumpy who tumbled downstairs, and yet after all came to the throne and married the princess?"

"Ivedy-Avedy," cried some; "Klumpy-Dumpy," cried the others. There was such a bawling and screaming!—the Fir tree alone was silent, and he thought to himself, "Am I not to bawl with the rest?—am I to do nothing whatever?" for he was one of the company, and had done what he had to do.

And the man told about Klumpy-Dumpy that tumbled down, who notwithstanding came to the throne, and at last married the princess. And the children clapped their hands, arid cried out, "Oh, go on! Do go on!" they waited to hear about Ivedy-Avedy too, but the little man only told them about Klumpy-Dumpy. The Fir tree stood quite still and absorbed in thought: the birds in the wood had never related the like of this. "Klumpy-Dumpy fell downstairs, and yet he married the princess! Yes, yes! that's the way of the world!" thought the Fir tree, and believed it all, because the man who told the story was so good-looking. "Well, well! who knows, perhaps I may fall downstairs too, and get a princess as wife!" And he looked forward with joy to the morrow, when he hoped to be decked out again with lights, play-things, fruits, and tinsel.

"I won't tremble to-morrow!" thought the Fir tree. "I will enjoy to the full all my splendor! To-morrow I shall hear again the story of Klumpy-Dumpy, and perhaps that of Ivedy-Avedy too." And the whole night the Tree stood still and in deep thought.

In the morning the servant and the housemaid came in.

"Now then the splendor will begin again," thought the Fir. But they dragged him out of the room, and up the stairs into the loft; and here, in a dark corner, where no daylight could enter, they left him. "What's the meaning of this?" thought the Tree. "What am I to do here? What shall I hear now, I wonder?" And he leaned against the wall lost in reverie. Time enough had he too for his reflections; for days and nights passed on, and nobody came up; and when at last somebody did come, it was only to put some great trunks in a corner out of the way. There stood the Tree quite hidden; it seemed as if he had been entirely forgotten.

"'Tis now winter out-of-doors!" thought the Tree. "The earth is hard and covered with snow; men cannot plant me now, and therefore I have been put up here under shelter till the springtime comes! How thoughtful that is! How kind man is, after all! If it only were not so dark here, and so terribly lonely! Not even a hare. And out in the woods it was so pleasant, when the snow was on the ground, and the hare leaped by; yes—even when he jumped over me; but I did not like it then. It is really terribly lonely here!"

"Squeak! squeak!" said a little Mouse at the same moment, peeping out of his hole. And then another little one came. They snuffed about the Fir tree, and rustled among the branches.

"It is dreadfully cold," said the Mouse. "But for that, it would be delightful here, old Fir, wouldn't it?"

"I am by no means old," said the Fir tree. "There's many a one considerably older than I am."

"Where do you come from," asked the Mice; "and what can you do?" They were so extremely curious. "Tell us about the most beautiful spot on the earth. Have you never been there? Were you never in the larder, where cheeses lie on the shelves, and hams hang from above; where one dances about on tallow candles; that place where one enters lean, and comes out again fat and portly?"

"I know no such place," said the Tree. "But I know the wood, where the sun shines, and where the little birds sing." And then he told all about his youth; and the little Mice had never heard the like before; and they listened and said:

"Well, to be sure! How much you have seen! How happy you must have been!"

"I!" said the Fir tree, thinking over what he had himself related. "Yes, in reality those were happy times." And then he told about Christmas Eve, when he was decked out with cakes and candles.

"Oh," said the little Mice, "how fortunate you have been, old Fir tree!"

"I am by no means old," said he. "I came from the wood this winter; I am in my prime, and am only rather short for my age."

"What delightful stories you know!" said the Mice; and the next night they came with four other little Mice, who were to hear what the Tree recounted; and the more he related, the more plainly he remembered all himself; and it appeared as if those times had really been happy times. "But they may still come — they may still come. Humpy-Dumpy fell downstairs, and yet he got a princess!" and he thought at the moment of a nice little Birch tree growing out in the woods; to the Fir, that would be a real charming princess.

"Who is Klumpy-Dumpy?" asked the Mice. So then the Fir tree told the whole fairy tale, for he could remember every single word of it; and the little Mice jumped for joy up to the very top of the Tree. Next night two more Mice came, and on Sunday two Rats, even; but they said the stories were not interesting, which vexed the little Mice; and they, too, now began to think them not so very amusing either.

"Do you know only one story?" asked the Rats.

"Only that one," answered the Tree. "I heard it on my happiest evening; but I did not then know how happy I was."

"It is a very stupid story! Don't you know one about bacon and tallow candles? Can't you tell any larder stories?"

"No," said the Tree.

"Then good-by," said the Rats and they went home.

At last the little Mice stayed away also; and the Tree sighed: "After all, it was very pleasant when the sleek little Mice sat round me and listened to what I told them. Now that too is over. But I will take good care to enjoy myself when I am brought out again."

But when was that to be? Why, one morning there came a quantity of people and set to work in the loft. The trunks were moved, the tree was pulled out and thrown — rather hard, it is true — down on the floor, but a man drew him toward the stairs, where the daylight shone.

"Now a merry life will begin again," thought the Tree. He felt the fresh air, the first sunbeam — and now he was out in the courtyard. All passed so quickly, there was so much going on around him, that the Tree quite forgot to look to himself. The court adjoined a garden, and all was in flower; the roses hung so fresh and odorous over the balustrade, the lindens were in blossom, the Swallows flew by, and said "Quirre-vit! my husband is come!" but it was not the Fir tree that they meant.

"Now, then, I shall really enjoy life," said he, exultingly, and spread out his branches; but, alas! they were all withered and yellow. It was in a corner that he lay, among weeds and nettles. The golden star of tinsel was still on the top of the Tree, and glittered in the sunshine.

In the courtyard some of the merry children were playing who had danced at Christmas round the Fir tree, and were so glad at the sight of him. One of the youngest ran and tore off the golden star.

"Only look what is still on the ugly old Christmas tree!" said he, trampling on the branches, so that they all cracked beneath his feet.

And the Tree beheld all the beauty of the flowers, and the freshness in the garden; he beheld himself, and wished he had remained in his dark corner in the loft: he thought of his first youth in the wood, of the Merry Christmas Eve, and of the little Mice who had listened with so much pleasure to the story of Humpy-Dumpy.

"'Tis over — 'tis past!" said the poor Tree. "Had I but rejoiced when I had reason to do so! But now 'tis past, 'tis past!"

And the gardener's boy chopped the Tree into small pieces; there was a whole heap lying there. The wood flamed up splendidly under the large brewing copper, and it sighed so deeply! Each sigh was like a shot.

The boys played about in the court, and the youngest wore the gold star on his breast which the Tree had had on the happiest evening of his life. However, that was over now — the Tree gone, the story at an end. All, all was over; every tale must end at last.

THE FLYING TRUNK

By Hans Christian Andersen

There was once a merchant, who was so rich that he could pave the whole street with gold, and almost have enough left for a little lane. But he did not do that; he knew how to employ his money differently. When he spent a shilling he got back a crown, such a clever merchant was he; and this continued till he died.

His son now got all this money; and he lived merrily, going to the masquerade every evening, making kites out of dollar notes, and playing at ducks and drakes on the seacoast with gold pieces instead of pebbles. In this way the money might soon be spent, and indeed it was so. At last he had no more than four shillings left, and no clothes to wear but a pair of slippers and an old dressing gown.

Now his friends did not trouble themselves any more about him as they could not walk with him in the street, but one of them, who was good-natured, sent him an old trunk, with the remark: "Pack up!" Yes, that was all very well, but he had nothing to pack, therefore he seated himself in the trunk.

That was a wonderful trunk. So soon as any one pressed the lock the trunk could fly. He pressed it, and whirr! away flew the trunk with him through the chimney and over the clouds farther and farther away. But as often as the bottom of the trunk cracked a little he was in great fear lest it might go to pieces, and then he would have flung a fine somersault! In that way he came to the land of the Turks. He hid the trunk in a wood under some dry leaves, and then went into the town. He could do that very well, for among the Turks all the people went about dressed like himself in dressing gown and slippers. Then he met a nurse with a little child.

"Here, you Turkish nurse," he began, "what kind of a great castle is that close by the town, in which the windows are so high up?"

"There dwells the Sultan's daughter," replied she. "It is prophesied that she will be very unhappy respecting a lover; and therefore nobody may go near her, unless the Sultan and Sultana are there too."

"Thank you!" said the Merchant's Son; and he went out into the forest, seated himself in his trunk, flew on the roof, and crept through the window into the Princess's room.

She was lying asleep on the sofa, and she was so beautiful that the Merchant's Son was compelled to kiss her. Then she awoke, and was startled very much; but he said he was a Turkish angel who had come down to her through the air, and that pleased her.

They sat down side by side, and he told her stories about her eyes; and he told her they were the most glorious dark lakes, and that thoughts were swimming about in them like mermaids. And he told her about her forehead; that it was a snowy mountain with the most splendid halls and pictures. And he told her about the stork who brings the lovely little children.

Yes, those were fine histories! Then he asked the Princess if she would marry him, and she said, "Yes," directly.

"But you must come here on Saturday," said she. "Then the Sultan and Sultana will be here to tea. They will be very proud that I am to marry a Turkish angel. But take care that you know a very pretty story, for both my parents are very fond indeed of stories. My mother likes them high-flown and moral, but my father likes them merry, so that one can laugh."

"Yes, I shall bring no marriage gift but a story," said he; and so they parted. But the Princess gave him a saber, the sheath embroidered with gold pieces and that was very useful to him.

Now he flew away, bought a new dressing gown, and sat in the forest and made up a story; it was to be ready by Saturday, and that was not an easy thing.

By the time he had finished it Saturday had come. The Sultan and his wife and all the court were at the 'Princess's to tea. He was received very graciously.

"Will you relate us a story?" said the Sultana; "one that is deep and edifying."

"Yes, but one that we can laugh at," said the Sultan.

"Certainly," he replied; and so began. And now listen well.

"There was once a bundle of Matches, and these Matches were particularly proud of their high descent. Their genealogical tree, that is to say, the great fir tree of which each of them was a little splinter, had been a great old tree out in the forest. The Matches now lay between a Tinder-box and an old Iron Pot; and they were telling about the days of their youth. 'Yes, when we were upon the green boughs,' they said, 'then we really were upon the green boughs! Every morning and evening there was diamond tea for us—I mean dew; we had sunshine all day long whenever the sun shone, and all the little birds had to tell stories. We could see very well that we were rich, for the other trees were only dressed out in summer, while our family had the means to wear green dresses in the winter as well. But then the woodcutter came, like a great revolution, and our family was broken up. The head of the family got an appointment as mainmast in a first-rate ship, which could sail round the world if necessary; the other branches went to other places, and now we have the office of kindling a light for the vulgar herd. That's how we grand people came to be in the kitchen.'

"'My fate was of different kind,' said the Iron Pot, which stood next to the Matches. 'From the beginning, ever since I came into the world, there has been a great deal of scouring and cooking done in me. I look after the practical part, and am the first here in the house. My only pleasure is to sit in my place after dinner, very clean and neat, and to carry on a sensible conversation with my comrades. But except the Waterpot, which is sometimes taken down into the courtyard, we always live within our four walls. Our only newsmonger is the Market Basket; but he speaks very uneasily about the government and the people. Yes, the other day there was an old pot that fell down, from fright, and burst. He's liberal, I can tell you!'—'Now you're talking too much,' the Tinder-box interrupted, and the steel struck against the flint, so that sparks flew out. 'Shall we not have a merry evening?'

"'Yes, let us talk about who is the grandest,' said the Matches.

"'No, I don't like to talk about myself,' retorted the Pot. 'Let us get up an evening entertainment. I will begin. I will tell a story from real life, something that everyone has experienced, so that we can easily imagine the situation, and take pleasure in it. On the Baltic, by the Danish shore—'

"'That's a pretty beginning!' cried all the Plates. 'That will be a story we shall like.'

"'Yes, it happened to me in my youth, when I lived in a family where the furniture was polished, the floors scoured, and new curtains were put up every fortnight.'

"'What an interesting way you have of telling a story!' said the Carpet Broom. 'One can tell directly that a man is speaking who has been in woman's society. There's something pure runs through it.'

"And the Pot went on telling the story, and the end was as good as the beginning.

"All the Plates rattled with joy, and the Carpet Broom brought some green parsley out of the dust hole, and put it like a wreath on the Pot, for he knew that it would vex the others. 'If I crown him to-day,' it thought, 'he will crown me tomorrow.'

"'Now I'll dance,' said the Fire Tongs; and they danced. Preserve us! how that implement could lift up one leg! The old chair-cushion burst to see it. 'Shall I be crowned too?' thought the Tongs; and indeed a wreath was awarded.

"'They're only common people, after all!' thought the Matches.

"Now the Tea Urn was to sing; but she said she had taken cold and could not sing unless she felt boiling within. But that was only affectation: she did not want to sing, except when she was in the parlor with the grand people.

"In the window sat an old Quill Pen, with which the maid generally wrote: there was nothing remarkable about this pen, except that it had been dipped too deep into the ink, but she was proud of that. 'If the Tea Urn won't sing,' she said, 'she may leave it alone. Outside hangs a nightingale in a cage, and he can sing. He hasn't had any education, but this evening we'll say nothing about that.'

"'I think it very wrong,' said the Teakettle—he was the kitchen singer, and half brother to the Tea Urn—'that that rich and foreign bird should be listened to. Is that patriotic? Let the Market Basket decide.'

"'I am vexed,' said the Market Basket. 'No one can imagine how much I am secretly vexed. Is that a proper way of spending the evening? Would it not be more sensible to put the house in order? Let each one go to his own place, and I will arrange the whole game. That would be quite another thing.'

'Yes, let us make a disturbance, cried they all. Then the door opened, and the maid came in, and they all stood still; not one stirred. But there was not one pot among them who did not know what he could do and how grand he was. 'Yes, if I had liked,' each one thought, 'it might have been a very merry evening.'

"The servant girl took the Matches and lighted the fire with them. mercy! how they sputtered and burst out into flame! 'Now everyone can see,' thought they, 'that we are the first. How we shine! what a light!'—and they burned out."

"That was a capital story," said the Sultana. "I feel myself quite carried away to the kitchen, to the Matches. Yes, now thou shalt marry our daughter."

"Yes, certainly," said the Sultan, "thou shalt marry our daughter on Monday."

And they called him thou, because he was to belong to the family.

The wedding was decided on, and on the evening before it the whole city was illuminated. Biscuits and cakes were thrown among the people, the street boys stood on their toes, called out "Hurrah!" and whistled on their fingers. It was uncommonly splendid.

"Yes, I shall have to give something as a treat," thought the Merchant's Son. So he bought rockets and crackers, and every imaginable sort of firework, put them all into his trunk, and flew up into the air.

"Crack!" how they went, and how they went off! All the Turks hopped up with such a start that their slippers flew about their ears; such a meteor they had never yet seen. Now they could understand that it must be a Turkish angel who was going to marry the Princess.

What stories people tell! Everyone whom he asked about it had seen it in a separate way; but one and all thought it fine.

"I saw the Turkish angel himself," said one. "He had eyes like glowing stars, and a beard like foaming water."

"He flew up in a fiery mantle," said another; "the most lovely little cherub peeped forth from among the folds."

Yes, they were wonderful things that he heard; and on the following day he was to be married.

Now he went back to the forest to rest himself in his trunk. But what had become of that? A spark from the fireworks had set fire to it, and the trunk was burned to ashes. He could not fly any more, and could not get to his bride.

She stood all day on the roof waiting; and most likely she is waiting still. But he wanders through the world, telling fairy tales; but they are not so merry as that one he told about the Matches.

THE DARNING NEEDLE

By Hans Christian Andersen

There was once a darning needle, who thought herself so fine, she imagined she was an embroidery needle.

"Take care, and mind you hold me tight!" she said to the Fingers that took her out. "Don't let me fall! If I fall on the ground I shall certainly never be found again, for I am so fine!"

"That's as it may be," said the Fingers; and they grasped her round the body.

"See, I'm coming with a train!" said the Darning Needle, and she drew a long thread after her, but there was no knot in the thread.

The Fingers pointed the needle just at the cook's slipper, in which the upper leather had burst, and was to be sewn together.

"That's vulgar work," said the Darning Needle. "I shall never get through. I'm breaking! I'm breaking!" And she really broke. "Did I not say so?" said the Darning Needle; "I'm too fine!"

"Now it's quite useless," said the Fingers; but they were obliged to hold her fast, all the same; for the cook dropped some sealing wax upon the needle, and pinned her handkerchief together with it in front.

"So, now I'm a breastpin!" said the Darning Needle. "I knew very well that I should come to honor: when one is something, one comes to something!"

And she laughed quietly to herself—and one can never see when a darning needle laughs. There she sat, as proud as if she was in a state coach, and looked all about her.

"May I be permitted to ask if you are of gold?" she inquired of the pin, her neighbor. "You have a very pretty appearance, and a peculiar head, but it is only little. You must take pains to grow, for it's not everyone that has sealing wax dropped upon him."

And the Darning Needle drew herself up so proudly that she fell out of the handkerchief right into the sink, which the cook was rinsing out.

"Now we're going on a journey," said the Darning Needle. "If I only don't get lost!"

But she really was lost.

"I'm too fine for this world," she observed, as she lay in the gutter. "But I know who I am, and there's always something in that!"

So the Darning Needle kept her proud behavior, and did not lose her good humor. And things of many kinds swam over her, chips and straws and pieces of old newspapers.

"Only look how they sail!" said the Darning Needle. "They don't know what is under them! I'm here, I remain firmly here. See, there goes a chip thinking of nothing in the world but of himself—of a chip! There's a straw going by now. How he turns! how he twirls about! Don't think only of yourself, you might easily run up against a stone. There swims a bit of newspaper. What's written upon it has long been forgotten, and yet it gives itself airs. I sit quietly and patiently here. I know who I am, and I shall remain what I am."

One day something lay close beside her that glittered splendidly; then the Darning Needle believed that it was a diamond; but it was a bit of broken bottle; and because it shone, the Darning Needle spoke to it, introducing herself as a breastpin.

"I suppose you are a diamond?" she observed.

"Why, yes, something of that kind."

And then each believed the other to be a very valuable thing; and they began speaking about the world, and how very conceited it was.

"I have been in a lady's box," said the Darning Needle, "and this lady was a cook. She had five fingers on each hand, and I never saw anything so conceited as those five fingers. And yet they were only there that they might take me out of the box and put me back into it."

"Were they of good birth?" asked the Bit of Bottle.

"No, indeed," cried the Darning Needle, "but very haughty. There were five brothers, all of the finger family. They kept very proudly together, though they were of different lengths: the outermost, the thumbling, was short and fat; he walked out in front of the ranks, and only had one joint in his back, and could only make a single bow; but he said that if he were hacked off a man, that man was useless for service in war. Daintymouth, the second finger, thrust himself into sweet and sour, pointed to sun and moon, and gave the impression when they wrote. Longman, the third, looked at all the others over his shoulder. Goldborder, the fourth, went about with a golden belt round his waist; and little Playman did nothing at all, and was proud of it. There was nothing but bragging among them, and therefore I went away."

"And now we sit here and glitter!" said the Bit of Bottle.

At that moment more water came into the gutter, so that it overflowed, and the Bit of Bottle was carried away.

"So he is disposed of," observed the Darning Needle. "I remain here, I am too fine. But that's my pride, and my pride is honorable." And proudly she sat there, and had many great thoughts. "I could almost believe I had been born of a sunbeam, I'm so fine! It really appears as if the sunbeams were always seeking for me under the water. Ah! I'm so fine that my mother cannot find me. If I had my old eye, which broke off, I think I should cry; but, no, I should not do that: it's not genteel to cry."

One day a couple of street boys lay grubbing in the gutter where they sometimes find old nails, farthings, and similar treasures. It was dirty work, but they took great delight in it.

"Oh!" cried one, who had pricked himself with the Darning Needle, there's a fellow for you!"

"I'm not a fellow; I'm a young lady!" said the Darning Needle.

But nobody listened to her. The sealing wax had come off, and she had turned black; but black makes one look slender, and she thought herself finer even than before.

"Here comes an eggshell sailing along!" said the boys; and they stuck the Darning Needle fast in the eggshell.

"White walls, and black myself! that looks well," remarked the Darning Needle. "Now one can see me. I only hope I shall not be seasick!" But she was not seasick at all. "It is good against seasickness, if one has a steel stomach, and does not forget that one is a little more than an ordinary person! Now my seasickness is over. The finer one is, the more one can bear."

"Crack!" went the eggshell, for a wagon went over her.

"Good heavens, how it crushes one!" said the Darning Needle. "I'm getting seasick now — I'm quite sick."

But she was not really sick, though the wagon went over her; she lay there at full length, and there she may lie.

PEN AND INKSTAND

By Hans Christian Andersen

The following remark was made in a poet's room, as the speaker looked at the inkstand that stood upon his table:

"It is marvelous all that can come out of that ink-stand! What will it produce next? Yes, it is marvelous!"

"So it is!" exclaimed the Inkstand. "It is incomprehensible! That is what I always say." It was thus the Inkstand addressed itself to the Pen, and to everything else that could hear it on the table. "It is really astonishing all that can come from me! It is almost incredible! I positively do not know myself what the next thing may be, when a person begins to dip into me. One drop of me serves for half a side of paper; and what may not then appear upon it? I am certainly something extraordinary. From me proceed all the works of the poets. These animated beings, whom people think they recognize—these deep feelings, that gay humor, these charming descriptions of nature—I do not understand them myself, for I know nothing about nature; but still it is all in me. From me have gone forth, and still go forth, these warrior hosts, these lovely maidens, these bold knights on snorting steeds, those droll characters in humbler life. The fact is, however, that I do not know anything about them myself. I assure you they are not my ideas."

"You are right there," replied the Pen. "You have few ideas, and do not trouble yourself much with thinking, if you did exert yourself to think, you would perceive that you ought to give something that was not dry. You supply me with the means of committing to paper what I have in me; I write with that. It is the pen that writes. Mankind do not doubt that; and most men have about as much genius for poetry as an old inkstand."

"You have but little experience," said the ink-stand. "You have scarcely been a week in use, and you are already half worn out. Do you fancy that you are a poet? You are only a servant: and I have had many of your kind before you came—many of the goose family, and of English manufacture. I know both quill pens and steel pens. I have had a great many in my service, and I shall have many more still, when he, the man who stirs me up, comes and puts down what he takes from me. I should like very much to know what will be the next thing he will take from me."

"Ink tub!" said the Pen.

Late in the evening the Poet returned home. He had been at a concert, had heard a celebrated violin player, and was quite enchanted with his wonderful performance. It had been a complete gush of melody that he had drawn from the instrument. Sometimes it seemed like the gentle murmur of a rippling stream, sometimes like the singing of birds, sometimes like the tempest sweeping through the mighty pine forests, he fancied he heard his own heart weep, but in the sweet tones that can be heard in a woman's charming voice. It seemed as if not only the strings of the violin made music, but its bridge, its pegs, and its sounding board. It was astonishing! The piece had been a most difficult one; but it seemed like play—as if the bow were but wandering capriciously over the strings. Such was the appearance of facility, that everyone might have supposed he could do it. The violin seemed to sound of itself, the bow to play of itself. These two seemed to do it all. One forgot the master who guided them, who gave them life and soul. Yes, they forgot the master; but the Poet thought of him. He named him, and wrote down his thoughts as follows:

"How foolish it would be of the violin and the bow, were they to be vain in their performance! And yet this is what so often we of the human species are. Poets, artists, those who make discoveries in science, military and naval commanders—we are all proud of ourselves; and yet we are all only the instruments in our Lord's hands. To Him alone be the glory! We have nothing to arrogate to ourselves."

This was what the Poet wrote; and he headed it with: "The Master and the Instruments."

"Well, madam," said the Pen to the Inkstand when they were again alone, "you heard him read aloud what I had written."

"Yes, what I gave you to write," said the Ink-stand. "It was a hit at you for your conceit. Strange that you cannot see that people make a fool of you! I gave you that hit pretty cleverly. I confess, though, it was rather malicious."

"Inkholder!" cried the Pen.

"Writing stick!" cried the Inkstand.

They both felt assured that they had answered well; and it is a pleasant reflection that one has made a smart reply—one sleeps comfortably after it. And they both went to sleep; but the Poet could not sleep. His thoughts welded forth like the tones from the violin, trilling like pearls, rushing like a storm through the forest. He recognized the feeling of his own heart—he perceived the gleam from the everlasting Master.

To Him alone be the glory!

CINDERELLA

Retold by Miss Mulock

There was once an honest gentleman who took for his second wife a lady, the proudest and most disagreeable in the whole country. She had two daughters exactly like herself in all things. He also had one little girl, who resembled her dead mother, the best woman in all the world. Scarcely had the second marriage taken place, than the stepmother became jealous of the good qualities of the little girl who was so great a contrast to her own two daughters. She gave her all the menial occupations of the house; compelled her to wash the floors and staircases; to dust the bedrooms, and clean the grates; and while her sisters occupied carpeted chambers hung with mirrors, where they could see themselves from head to foot, this poor little damsel was sent to sleep in an attic, on an old straw mattress, with only one chair and not a looking-glass in the room.

She suffered all in silence, not daring to complain to her father, who was entirely ruled by his new wife. When her daily work was done, she used to sit down in the chimney corner among the ashes; from which the two sisters gave her the nickname of Cinderella. But Cinderella, however, shabbily clad, was handsomer than they were with all their fine clothes.

It happened that the king's son gave a series of balls, to which were invited all the rank and fashion of the city, and among the rest the two elder sisters. They were very proud and happy, and occupied their whole time in deciding what they should wear; a source of new trouble to Cinderella, whose duty it was to get up their fine linen and laces, and who never could please them however much she tried. They talked of nothing but their clothes.

"I," said the elder, "shall wear my velvet gown and my trimmings of English lace."

"And I," added the younger, "will have but my ordinary silk petticoat, but I shall adorn it with an upper skirt of flowered brocade, and shall put on my diamond tiara, which is a great deal finer than anything of yours."

Here the elder sister grew angry, and the dispute began to run so high that Cinderella, who was known to have excellent taste, was called upon to decide between them. She gave them the best advice she could, and gently and submissively offered to dress them herself, and especially to arrange their hair, an accomplishment in which she excelled many a noted coiffeur. The important evening came, and she exercised all her skill to adorn the two young ladies. While she was combing out the elder's hair, this ill-natured girl said sharply, "Cinderella, do you not wish you were going to the ball?"

"Ah, madam" (they obliged her always to say madam), "you are only mocking me; it is not my fortune to have any such pleasure."

"You are right; people would only laugh to see a little cinder wench at a ball."

Any other than Cinderella would have dressed the hair all awry, but she was good, and dressed it perfectly even and smooth, and as prettily as she could.

The sisters had scarcely eaten for two days, and had broken a dozen staylaces a day, in trying to make themselves slender; but to-night they broke a dozen more, and lost their tempers over and over again before they had completed their toilet. When at last the happy moment arrived, Cinderella followed them to the coach; after it had whirled them away, she sat down by the kitchen fire and cried.

Immediately her godmother, who was a fairy, appeared beside her. "What are you crying for, my little maid?"

"Oh, I wish—I wish—" Her sobs stopped her.

"You wish to go to the ball; isn't it so?"

Cinderella nodded.

"Well then, be a good girl, and you shall go. First run into the garden and fetch me the largest pumpkin you can find."

Cinderella did not comprehend what this had to do with her going to the ball, but being obedient and obliging, she went. Her godmother took the pumpkin, and having scooped out all its inside, struck it with her wand; it became a splendid gilt coach, lined with rose-colored satin.

"Now fetch me the mousetrap out of the pantry, my dear."

Cinderella brought it; it contained six of the fattest, sleekest mice. The fairy lifted up the wire door, and as each mouse ran out she struck it and changed it into a beautiful black horse.

"But what shall I do for your coachman, Cinderella?"

Cinderella suggested that she had seen a large black rat in the rat trap, and he might do for want of better.

"You are right; go and look again for him."

He was found; and the fairy made him into a most respectable coachman, with the finest whiskers imaginable. She afterward took six lizards from behind the pumpkin frame, and changed them into six footmen, all in splendid livery, who immediately jumped up behind the carriage, as if they had been footmen all their days. "Well, Cinderella, now you can go to the ball."

"What, in these clothes?" said Cinderella piteously, looking down on her ragged frock.

Her godmother laughed, and touched her also with the wand; at which her wretched threadbare jacket became stiff with gold, and sparkling with jewels; her woolen petticoat lengthened into a gown of sweeping satin, from underneath which peeped out her little feet, no longer bare, but covered with silk stockings, and the prettiest glass slippers in the world. "Now, Cinderella, depart; but remember, if you stay one instant after midnight, your carriage will become a pumpkin, your coachman a rat, your horses mice, and your footmen lizards; while you, yourself, will be the little cinder wench you were an hour ago."

Cinderella promised without fear, her heart was so full of joy.

Arrived at the palace, the king's son, whom some one, probably the fairy, had told to await the coming of an uninvited princess, whom nobody knew, was standing at the entrance, ready to receive her. He offered her his hand, and led her with the utmost courtesy through the assembled guests, who stood aside to let her pass, whispering to one another, "Oh, how beautiful she is!" It might have turned the head of anyone but poor Cinderella, who was so used to be despised, that she took it all as if it were something happening in a dream.

Her triumph was complete; even the old king said to the queen, that never since her majesty's young days had he seen so charming and elegant a person. All the court ladies scanned her eagerly, clothes and all, determining to have theirs made next day of exactly the same pattern. The king's son himself led her out to dance, and she danced so gracefully that he admired her more and more. Indeed, at supper, which was fortunately early, his admiration quite took away his appetite. For Cinderella, herself, with an involuntary shyness, sought out her sisters; placed herself beside them and offered them all sorts of civil attentions, which coming as they supposed from a stranger, and so magnificent a lady, almost overwhelmed them with delight.

While she was talking with them, she heard the clock strike a quarter to twelve, and making a courteous adieu to the royal family, she reentered her carriage, escorted tenderly by the king's son, and arrived in safety at her own door. There she found her godmother, who smiled approval; and of whom she begged permission to go to a second ball, the following night, to which the queen had earnestly invited her.

While she was talking, the two sisters were heard knocking at the gate, and the fairy godmother vanished, leaving Cinderella sitting in the chimney corner, rubbing her eyes and pretending to be very sleepy.

"Ah," cried the eldest sister maliciously, "it has been the most delightful ball, and there was present the most beautiful princess I ever saw, who was so exceedingly polite to us both."

"Was she?" said Cinderella indifferently; "and who might she be?"

"Nobody knows, though everybody would give their eyes to know, especially the king's Son."

"Indeed!" replied Cinderella, a little more interested; "I should like to see her. Miss Javotte" — that was the elder sister's name — "will you not let me go to-morrow, and lend me your yellow gown that you wear on Sundays?"

"What, lend my yellow gown to a cinder wench! I am not so mad as that;" at which refusal Cinderella did not complain, for if her sister really had lent her the gown, she would have been considerably embarrassed.

The next night came, and the two young ladies, richly dressed in different toilets, went to the ball.

Cinderella, more splendidly attired and beautiful than ever, followed them shortly after. "Now remember twelve o'clock," was her godmother's parting speech; and she thought she certainly should. But the prince's attentions to her were greater even than the first evening, and in the delight of listening to his pleasant conversation, time slipped by unperceived. While she was sitting beside him in a lovely alcove, and looking at the moon from under a bower of orange blossoms, she heard a clock strike the first stroke of twelve. She started up, and fled away as lightly as a deer.

Amazed, the prince followed, but could not catch her. Indeed he missed his lovely princess altogether, and only saw running out of the palace doors, a little dirty lass whom he had never beheld before, and of whom he certainly would never have taken the least notice. Cinderella arrived at home breathless and weary, ragged and cold, without carriage, or footman or coachman; the only remnant of her past magnificence being one of her little glass slippers — the other she had dropped in the ballroom as she ran away.

When the two sisters returned, they were full of this strange adventure, how the beautiful lady had appeared at the ball more beautiful than ever, and enchanted everyone who looked at her; and how as the clock was striking twelve she had suddenly risen up and fled through the ballroom, disappearing no one knew how or where, and dropping one of her glass slippers behind her in her flight. How the king's son had remained inconsolable, until he chanced to pick up the little glass slipper, which he carried away in his pocket, and was seen to take it out continually, and look at it affectionately, with the air of a man very much in love; in fact, from his behavior during the remainder of the evening, all the court and royal family were convinced that he had become desperately enamored of the wearer of the little glass slipper.

Cinderella listened in silence, turning her face to the kitchen fire, and perhaps it was that which made her look so rosy, but nobody ever noticed or admired her at home, so it did not signify, and next morning she went to her weary work again just as before.

A few days after, the whole city was attracted by the sight of a herald going round with a little glass slipper in his hand, publishing with a flourish of trumpets, that the king's son ordered this to be fitted on the foot of every lady in the kingdom, and that he wished to marry the lady whom it fitted best, or to whom it and the fellow slipper belonged. Princesses, duchesses, countesses, and simple gentlewomen all tried it on, but being a fairy slipper, it fitted nobody; and besides, nobody could produce its fellow slipper, which lay all the time safely in the pocket of Cinderella's old linsey gown.

At last the herald came to the house of the two sisters, and though they well knew neither of themselves was the beautiful lady, they made every attempt to get their clumsy feet into the glass slipper, but in vain.

"Let me try it on," said Cinderella from the chimney corner.

"What, you?" cried the others, bursting into shouts of laughter; but Cinderella only smiled, and held out her hand.

Her sisters could not prevent her, since the command was that every young maiden in the city should try on the slipper, in order that no chance might be left untried, for the prince was nearly breaking his heart; and his father and mother were afraid that though a prince, he would actually die for love of the beautiful unknown lady.

So the herald bade Cinderella sit down on a three-legged stool in the kitchen, and himself put the slipper on her pretty little foot, which it fitted exactly; she then drew from her pocket the fellow slipper, which she also put on, and stood up—for with the touch of the magic shoes all her dress was changed likewise—no longer the poor despised cinder wench, but the beautiful lady whom the king's son loved.

Her sisters recognized her at once. Filled with astonishment, mingled with no little alarm, they threw themselves at her feet, begging her pardon for all their former unkindness. She raised and embraced them; told them she forgave them with all her heart, and only hoped they would love her always. Then she departed with the herald to the king's palace, and told her whole story to his majesty and the royal family, who were not in the least surprised, for everybody believed in fairies, and everybody longed to have a fairy godmother.

For the young prince, he found her more lovely and lovable than ever, and insisted upon marrying her immediately. Cinderella never went home again, but she sent for her two sisters to the palace, and with the consent of all parties married them shortly after to two rich gentlemen of the court.

LITTLE RED RIDING-HOOD

By Charles Perrault

Once upon a time there lived in a certain village a little country girl, the prettiest creature ever seen. Her mother was very fond of her, and her grandmother doted on her still more. This good woman had made for her a little red riding-hood, which became the girl so well that everybody called her Little Red Riding-Hood.

One day her mother, having made some custards, said to her:

"Go, my dear, and see how thy grandmamma does, for I hear she has been very ill; carry her a custard and this little pot of butter."

Little Red Riding-Hood set out immediately to go to her grandmother, who lived in another village.

As she was going through the wood she met with Gaffer Wolf, who had a very great mind to eat her up, but he durst not, because of some fagot makers hard by in the forest. He asked her whither she was going. The poor child, who did not know that it was dangerous to stop and listen to a wolf, said to him:

"I am going to see my grandmamma and carry her a custard and a little pot of butter from my mamma."

"Does she live far off?" said the Wolf.

"Oh! yes," answered Little Red Riding-Hood; "it is beyond that mill you see there, at the first house in the village."

"Well," said the Wolf, "I'll go and see her, too. I'll go this way and you go that, and we shall see who will be there soonest."

The Wolf began to run as fast as he could, taking the nearest way, and the little girl went by the longest, diverting herself in gathering nuts, running after butterflies, and making nosegays of such little flowers as she met with. The Wolf was not long before he got to the old woman's house. He knocked at the door—tap, tap.

"Who's there?"

"Your grandchild, Little Red Riding-Hood," replied the Wolf, imitating her voice; "who has brought you a custard and a little pot of butter sent you by mamma."

The good grandmother, who was in bed, because she was ill, cried out:

"Pull the bobbin, and the latch will go up."

The Wolf pulled the bobbin, and the door opened, and he fell upon the good woman and ate her up in a moment, for it was above three days that he had not touched a bit. He then shut the door and went into the grandmother's bed, expecting Little Red Riding-Hood, who came some time afterward and knocked at the door — tap, tap.

"Who's there?"

Little Red Riding-Hood, hearing the big voice of the Wolf, was at first afraid; but believing her grandmother had got a cold and was hoarse, answered:

'Tis your grandchild, Little Red Riding-Hood, who has brought you a custard and a little pot of butter mamma sends you."

The Wolf cried out to her, softening his voice as much as he could:

"Pull the bobbin and the latch will go up."

Little Red Riding-Hood pulled the bobbin and the door opened.

The wolf, seeing her come in, said to her, hiding himself under the bedclothes:

"Put the custard and the little pot of butter upon the stool, and come and lie down with me."

Little Red Riding-Hood undressed herself and went into bed, where, being greatly amazed to see how her grandmother looked in her night clothes, she said to her:

"Grandmamma, what great arms you've got!"

"That is the better to hug thee, my dear."

"Grandmamma, what great legs you've got!"

"The better to run, my child."

"Grandmamma, what great ears you've got!"

"The better to hear, my child!"

"Grandmamma, what great eyes you've got!"

"The better to see, my child."

"Grandmamma, what great teeth you've got!"

"To eat thee up!"

And saying these words, the wicked Wolf fell upon Little Red Riding-Hood and ate her all up.

THE STORY OF THE THREE BEARS

By Robert Southey

Once upon a time there were three Bears, who lived together in a house of their own in a wood. One of them was a Little, Small, Wee Bear; and one was a Middle-sized Bear, and the other was a Great, Huge Bear. They had each a pot for their porridge, a little pot for the Little, Small, Wee Bear; and a middle-sized pot for the Middle Bear; and a great pot for the Great, Huge Bear. And they had each a chair to sit in: a little chair for the Little, Small, Wee Bear; and a middle-sized chair for the Middle Bear; and a great chair for the Great, Huge Bear. And they had each a bed to sleep in: a little bed for the Little, Small, Wee Bear; and a middle-sized bed for the Middle Bear; and a great bed for the Great, Huge Bear.

One day, after they had made the porridge for their breakfast and poured it into their porridge pots, they walked out into the wood while the porridge was cooling, that they might not burn their mouths by beginning too soon to eat it. And while they were walking a little old woman came to the house. She could not have been a good, honest, old woman; for, first, she looked in at the window, and then she peeped in at the keyhole, and, seeing nobody in the house, she lifted the latch. The door was not fastened, because the bears were good bears, who did nobody any harm, and never suspected that anybody would harm them. So the little old woman opened the door and went in; and well pleased she was when she saw the porridge on the table. If she had been a good little old woman she would have waited till the bears came home, and then, perhaps, they would have asked her to breakfast, for they were good hears—a little rough or so, as the manner of bear's is, but for all that very good-natured and hospitable. But she was an impudent, bad old woman, and set about helping herself.

So first she tasted the porridge of the Great Huge Bear, and that was too hot for her; and she said a bad word about that. And then she tasted the porridge of the Middle Bear, and that was too cold for her; and she said a bad word about that, too. And then she went to the porridge of the Little, Small, Wee Bear, and tasted that, and that was neither too hot nor too cold, but just right; and she liked it so well that she ate it all up; but the naughty old woman said a bad word about the little porridge pot, because it did not hold enough for her.

Then the little old woman sat down in the chair of the Great, Huge Bear, and that was too hard for her. And then she sat down in the chair of the Middle Bear, and that was too soft for her. And then she sat down in the chair of the Little Small, Wee Bear, and that was neither too hard nor too soft, but just right. So she seated herself in it, and there she sat till the bottom of the chair came out, and down came she, plump upon the ground. And the naughty old woman said wicked words about that, too.

Then the little old woman went upstairs into the bedchamber in which the three Bears slept. And first she lay down upon the bed of the Great, Huge Bear, but that was too high at the head for her. And next she lay down upon the bed of the Middle Bear, and that was too high at the foot for her. And then she lay down upon the bed of the Little, Small, Wee Bear, and that was neither too high at the head nor at the foot, but just right. So she covered herself up comfortably, and lay there till she fell asleep. By this time the three Bears thought their porridge would be cool enough, so they came home to breakfast. Now the little old woman had left the spoon of the Great, Huge Bear standing in his porridge.

"SOMEBODY HAS BEEN AT MY PORRIDGE!"

said the Great, Huge Bear, in his great gruff voice. And when the Middle Bear looked at his, he saw that the spoon was standing in it, too. They were wooden spoons; if they had been silver ones the naughty old woman would have put them in her pocket.

"SOMEBODY HAS BEEN AT MY PORRIDGE!"

said the middle Bear, in his middle voice.

Then the Little, Small, Wee Bear looked at his, and there was the spoon in the porridge pot, but the porridge was all gone.

"SOMEBODY HAS BEEN AT MY PORRIDGE,
AND HAS EATEN IT ALL UP!"

said the Little, Small, Wee Bear, in his little, small, wee voice.

Upon this the three Bears, seeing that some one had entered their house and eaten up the Little, Small, Wee Bear's breakfast, began to look about them. Now the little old woman had not put the hard cushion straight when she rose from the chair of the Great, Huge Bear.

"SOMEBODY HAS BEEN SITTING IN MY CHAIR!"

said the Great, Huge Bear, in his great, rough, gruff voice.

And the little old woman had squatted down the soft cushion of the Middle Bear.

"SOMEBODY HAS BEEN SITTING IN MY CHAIR!"

said the Middle Bear, in his middle voice.

And you know what the little old woman had done to the third chair.

"SOMEBODY HAS BEEN SITTING IN MY CHAIR,
AND HAS SAT THE BOTTOM OUT OF IT!"

said the Little, Small, Wee Bear, in his little, small, wee voice.

Then the three bears thought it necessary that they should make further search; so they went upstairs into their bedchamber. Now the little old woman had pulled the pillow of the Great, Huge Bear out of its place.

"SOMEBODY HAS BEEN LYING IN MY BED!"

said the Great, Huge Bear, in his great, rough, gruff voice.

And the little old woman had pulled the bolster of the Middle Bear out of its place.

"SOMEBODY HAS BEEN LYING IN MY BED!"

said the Middle Bear, in his middle voice.

And when the Little, Small, Wee Bear came to look at his bed, there was the bolster in its place, and upon the pillow was the little old woman's ugly, dirty head—which was not in its place, for she had no business there.

"SOMEBODY HAS BEEN LYING IN MY BED—AND HERE SHE IS!"

said the Little, Small, Wee Bear, in his little, small, wee voice.

The little old woman had heard in her sleep the great, rough, gruff voice of the Great, Huge Bear, but she was so fast asleep that it was no more to her than the moaning of wind or the rumbling of thunder. And she had heard the middle voice of the Middle Bear, but it was only as if she had heard some one speaking in a dream. But when she heard the little, small, wee voice of the Little, Small, Wee Bear, it was so sharp and so shrill that it awakened her at once. Up she started, and when she saw the three bears on one side of the bed she tumbled herself out at the other and ran to the window. Now the window was open, because the Bears, like good, tidy bears as they were, always opened their bedchamber window when they got up in the morning. Out the little old woman jumped, and whether she broke her neck in the fall or ran into the wood and was lost there, or found her way out of the wood and was taken up by the constable and sent to the House of Correction for a vagrant as she was, I cannot tell. But the three Bears never saw anything more of her.

PUSS IN BOOTS

By Charles Perrault

A miller, dying, divided all his property between his three children. This was very easy, as he had nothing to leave but his mill, his ass, and his cat; so he made no will, and called in no lawyer. The eldest son had the mill; the second, the ass; and the youngest, nothing but the cat. The young fellow was quite downcast at so poor a lot. "My brothers," said he, "by putting their property together, may gain an honest living, but there is nothing left for me except to die of hunger, unless, indeed, I were to kill my cat and eat him, and make a muff of his skin."

The cat, who heard all this, sat up on his four paws, and looking at him with a grave and wise air, said: "Master, I think you had better not kill me; I shall be much more useful to you alive."

"How so?" asked his master.

"You have but to give me a sack and a pair of boots, such as gentlemen wear when they go shooting, and you will find you are not so ill off as you suppose."

Now, though the young man did not much depend upon the cat's words, still he thought it rather surprising that a cat should speak at all. And he had before now seen him play a great many cunning tricks in catching rats and mice, so that it seemed advisable to trust him a little further; especially as — poor young fellow — he had nobody else to trust.

When the cat got his boots, he drew them on with a grand air, and slinging his sack over his shoulder, and drawing the cords of it round his neck, he marched bravely to a rabbit warren hard by, with which he was well acquainted. Then, putting some bran and lettuces into his bag, and stretching himself out beside it as if he were dead, he waited till some fine, fat young rabbit, ignorant of the wickedness and deceit of the world, should peep into the sack to eat the food that was inside. This happened very shortly, for there are plenty of foolish young rabbits in every warren; and when one of them, who really was a splendid fat fellow, put his head inside, Master Puss drew the cords immediately, and took him and killed him without mercy. Then, very proud of his prey, he marched direct to the palace, and begged to speak with the King.

He was told to ascend to the apartment of his majesty, where, making a low bow, he said: "Sire, here is a magnificent rabbit, killed in the warren, which belongs to my lord the Marquis of Carabas, and which he told me to offer humbly to your majesty."

"Tell your master," replied the King, politely, "that I accept his present, and am very much obliged to him."

Another time, Puss went out and hid himself and his sack in a wheat field, and there caught two splendid fat partridges in the same manner as he had done the rabbit. When he presented them to the King, with a similar message as before, his majesty was so pleased that he ordered the cat to be taken down into the kitchen and given something to eat and drink; where, while enjoying himself, the faithful animal did not cease to talk in the most cunning way of the large preserves and abundant game which belonged to his lord the Marquis of Carabas.

One day, hearing that the King was intending to take a drive along the riverside with his daughter, the most beautiful princess in the world, Puss said to his master: "Sir, if you would only follow my advice, your fortune is made."

"Be it so," said the miller's son, who was growing disconsolate, and cared very little what he did: "Say your say, cat."

"It is but little," replied Puss, looking wise, as cats can. "You have only to go and bathe in the river at a place which I shall show you, and leave all the rest to me. Only remember that you are no longer yourself, but my lord the Marquis of Carabas."

"Just so," said the miller's son, "it's all the same to me;" but he did as the cat told him.

While he was bathing, the King and all the court passed by, and were startled to hear loud cries of "Help! help! my lord the Marquis of Carabas is drowning." The King put his head out of the carriage, and saw nobody but the cat, who had at different times brought him so many presents of game; however, he ordered his guards to fly quickly to the succor of my lord the Marquis of Carabas. While they were pulling the unfortunate marquis out of the water, the cat came up, bowing, to the side of the King's carriage, and told a long and pitiful story about some thieves who, while his master was bathing, had come and carried away all his clothes, so that it would be impossible for him to appear before his majesty and the illustrious princess.

"Oh, we will soon remedy that," answered the King, kindly and immediately ordered one of the first officers of the household to ride back to the palace with all speed, and bring thence a supply of fine clothes for the young gentleman, who kept out of sight until they arrived. Then, being handsome and well-made, his new clothes became him so well, that he looked as if he had been a marquis all his days, and advanced with an air of respectful ease to offer his thanks to his majesty.

The King received him courteously, and the princess admired him very much. Indeed, so charming did he appear to her, that she hinted to her father to invite him into the carriage with them, which, you may be sure the young man did not refuse. The cat, delighted at the success of his scheme, went away as fast as he could, and ran so swiftly that he kept a long way ahead of the royal carriage. He went on and on, till he came to some peasants who were mowing in a meadow. "Good people," said he, in a very firm voice, "the King is coming past here shortly, and if you do not say that the field you are mowing belongs to my lord the Marquis of Carabas, you shall all be chopped as small as mincemeat."

So when the King drove by, and asked whose meadow it was where there was such a splendid crop of hay, the mowers all answered, trembling, that it belonged to my lord the Marquis of Carabas.

"You have very fine land, marquis," said his majesty to the miller's son, who bowed, and answered that "it was not a bad meadow, take it altogether."

Then the cat came to a wheat field, where the reapers were reaping with all their might. He bounced in upon them: "The King is coming past to-day, and if you do not tell him that this wheat belongs to my lord the Marquis of Carabas, I will have you everyone chopped as small as mincemeat." The reapers, very much alarmed, did as they were bid, and the King congratulated the marquis upon possessing such beautiful fields, laden with such an abundant harvest.

They drove on—the cat always running before and saying the same thing to everybody he met, that they were to declare that the whole country belonged to his master; so that even the King was astonished at the vast estate of my lord the Marquis of Carabas.

But now the cat arrived at a great castle where dwelt an Ogre, to whom belonged all the land through which the royal carriage had been driving. This Ogre was a cruel tyrant, and his tenants and servants were terribly afraid of him, which accounted for their being so ready to say whatever they were told to say by the cat, who had taken pains to inform himself all about the Ogre. So, putting on the boldest face he could assume, Puss marched up to the castle with his boots on, and asked to see the owner of it, saying that he was on his travels, but did not wish to pass so near the castle of such a noble gentleman without paying his respects to him. When the Ogre heard this message, he went to the door, received the cat as civilly as an Ogre can, and begged him to walk in and repose himself.

"Thank you, sir," said the cat; "but first I hope you will satisfy a traveler's curiosity. I have heard in far countries of your many remarkable qualities, and especially how you have the power to change yourself into any sort of beast you choose—a lion, for instance, or an elephant."

"That is quite true," replied the Ogre; "and lest you should doubt it I will immediately become a lion."

He did so; and the cat was so frightened that he sprang up to the roof of the castle and hid himself in the gutter—a proceeding rather inconvenient on account of his boots, which were not exactly fitted to walk with on tiles. At length, perceiving that the Ogre had resumed his original form, he came down again, and owned that he had been very much frightened.

"But, sir," said he, "it may be easy enough for such a big gentleman as you to change himself into a large animal; I do not suppose you could become a small one—a rat, or mouse, for instance. I have heard that you can; still, for my part, I consider it quite impossible."

"Impossible!" cried the other, indignantly. "You shall see!" and immediately the cat saw the Ogre no longer, but a little mouse running along on the floor.

This was exactly what Puss wanted; and he fell upon him at once and ate him up. So there was an end to the Ogre.

By this time the King had arrived opposite the castle, and had a strong wish to go into it. The cat, hearing the noise of the carriage wheels, ran forward in a great hurry, and, standing at the gate, said, in a loud voice: "Welcome, sire, to the castle of my lord the Marquis of Carabas."

"What!" cried his majesty, very much surprised, "does the castle also belong to you? Truly, marquis, you have kept your secret well up to the last minute. I have never seen anything finer than this courtyard and these battlements. Let us go in, if you please."

The marquis, without speaking, offered his hand to the princess to help her to descend, and, standing aside that the King might enter first, followed his majesty to the great hall, where a magnificent dinner was laid out, and where, without more delays they all sat down to feast.

Before the banquet was over, the King, charmed with the good qualities of the Marquis of Carabas, said, bowing across the table at which the princess and the miller's son were talking very confidentially together: "It rests with you, marquis, whether you will marry my daughter."

"I shall be only too happy," said the marquis, and the princess's cast-down eyes declared the same.

So they were married the very next day, and took possession of the Ogre's castle, and of everything that had belonged to him.

As for the cat, he became at once a great lord, and had nevermore any need to run after mice, except for his own diversion.

JACK THE GIANT-KILLER

Retold by Joseph Jacobs

In the reign of the famous King Arthur there lived in Cornwall a lad named Jack, who was a boy of a bold temper and took delight in hearing or reading of conjurers, giants, and fairies; and used to listen eagerly to the deeds of the knights of King Arthur's Round Table.

In those days there lived on St. Michael's Mount, off Cornwall, a huge Giant, eighteen feet high and nine feet round; his fierce and savage looks were the terror of all who beheld him.

He dwelt in a gloomy cavern on the top of the mountain, and used to wade over to the mainland in search of prey, when he would throw half a dozen oxen upon his back, and tie three times as many sheep and hogs round his waist, and march back to his own abode.

The Giant had done this for many years when Jack resolved to destroy him.

Jack took a horn, a shovel, a pickaxe, his armor, and a dark lantern, and one winter's evening he went to the mount. There he dug a pit twenty-two feet deep and twenty broad. He covered the top over so as to make it look like solid ground. He then blew such a blast on his horn that the Giant awoke and came out of his den, crying out: "You saucy villain, you shall pay for this! I'll broil you for my breakfast!"

He had just finished, when, taking one step farther, he tumbled headlong into the pit, and Jack struck him a blow on the head with his pickaxe which killed him. Jack then returned home to cheer his friends with the news.

Another Giant, called Blunderbore, vowed to be revenged on Jack if ever he should have him in his power.

This Giant kept an enchanted castle in the midst of a lonely wood, and some time after the death of Cormoran, Jack was passing through a wood, and, being weary, sat down and went to sleep.

The Giant, passing by and seeing Jack, carried him to his castle, where he locked him up in a large room, the floor of which was covered with the bodies, skulls, and bones of men and women.

Soon after, the Giant went to fetch his brother, who was likewise a Giant, to take a meal off his flesh, and Jack saw with terror through the bars of his prison the two Giants approaching.

Jack, perceiving in one corner of the room a strong cord, took courage, and making a slip-knot at each end, he threw them over their heads, and tied it to the window-bars; he then pulled till he had choked them. When they were black in the face he slid down the rope and stabbed them to the heart.

Jack next took a great bunch of keys from the pocket of Blunderbore and went into the castle again. He made a strict search through all the rooms, and in one of them found three ladies tied up by the hair of their heads and almost starved to death. They told him that their husbands had been killed by the Giants, who had then condemned them to be starved to death.

"Ladies," said Jack, "I have put an end to the monster and his wicked brother, and I give you this castle and all the riches it contains to make some amends for the dreadful pains you have felt." He then very politely gave them the keys of the castle and went farther on his journey to Wales.

As Jack had but little money, he went on as fast as possible. At length he came to a handsome house.

Jack knocked at the door, when there came forth a Welsh Giant. Jack said he was a traveler who had lost his way, on which the Giant made him welcome and let him into a room where there was a good bed to sleep in.

Jack took off his clothes quickly, but though he was weary he could not go to sleep. Soon after this he heard the Giant walking backward and forward in the next room and saying to himself:

> "Though here you shall lodge with me this night,
> You shall not see the morning light;
> My club shall dash your brains out quite!"

"Say you so?" thought Jack. "Are these your tricks upon travelers? But I hope to prove as cunning as you are." Then, getting out of bed, he groped about the room and at last found a thick tog of wood. He laid it in his own place in the bed, and then hid himself in a dark corner of the room.

The Giant, about midnight, entered the apartment, and with his bludgeon struck many blows on the bed, in the very place where Jack had laid the log; and then he went back to his own room, thinking he had broken all Jack's bones.

Early in the morning Jack put a bold face upon the matter and walked into the Giant's room to thank him for his lodging. The Giant started when he saw him, and began to stammer out: "Oh! dear me; is it you? Pray, how did you sleep last night? Did you hear or see anything in the dead of the night?"

"Nothing worth speaking of," said Jack, carelessly; "a rat, I believe, gave me three or four slaps with its tail, and disturbed me a little; but I soon went to sleep again."

The Giant wondered more and more at this; yet he did not answer a word, but went to bring two great bowls of hasty-pudding for their breakfast. Jack wanted to make the Giant believe that he could eat as much as himself so he contrived to button a leathern bag inside his coat and slip the hasty-pudding into this bag while he seemed to put it into his mouth.

When breakfast was over he said to the Giant: "Now I will show you a fine trick. I can cure all wounds with a touch; I could cut off my head in one minute, and the next put it sound again on my shoulders. You shall see an example." He then took hold of the knife, ripped up the leathern bag, and all the hasty-pudding tumbled out upon the floor.

"Ods splutter hur nails!" cried the Welsh Giant, who was ashamed to be outdone by such a little fellow as Jack, "hur can do that hurself;" so he snatched up the knife, plunged it into his own stomach, and in a moment dropped down dead.

Jack, having hitherto been successful in all his undertakings, resolved not to be idle in future; he therefore furnished himself with a horse, a cap of knowledge, a sword of sharpness, shoes of swiftness, and an invisible coat, the better to perform the wonderful enterprises that lay before him.

He traveled over high hills, and on the third day he came to a large and spacious forest through which his road lay. Scarcely had he entered the forest when he beheld a monstrous Giant dragging along by the hair of their heads a handsome Knight and his lady. Jack alighted from his horse, and tying him to an oak-tree, put on his invisible coat, under which he carried his sword of sharpness.

When he came up to the Giant he made several strokes at him, but could not reach his body, but wounded his thighs in several places; and at length, putting both hands to his sword and aiming with all his might, he cut off both his legs. Then Jack, setting his foot upon his neck, plunged his sword into the Giant's body, when the monster gave a groan and expired.

The Knight and his lady thanked Jack for their deliverance, and invited him to their house to receive a proper reward for his services. "No," Said Jack, "I cannot be easy till I find out this monster's habitation." So taking the Knight's directions, he mounted his horse and soon after came in sight of another Giant, who was sitting on a block of timber waiting for his brother's return.

Jack alighted from his horse, and, putting on his invisible coat, approached and aimed a blow at the Giant's head, but missing his aim he only cut off his nose. On this the Giant seized his club and laid about him most unmercifully.

"Nay," said Jack, "if this be the case I'd better dispatch you!" So jumping upon the block, he stabbed him in the back, when he dropped down dead.

Jack then proceeded on his journey, and traveled over hills and dales till, arriving at the foot of a high mountain, he knocked at the door of a lonely house, when an old man let him in.

When Jack was seated the hermit thus addressed him: "My son, on the top of this mountain is an enchanted castle, kept by the Giant Galligantus and a vile magician. I lament the fate of a duke's daughter, whom they seized as she was walking in her father's garden, and brought hither transformed into a deer."

Jack promised that in the morning, at the risk of his life, he would break the enchantment; and after a sound sleep he rose early, put on his invisible coat, and got ready for the attempt.

When he had climbed to the top of the mountain he saw two fiery griffins; but he passed between them without the least fear of danger, for they could not see him because of his invisible coat. On the castle gate he found a golden trumpet, under which were written these lines:

Whoever can this trumpet blow
Shall cause the giant's overthrow.

As soon as Jack had read this he seized the trumpet and blew a shrill blast, which made the gates fly open and the very castle itself tremble.

The Giant and the conjurer now knew that their wicked course was at an end, and they stood biting their thumbs and shaking within fear. Jack, with his sword of sharpness, soon killed the Giant, and the magician was then carried away by a whirlwind; and every knight and beautiful lady who had been changed into birds and beasts returned to their proper shapes. The castle vanished away like smoke, and the head of the Giant Galligantus was sent to King Arthur.

The knights and ladies rested that night at the old man's hermitage, and next day they set out for the Court. Jack then went up to the King and gave his Majesty an account of all his fierce battles.

Jack's fame had now spread through the whole country, and at the King's desire the Duke gave him his daughter in marriage, to the joy of all his kingdom. After this the King gave him a large estate, on which he and his lady lived the rest of their days in joy and contentment.

TOM THUMB

Retold by Joseph Jacobs

In the days of the great Prince Arthur, there lived a mighty magician, named Merlin, the most learned and skillful enchanter the world has ever seen.

This famous magician, who could take any form he pleased, was travelling about as a poor beggar, and being very tired he stopped at the cottage of a Ploughman to rest himself, and asked for some food.

The countryman bade him welcome, and his wife, who was a very good-hearted woman, brought him some milk in a wooden bowl and some coarse brown bread on a platter.

Merlin was much pleased with the kindness of the Ploughman and his wife; but he could not help noticing that though everything was neat and comfortable in the cottage, they both seemed to be very unhappy. He therefore asked them why they were so melancholy, and learned that they were miserable because they had no children.

The Poor Woman said, with tears in her eves: "I should be the happiest creature in the world if I had a son although he was no bigger than my husband's thumb."

Merlin was so much amused with the idea of a boy no bigger than a man's thumb that he determined to grant the Poor Woman's wish. Accordingly, in a short time after, the Ploughman's wife had a son, who, wonderful to relate! was not a bit bigger than his father's thumb.

The Queen of the fairies, wishing to see the little fellow, came in at the window, while the mother was sitting up in bed admiring him. The Queen kissed the child, and, giving it the name of Tom Thumb, sent for some of the fairies, who dressed her little godson according to her orders:

An oak-leaf hat he had for his crown;
His shirt of web by spiders spun;
With jacket wove of thistle's down;
His trousers were of feathers done.
His stockings, of apple rind, they tie

With eyelash from his mother's eye:
His shoes were made of mouse's skin,
Tann'd with the downy hair within.

Tom never grew any larger than his father's thumb, but as he got older he became very cunning and full of tricks. When he was old enough to play with the boys, and had lost all his own cherry stones, he used to creep into the bags of his play-fellows, fill his pockets, and, getting out without their noticing him, would again join in the game.

One day, as he was coming out of a bag of cherry stones, where he had been stealing as usual, the boy to whom it belonged chanced to see him. "Ah, ah! my little Tommy," said the boy, "so I have caught you stealing my cherry stones at last, and you shall be rewarded for your thievish tricks." On saying this, he drew the string tight round his neck, and gave the bag such a hearty shake that poor little Tom's legs, thighs and body were sadly bruised. He roared out with pain and begged to be let out, promising never to steal again.

A short time afterwards his mother was making a batter pudding, and Tom, being anxious to see how it was made, climbed up to the edge of the bowl; but his foot slipped, and he plumped over head and ears into the batter, without his mother noticing him, who stirred him into the pudding-bag, and put him in the pot to boil.

The batter filled Tom's mouth, and prevented him from crying; but, upon feeling the hot water, he kicked and struggled so much in the pot that his mother thought that the pudding was bewitched, and, pulling it out of the pot, she threw it outside the door. A poor tinker, who was passing by, lifted up the pudding, put it in his bag, and walked off. As Tom had now got his mouth cleared of the batter, he began to cry aloud, which so frightened the tinker that he flung down the pudding and ran away. The pudding being broke to pieces by the fall, Tom crept out covered all over with the batter, and walked home. His mother, who was very sorry to see her darling in such a woeful state, put him into a teacup and soon washed off the batter; after which she kissed him and laid him in bed.

Soon after the adventure of the pudding, Tom's mother went to milk her cow in the meadow, and she took him along with her. As the wind was very high, for fear of being blown away, she tied him to a thistle with a piece of fine thread. The cow soon observed Tom's oak-leaf hat, and liking the appearance of it, took poor Tom and the thistle at one mouthful. While the cow was chewing the thistle Tom was afraid of her great teeth, which threatened to crush him in pieces, and he roared out as loud as he could: "Mother, mother!"

"Where are you, Tommy, my dear Tommy?" said his mother.

"Here, mother," replied he, "in the red cow's mouth."

His mother began to cry and wring her hands; but the cow, surprised at the odd noise in her throat, opened her mouth and let Tom drop out. Fortunately his mother caught him in her apron as he was falling to the ground, or he would have been dreadfully hurt. She then put Tom in her bosom and ran home with him.

Tom's father made him a whip of barley straw to drive the cattle with, and having one day gone into the fields, Tom slipped a foot and rolled into the furrow. A raven, which was flying over, picked him up and flew with him over the sea, and there dropped him.

A large fish swallowed Tom the moment he fell into the sea, which was soon after caught and bought for the table of King Arthur. When they opened the fish in order to cook it, every one was astonished at finding such a little boy, and Tom was quite delighted at being free again. They carried him to the King, who made Tom his dwarf, and he soon became a great favorite at court; for by his tricks and gambols he not only amused the King and Queen, but also the Knights of the Round Table.

It is said that when the King rode out on horseback he often took Tom along with him, and if a shower came on he used to creep into his Majesty's waistcoat pocket, where he slept till the rain was over.

King Arthur one day asked Tom about his parents, wishing to know if they were as small as he was, and whether they were well off. Tom told the King that his father and mother were as tall as anybody about the court, but in rather poor circumstances. On hearing this, the King carried Tom to his treasury, the place where he kept all his money, and told him to take as much money as he could carry home to his parents, which made the poor little fellow caper with joy. Tom went immediately to procure a purse which was made of a water-bubble, and then returned to the treasury, where he received a silver three-penny piece to put into it.

Our little hero had some difficulty in lifting the burden upon his back; but he at last succeeded in getting it placed and set forward on his journey. Without meeting with any accident, and after resting himself more than a hundred times by the way, in two days and two nights he reached his father's house in safety.

Tom had traveled forty-eight hours with a huge silver piece on his back, and was almost tired to death, when his mother ran out to meet him and carried him into the house. But he soon returned to court.

As Tom's clothes had suffered much in the batter pudding and the inside of the fish, his Majesty ordered him a new suit of clothes, and to be mounted as a knight on a mouse.

Of Butterfly's wings his shirt was made,
   His boots of chicken's hide;
And by a nimble fairy blade,
Well learned in the tailoring trade,
   His clothing was supplied.
   A needle dangled by his side;
   A dapper mouse he used to ride,
   Thus strutted Tom in stately pride!

It was certainly very amusing to see him in this dress and mounted on the mouse, as he rode out a-hunting with the King and nobility, who were all ready to expire with laughter at Tom and his fine prancing charioteer.

The King was so charmed with his address that he ordered a little chair to be made, in order that Tom might sit upon his table, and also a palace of gold, a span high, with a door an inch wide, to live in. He also gave him a coach, drawn by six small mice.

The Queen was so enraged at the honors conferred on Sir Thomas that she resolved to ruin him, and told the King that the little knight had been saucy to her.

The King sent for Tom in great haste, but being fully aware of the danger of royal anger, he crept into an empty snail shell, where he lay for a long time until he was almost starved with hunger; at last he ventured to peep out, and seeing a fine large butterfly on the ground, near the place of his concealment, he got close to it and jumping astride on it was carried up into the, air. The butterfly flew with him from tree to tree and from field to field, at last returned to the court, where the King and nobility all strove to catch him; but at last poor Tom fell from his seat into a watering-pot, in which he was almost drowned.

When the Queen saw him she was in a rage, and said he should be beheaded; and he was again put into a mouse trap until the time of his execution.

However, a cat, observing something alive in the trap, patted it about till the wires broke, and set Thomas at liberty.

The King received Tom again into favor, which he did not live to enjoy, for a large spider one day attacked him; and although he drew his sword and fought well, yet the spider's poisonous breath at last overcame him.

King Arthur and his whole court were so sorry at the loss of their little favorite that they went into mourning and raised a fine white marble monument over his grave with the following epitaph:

Here lies Tom Thumb, King Arthur's knight,
Who died by a spider's cruel bite.
He was well known in Arthur's court,
Where he afforded gallant sport;
He rode a tilt and tournament,
And on a mouse a-hunting went.
Alive he filled the court with mirth;
His death to sorrow soon gave birth.
Wipe, wipe your eyes, and shake your head
And cry, — Alas! Tom Thumb is dead!

BLUE BEARD

By Charles Perrault

There was once a man who had fine houses, both in town and country, a deal of silver and gold plate, embroidered furniture, and coaches gilded all over with gold. But this man was so unlucky as to have a blue beard, which made him so ugly that all the women and girls ran away from him.

One of his neighbors, a lady of quality, had two daughters who were perfect beauties. He asked her for one of them in marriage, but neither of them could bear the thought of marrying a man who had a blue beard. Besides, he had already been married several times, and nobody ever knew what became of his wives.

In the hope of making them like him, Blue Beard took them, with their mother and three or four ladies of their acquaintance, and other young people of the neighborhood, to one of his country houses, where they stayed a whole week.

There were parties of pleasure, hunting, fishing, dancing, mirth, and feasting all the time. Nobody went to bed, but all passed the time in merry-making and joking with one another. Everything succeeded so well that the youngest daughter began to think the master of the house was a very civil gentleman. And his beard not so very blue after all.

As soon as they returned home, the marriage took place. About a month afterward Blue Beard told his wife that he was obliged to take a journey for six weeks, about affairs of great consequence, desiring her to amuse herself in his absence, to send for her friends and acquaintances, to carry them in to the country if she pleased, and to have a good time wherever she was.

"Here," said he, "are the keys of the two great wardrobes wherein I have my best furniture; these are of my silver and gold plate, which is not every day in use; these open my strong boxes, which hold my money, both gold and silver; these my caskets of jewels; and this is the master key to all my apartments. This little one here is the key of the closet at the end of the great gallery on the ground floor. Open them all; go into all and every one of them, except that little closet, which I forbid you; if you happen to open it, there's nothing but what you may expect from my just anger and resentment."

She promised to observe exactly whatever he ordered; so, having embraced her, he got into his coach and proceeded on his journey.

Her neighbors and good friends did not wait to be sent for, so great was their impatience to see all the rich furniture of her house. They ran through all the rooms, closets, and wardrobes, which were all so fine and rich that they seemed to surpass one another.

After that they went up into the two great rooms, where were the best and richest furniture; they could not sufficiently admire the number and beauty of the tapestries, beds, couches, cabinets, stands, tables, and looking-glasses, in which you might see yourself from head to foot; some of them were framed with glass, others with silver, plain and gilded, the finest and most magnificent ever seen.

They ceased not to compliment and envy their friend, but she was so much pressed by her curiosity to open the closet on the ground floor that, without considering that it was very uncivil to leave her company, she went down a little back staircase with such haste that she had twice or thrice like to have broken her neck.

Arriving at the closet door, she hesitated, thinking of her husband's orders and considering what unhappiness might attend her if she was disobedient; but the temptation was so strong she could not overcome it. She took the little key and opened it, trembling, but could not at first see anything plainly because the windows were shut. After some moments she began to perceive that the floor was all covered with blood, in which lay the bodies of several dead women, ranged against the walls. (These were the wives whom Blue Beard had married and murdered, one after another.) She thought she would die for fear, and the key, which she pulled out of the lock, fell out of her hand.

After having somewhat recovered from the shock, she took up the key, locked the door, and went upstairs to her bedroom to rest. Having observed that the key of the closet was stained with blood, she tried two or three times to wipe it off, but the stain would not come out; in vain did she wash it, and even rub it with soap and sand, the blood still remained, for the key was magical; when the blood was removed from one side it came again on the other.

Blue Beard returned from his journey the same evening, and said he had received letters upon the road informing him that the affair he went about was ended to his advantage. His wife did all she could to convince him she was extremely glad of his speedy return.

Next morning he asked her for the keys, which she gave him, but with such a trembling hand that he easily guessed what had happened.

"What!" said he, "is not the key of my closet among the rest?"

"I must certainly," said she, "have left it above upon the table."

"Fail not," said Blue Beard, "to bring it to me presently."

After several goings backward and forward she was forced to bring him the key. Blue Beard attentively considered it and said to his wife:

"How comes this blood upon the key?"

"I do not know," cried the poor woman, paler than death.

"You do not know!" replied Blue Beard. "I very well know. You were resolved to go into the closet, were you not? Very well, madam; you shall go in and take your place among the ladies you saw there."

Upon this she threw herself at her husband's feet, and begged his pardon with all the signs of a true repentance, vowing that she would never again be disobedient. She would have melted a rock, so beautiful and sorrowful was she; but Blue Beard had a heart harder than any rock!

"You must die, madam," said he, "and that; very soon."

"Since I must die," answered she, her eyes bathed in tears, "give me some little time to say my prayers."

"I give you," replied Blue Beard, "half a quarter of an hour, but not one moment more."

When she was alone she called out to her sister:

"Sister Anne, go up, I beg you, on top of the tower and see if my brothers are not coming; they promised me that they would come to-day, and if you see them, give them a sign to make haste."

Sister Anne went up on the top of the tower, and the poor afflicted wife cried out from time to time:

"Anne, sister Anne, do you see anyone coming?"

And sister Anne replied:

"I see nothing but the sun, which makes a dust, and the grass, which looks green."

In the meanwhile Blue Beard, holding a great saber in his hand, cried out as loud as he could bawl to his wife:

"Come down instantly, or I shall come up after you."

"One moment longer, if you please," said his wife; and then she cried out softly: "Anne, sister Anne, dost thou see anybody coming?"

And sister Anne answered:

"I see nothing but the sun, which makes a dust, and the grass, which is green."

"Come down quickly," shouted Blue Beard, "or I will come up after you."

"I am coming," answered his wife; and then she cried: "Anne, sister Anne, dost thou not see any one coming?"

"I see," replied sister Anne, "a great dust, which comes on this side."

"Are they my brothers?"

"Alas! no, my dear sister, I see a flock of sheep."

"Will you not come down?' roared Blue Beard.

"One moment longer," said his wife, and then she cried out: "Anne, sister Anne, dost thou see nobody coming?"

"I see," said she, "two horsemen, but they are yet a great way off."

"God be praised!" replied the poor wife joyfully; "they are my brothers; I will make them a sign, as well as I can, for them to make haste."

Then Blue Beard bawled out so loud that he made the whole house tremble. The distressed wife came down and threw herself at his feet, all in tears, with her hair about her shoulders.

"That will not help you," says Blue Beard; "you must die;" then, taking hold of her hair with one hand, and lifting up the sword with the other, he was going to cut off her head. The poor lady, turning to him and looking at him with dying eyes, begged him to give her one little moment more.

"No, no," said he; "say your prayers," and was just about to strike...

At this very instant there was such a loud knocking at the gate that Blue Beard looked up in alarm. The gate was opened and two horsemen entered, who drew their swords and ran directly at Blue Beard. He knew them to be his wife's brothers, one a dragoon, the other a musketeer; so that he quickly ran to save himself; but the two brothers pursued so close that they overtook him before he could get to the steps of the porch, and ran their swords through his body and left him dead. The poor wife was almost as dead as her husband, and had not strength enough to rise and welcome her brothers.

Blue Beard had no heirs, and so his wife became mistress of all his estate. She made use of one part of it to marry her sister Anne to a young gentleman who had loved her a long while; another part to buy captains' commissions for her brothers, and the rest to marry herself to a very worthy gentleman, who made her forget the unhappy time she had passed with Blue Beard.

THE BRAVE LITTLE TAILOR

Anonymous

One summer's day a little Tailor sat on his table by the window in the best of spirits and sewed for dear life. As he was sitting thus a peasant woman came down the street, calling out: "Good jam to sell! good jam to sell!" This sounded sweetly in the Tailor's ears; he put his little head out of the window and shouted: "Up here, my good woman, and you'll find a willing customer!" The woman climbed up the three flights of stairs with her heavy basket to the tailor's room, and he made her spread out the pots in a row before him. He examined them all, lifted them up and smelt them, and said at last: "This jam seems good; weigh me four ounces of it, my good woman; and even if it's a quarter of a pound I won't stick at it." The woman, who had hoped to find a good market, gave him what he wanted, but went away grumbling wrathfully. "Now Heaven shall bless this jam for my use," cried the little Tailor, "and it shall sustain and strengthen me." He fetched some bread out of a cupboard, cut a round off the loaf, and spread the jam on it. "That will taste good," he said; "but I'll finish that waistcoat first before I take a bite." He placed the bread beside him, went on sewing, and out of the lightness of his heart kept on making his stitches bigger and bigger. In the meantime the smell of the sweet jam rose to the ceiling, where swarms of flies were gathered, and attracted them to such an extent that they swarmed on to it in masses. "Ha! who invited you?" said the Tailor, and chased the unwelcome guests away. But the flies, who didn't understand English, refused to let themselves be warned off, and returned again in even greater numbers. At last the Tailor, losing all patience, reached out of his chimney-corner for a duster, and exclaiming, "Wait, and I'll give it to you!" he beat them mercilessly with it. When he left off he counted the slain, and no fewer than seven lay dead before him with outstretched legs. "What a brave fellow I am!" said he, and was filled with admiration at his own courage. "The whole town must know about this;" and in great haste the little Tailor cut out a girdle, hemmed it, and embroidered on it in big letters, "Seven at a blow." "What did I say, the town? no, the whole world shall hear of it," he said; and his heart beat for joy as a lamb wags his tail.

The Tailor strapped the girdle round his waist and set out into the wide world, for he considered his workroom too small a field for his bravery. Before he set forth he looked round about him, to see if there was anything in the house he could take with him on his journey; but he found nothing except an old cheese, which he took possession of. In front of the house he observed a bird that had been caught in some bushes, and this he put into his wallet beside the cheese. Then he went on his way merrily, and being light and quick he never felt tired. His way led up a hill on the top of which sat a powerful Giant, who was calmly surveying the landscape. The little Tailor went up to him, and greeting him cheerfully said: "Good-day, friend; there you sit at your ease viewing the whole wide world. I'm just on my way there. What do you say to accompanying me?" The Giant looked contemptuously at the Tailor, and said: "What a poor, wretched little creature you are!" "That's a good joke," answered the little Tailor, and unbuttoning his coat he showed the Giant the girdle. "There, now, you can read what sort of a fellow I am." The Giant read: "Seven at a blow," and thinking they were human beings the Tailor had slain, he had a certain respect for the little man. But first he thought he'd test him; so taking up a stone in his hand, he squeezed it till some drops of water ran out. "Now you do the same," said the Giant, "if you really wish to be thought strong." "Is that all?" said the little Tailor; "that's child's play to me." So he dived into his wallet, brought out the cheese, and pressed it till the whey ran out. "My squeeze was better than yours," said he. The Giant didn't know what to say, for he couldn't have believed it of the little fellow. To prove him again, the Giant lifted a stone and threw it so high that the eye could hardly follow it. "Now, my little dwarf, let me see you do that." "Well thrown," said the Tailor; "but, after all, your stone fell to the ground; I'll throw one that won't come down at all." He dived into his wallet again, and grasping the bird in his hand he threw it up into the air. The bird, enchanted to be free, soared up into the sky, and flew away never to return. "Well, what do you think of that little piece of business, friend?" asked the Tailor. "You can certainly throw," said the Giant; "but now let's see if you can carry a proper weight." With these words he led the Tailor to a huge oak-tree which had been felled to the ground, and said: "If you are strong enough, help me carry the tree out of the wood." "Most certainly," said the little Tailor: "just you take the trunk on your shoulder; I'll bear the top and branches, which is certainly the heaviest part." The Giant laid the trunk on his shoulder, but the Tailor sat at his ease among the branches; and the Giant, who couldn't see what was going on behind him, had to carry the whole tree, and the little Tailor into the bargain. There he sat behind in the best of spirits, lustily whistling a tune, as if carrying the tree were mere sport. The Giant after dragging the heavy weight for some time, could get on no farther, and shouted out: "Hi! I must let the tree fall." The Tailor sprang nimbly down, seized the tree with both hands as if he had carried it the whole way, and said to the Giant: "Fancy a big lazy fellow like you not being able to carry a tree!"

They continued to go on their way together, and as they passed by a cherry-tree the Giant grasped the top of it, where the ripest fruit hung, gave the branches into the Tailor's hand, and bade him eat. But the little Tailor was far too weak to hold the tree down, and when the Giant let go the tree swung back into the air, bearing the little Tailor with it. When he had fallen to the ground again without hurting himself, the Giant said: "What! do you mean to tell me you haven't the strength to hold down a feeble twig?" "It wasn't strength that was wanting," replied time Tailor; "do you think that would have been anything for a man who has killed seven at a blow? I jumped over the tree because the huntsmen are shooting among the branches near us. Do you do the like if you dare." The Giant made an attempt, but couldn't get over the tree, and stuck fast in the branches, so that here, too, the little Tailor had the better of him.

"Well, you're a fine fellow, after all," said the Giant; "come and spend the night with us in our cave." The little Tailor willingly consented to do this, and following his friend they went on till they reached a cave where several other giants were sitting round a fire, each holding a roast sheep in his hand, of which he was eating. The little Tailor looked about him, and thought: "Yes, there's certainly more room to turn round in here than in my workshop." The Giant showed him a bed, and bade him lie down and have a good sleep. But the bed was too big for the little Tailor, so he didn't get into it, but crept away into the corner. At midnight, when the Giant thought the little Tailor was fast asleep, he rose up, and taking his big iron walking-stick, he broke the bed in two with a blow, and thought he had made an end of the little grasshopper. At early dawn the Giants went off to the wood, and quite forgot about the little Tailor, till all of a sudden they met him trudging along in the most cheerful manner. The Giants were terrified at seeing him, and, fearing lest he should slay them, they all took to their heels as fast as they could.

The Little Tailor continued to follow his nose, and after he had wandered about for a long time he came to the courtyard of a royal palace, and feeling tired he lay down on the grass and fell asleep. While he lay there the people came, and looking him all over read on his girdle, "Seven at a blow." "Oh!" they said, "what can this great hero of a hundred fights want in our peaceful land? He must indeed be a mighty man of valor." They went and told the King about him, and said what a weighty and useful man he'd be in time of war and that it would be well to secure him at any price. This counsel pleased the King, and he sent one of his courtiers down to the little Tailor, to offer him, when he awoke, a commission in their army. The messenger remained standing by the sleeper, and waited till he stretched his limbs and opened his eyes, when he tendered his proposal. "That's the very thing I came here for," he answered; "I am quite ready to enter the King's service." So he was received with all honor, and given a special house of his own to live in.

But the other officers were angry at the success of the little Tailor, and wished him a thousand miles away. "What's to come of it all?" they asked one another; "if we quarrel with him, he'll let out at us, and at every blow seven will fall. There'll soon be an end of us." So they resolved to go in a body to the King, and all to send in their papers. "We are not made," they said. "to hold out against a man who kills seven at a blow." The King was grieved at the thought of losing all his faithful servants for the sake of one man, and he wished heartily that he had never set eyes on him, or that he could get rid of him. But he didn't dare to send him away, for he feared he might kill him and place himself on the throne. He thought long and deeply over the matter, and finally came to a conclusion. He sent for the Tailor and told him that, seeing what a great and warlike hero he was, he was about to make him an offer. In a certain wood of his kingdom there dwelt two Giants who did much harm by the way they robbed, murdered, burnt, and plundered everything about them; "no one could approach them without endangering his life. If he could overcome and kill these two giants he should have the King's only daughter for a wife, and half his kingdom into the bargain; he might have a hundred horsemen, too, to back him up." "That's the very thing for a man like me," thought the little Tailor; "one doesn't get the offer of a beautiful princess and half a kingdom every day." "Done with you," he answered; "I'll soon put an end to the Giants. But I haven't the smallest need of your hundred horsemen; a fellow who can slay seven men at a blow need not be afraid of two."

The little Tailor set out, and the hundred horsemen followed him. When he came to the outskirts of the wood he said to his followers: "You wait here, I'll manage the Giants by myself;" and he went on into the wood, casting his sharp little eyes right and left about him. After a while he spied the two Giants lying asleep under a tree, snoring till the very boughs bent with the breeze. The little Tailor lost no time in filling his wallet with stones, and then climbed up the tree under which they lay. When he got to about the middle of it he slipped along a branch till he sat just above the sleepers, when he threw down one stone after the other on the nearest Giant. The Giant felt nothing for a long time, but at last he woke up, and pinching his companion said: "What did you strike me for?" "I didn't strike you," said the other; "you must be dreaming." They both lay down to sleep again, and the Tailor threw down a stone on the second Giant, who sprang up and cried: "What's that for? Why did you throw something at me?" "I didn't throw anything," growled the first one. They wrangled on for a time, till as both were tired, they made up the matter and fell asleep again. The little Tailor began his game once more, and flung the largest stone he could find in his wallet with all his force, and hit the first Giant on the chest. "This is too much of a good thing!" he yelled, and springing up like a madman, he knocked his companion against the tree till he trembled. He gave, however, as good as he got, and they became so enraged that they tore up trees and beat each other with them, till they both fell dead at once on the ground. Then the little Tailor jumped down. "It's a mercy," he said, "that they didn't root up the tree on which I was sitting, or I should have had to jump like a squirrel on to another, which, nimble though I am, would have been no easy job." He drew his sword and gave each of the Giants a very fine thrust or two on the breast, and then went to the horsemen and said: "The deed is done; I've put an end to the two of them; but I assure you it has been no easy matter, for they even tore up trees in their struggle to defend themselves; but all that's of no use against one who slays seven men at a blow." "Weren't you wounded?" asked the horsemen. "No fear," answered the Tailor; "they haven't touched a hair of my head." But the horsemen wouldn't believe him till they rode into the wood and found the Giants weltering in their blood, and the trees lying around, torn up by the roots.

The little Tailor now demanded the promised reward, but the King repented his promise, and pondered once more how he could rid himself of the hero. "Before you obtain the hand of my daughter and half my kingdom," he said to him, "you must do another deed of valor. A unicorn is running about loose in the wood and doing much mischief; you must first catch it." "I'm even less afraid of one unicorn than of two Giants; seven at a blow, that's my motto." He took a piece of cord and an axe with him, went out to the wood, and again told the men who had been sent with him to remain outside. He hadn't to search long, for the unicorn soon passed by, and, on perceiving the Tailor, dashed straight at him as though it were going to spike him on the spot. "Gently, gently," said he; "not so fast, my friend;" and standing still he waited till the beast was quite near, when he sprang lightly behind a tree; the unicorn ran with all its force against the tree, and rammed its horn so firmly into the trunk that it had no strength left to pull it out again, and was thus successfully captured. "Now, I've caught my bird," said the Tailor, and he came out from behind the tree, placed the cord round its neck first, then struck the horn out of the tree within his axe, and when everything was in order led the beast Before the King.

Still the King didn't want to give him the promised reward and made a third demand. The Tailor was to catch a wild boar for him that did a great deal of harm in the wood; and he might have the huntsmen to help him. "Willingly," said the Tailor; "that's mere child's play." But he didn't take the huntsmen into the wood with him, and they were well enough pleased to remain behind, for the wild boar had often received them in a manner which did not make them desire its further acquaintance. As soon as the boar perceived the Tailor it ran at him with foaming mouth and gleaming teeth, and tried to knock him down; but our alert little friend ran into a chapel that stood near, and got out of the window with a jump. The boar pursued him into the church, but the Tailor skipped round to the door and closed it securely. So the raging beast was caught, for it was far too heavy and unwieldy to spring out of the window. The little Tailor summoned the huntsmen together, that they might see the Prisoner with their own eyes. Then the hero betook himself to the King, who was obliged now, whether he liked it or not, to keep his promise, and hand him over his daughter and half his kingdom. Had he known that no hero-warrior, but only a little tailor, stood before him, it would have gone even more to his heart. So the wedding was celebrated with much splendor and little joy, and the Tailor became a King.

After a time the Queen heard her husband saying one night in his sleep: "My lad, make that waistcoat and patch these trousers, or I'll box your ears." Thus she learned in what rank the young gentleman had been born, and next day she poured forth her woes to her father, and begged him to help her to get rid of a husband who was nothing more nor less than a tailor. The King comforted her, and said: "Leave your bedroom door open tonight; my servants shall stand outside, and when your husband is fast asleep they shall enter, bind him fast, and carry him on to a ship, which shall sail away out into the wide ocean." The Queen was well satisfied with the idea, but the armor-bearer, who had overheard everything, being much attached to his young master, went straight to him and revealed the whole plot. "I'll soon put a stop to the business," said the Tailor. That night he and his wife went to bed at the usual time; and when she thought he had fallen asleep she got up, opened the door, and then lay down again. The little Tailor, who had only pretended to be asleep, began to call out in a clear voice: "My lad, make that waistcoat and patch these trousers, or I'll box your ears. I have killed seven at a blow, slain two giants, led a unicorn captive, and caught a wild boar, then why should I be afraid of those men standing outside my door?" The men, when they heard the Tailor saying these words, were so terrified that they fled as if pursued by a wild army, and didn't dare go near him again. So the little Tailor was and remained a King all the days of his life.

THE SLEEPING BEAUTY IN THE WOOD

By Charles Perrault

There was once in a distant country a King and Queen whose only sorrow was that they had no children. At last the Queen gave birth to a little daughter and the King showed his joy by giving a christening feast so grand that the like of it was never known. He asked all the fairies in the land—there were seven found in the kingdom—to stand godmothers to the little Princess; hoping that each might bestow on her some good gift.

After the christening all the guests returned to the palace, where there was placed before each fairy godmother a magnificent covered dish, and a knife, fork, and spoon of pure gold, set with precious stones. But, as they all were sitting down at table there entered an old fairy who had not been invited, because it was more than fifty years since she had gone out of a certain tower, and she was thought to be dead or enchanted. The King ordered a cover to be placed for her, but it was of common earthenware, for he had ordered from his jeweler only seven gold dishes, for the seven fairies aforesaid. The old fairy thought herself neglected, and muttered angry threats, which were overheard by one of the younger fairies, who chanced to sit beside her. This good godmother, afraid of harm to the pretty baby, hastened to hide herself behind the hangings in the hall. She did this because she wished to speak last and repair any evil the old fairy might intend.

The fairies now offered their good wishes, which, unlike most wishes, were sure to come true. The first wished that the little Princess should grow up the fairest woman in the world; the second, that she should have wit like an angel; the third, that she should be perfectly graceful; the fourth, that she should sing like a nightingale; the fifth, that she should dance perfectly well; the sixth, that she should play all kinds of music perfectly. Then the old fairy's turn came. Shaking her head spitefully, she uttered the wish that when the baby grew up into a young lady, and learned to spin, she might prick her finger with a spindle and die of the wound.

This terrible prophecy made all the company tremble; and every one fell to crying. Upon which the wise young fairy appeared from behind the curtains and said: "Assure yourselves O King and Queen; the Princess shall not die. I have no power to undo what my elder has done. The Princess must pierce her finger with a spindle and she shall then sink, not into the sleep of death, but into a sleep that will last a hundred years. After that time is ended, the son of a King shall come and awake her."

Then all the fairies vanished.

The King, in the hope of avoiding his daughter's doom, issued an edict forbidding all persons to spin, and even to have spinning wheels in their houses, on pain of instant death. But it was in vain. One day when she was just fifteen years of age, the King and Queen left their daughter alone in one of their castles, where, wandering about at her will, she came to a little room in the top of a tower, and there found a very old woman, who had not heard of the King's edict, busy with her spinning wheel.

"What are you doing, good old woman?" said the Princess.

"I'm spinning my pretty child."

"Ah, how pretty! Let me try if I can spin also."

She had no sooner taken up the spindle than, being hasty and unhandy, she pierced her finger with the point. Though it was so small a wound, she fainted away at once and dropped on the floor. The poor old woman called for help; shortly came the ladies-in-waiting, who tried every means to restore their young mistress; but all in vain. She lay, beautiful as an angel, the color still lingering in her lips and cheeks, her fair bosom softly stirred with her breath; only her eyes were fast closed. When the King, her father, and the Queen, her mother, beheld her thus, they knew that all had happened as the cruel fairy meant, and that their daughter would sleep for one hundred years. They sent away all the physicians and attendants, and themselves sorrowing laid her upon a bed in the finest apartment in the palace. There she slept and looked like a sleeping angel still.

When this misfortune happened, the kindly young fairy who had saved the Princess by changing her sleep of death into this sleep of a hundred years, was twelve thousand leagues away, in the kingdom of Mataquin. But, being informed of everything by a little dwarf who wore seven-league boots, she arrived speedily in a chariot of fire drawn by dragons. The King handed her out of the chariot, and she approved of all he had done. Then, being a fairy of great common sense and foresight, she thought that the Princess, awakening after a hundred years in this old castle, might not know what to do with herself if she found herself alone. Accordingly, she touched with her magic wand everybody and everything in the palace except the King and Queen: governesses, ladies of honor, waiting maids, gentlemen ushers, cooks, kitchen girls, pages, footmen; even the horses that were in the stables, and the grooms that attended them, she touched each and all. Nay, the dogs, too, in the outer court, and the little fat lapdog, Mopsey, who had laid himself down beside his mistress on her splendid bed, were also touched, and they, like all the rest, fell fast asleep in a moment. The very spits that were before the kitchen fire fell asleep, and the fire itself, and everything became as still as if it were the middle of the night, or as if the palace were a palace of the dead.

The King and Queen, having kissed their daughter, went out of the castle, giving orders that it was to be approached no more. The command was unnecessary, for in one quarter of an hour there sprang up around it a wood so thick and thorny that neither beasts nor men could attempt to penetrate there. Above this dense mass of forest could only be seen the top of the high tower where the lovely Princess slept.

When a hundred years were gone the King had died, and his throne had passed to another royal family. The reigning King's son, being one day out hunting, was stopped in the chase by this great wood, inquired what wood it was and what were those towers which he saw appearing out of the midst of it. Every one answered as he had heard. Some said it was an old castle haunted by spirits. Others said it was the abode of witches and enchanters. The most common story was that an Ogre lived there, a giant with long teeth and claws, who carried away naughty little boys and girls and ate them up. The Prince did not know what to think. At length an old peasant was found who remembered having heard his grandfather say to his father that in this tower was a Princess, beautiful as the day, who was doomed to sleep there for one hundred years, until awakened by a king's son, who was to marry her.

At this the young Prince, who had the spirit of a hero, determined to find out the truth for himself.

Spurred on by love and honor, he leaped from his horse and began to force his way through the thick wood. To his amazement the stiff branches all gave way, and the ugly thorns drew back of their own accord, and the brambles buried themselves in the earth to let him pass. This done, they closed behind him, allowing none to follow. Nevertheless, he pushed boldly on alone.

The first thing he saw was enough to freeze him with fear. Bodies of men and horses lay extended on the ground; but the men had faces, not death white, but red as roses, and beside them were glasses half filled with wine, showing that they had gone to sleep drinking. Next he entered a large court paved with marble, where stood rows of guards presenting arms, but as still as if cut out of stone; then he passed through many chambers where gentlemen and ladies, all in the dress of the past century, slept at their ease, some standing, some sitting. The pages were lurking in corners, the ladies of honor were stooping over their embroidery frames or listening to the gentlemen of the court; but all were as silent and as quiet as statues. Their clothes, strange to say, were fresh and new as ever; and not a particle of dust or spider web had gathered over the furniture, though it had not known a broom for a hundred years. Finally, the astonished Prince came to an inner chamber, where was the fairest sight his eyes ever beheld.

A young girl of wonderful beauty lay asleep on an embroidered bed, and she looked as if she had only just closed her eyes. Trembling, the Prince approached and knelt beside her. Some say he kissed her; but as nobody saw it, and she never told, we cannot be quite sure of the fact. However, as the end of the enchantment had come, the Princess waked at once, and, looking at him with eyes of the tenderest regard, said, sleepily: "Is it you, my Prince? I have waited for you very long."

Charmed with these words, and still more by the tone in which they were uttered, the Prince assured her that he loved her more than his life. For a long time did they sit talking, and yet had not said half enough. Their only interruption was the little dog Mopsey, who had awakened with his mistress, and now began to be jealous that the Princess did not notice him as much as she was wont to do.

Meanwhile all the attendants, whose enchantment was also broken, not being in love, were ready to die of hunger after their fast of a hundred years. A lady of honor ventured to say that dinner was served, whereupon the Prince handed his beloved Princess at once to the great hall. She did not wait to dress for dinner, being already perfectly and magnificently attired, though in a fashion somewhat out of date. However, her lover had the politeness not to notice this, nor to remind her that she was dressed exactly like his grandmother whose portrait still hung on the palace walls.

During dinner a concert by the attendant musicians took place, and, considering they had not touched their instruments for a century, they played the old tunes extremely well. They ended with a wedding march, for that very evening the Prince and Princess were married.

After a few days they went together out of the castle and enchanted wood, both of which immediately vanished, and were nevermore beheld by mortal eyes. The Princess was restored to her ancestral kingdom, and after a few years the Prince and she became King and Queen, and ruled long and happily.

THE FAIR ONE WITH GOLDEN LOCKS

Retold by Miss Mulock

There was once a King's daughter so beautiful that they named her the Fair One with Golden Locks. These golden locks were the most remarkable in the world, soft and fine, and falling in long waves down to her very feet. She wore them always thus, loose and flowing, surmounted with a wreath of flowers; and though such long hair was sometimes rather inconvenient, it was so exceedingly beautiful, shining in the sun like ripples of molten gold, that everybody agreed she fully deserved her name.

Now there was a young King of a neighboring country, very handsome, very rich, and wanting nothing but a wife to make him happy. He heard so much of the various perfections of the Fair One with Golden Locks, that at last, without even seeing her, he fell in love with her so desperately that he could neither eat nor drink, and resolved to send an ambassador at once to demand her in marriage. So he ordered a magnificent equipage—more than a hundred horses and a hundred footmen—in order to bring back to him the Fair One with Golden Locks, who, he never doubted, would be only too happy to become his Queen. Indeed, he felt so sure of her that he refurnished the whole palace, and had made by all the dressmakers of the city, dresses enough to last a lady a lifetime. But, alas! when the ambassador arrived and delivered his message, either the princess was in bad humor, or the offer did not appear to be to her taste; for she returned her best thanks to his majesty, but said she had not the slightest wish or intention to get married. She also, being a prudent damsel, declined receiving any of the presents which the King had sent her; except that, not quite to offend his majesty, she retained a box of English pins, which were in that country of considerable value.

When the ambassador returned, alone and unsuccessful, all the court was very much affected, and the King himself began to weep with all his might. Now, there was in the palace household a young gentleman named Avenant, beautiful as the sun, besides being at once so amiable and so wise that the King confided to him all his affairs; and every one loved him, except those people—to be found in all courts—who were envious of his good fortune. These malicious folk hearing him say gaily: "If the King had sent me to fetch the Fair One with Golden Locks, I know she would have come back with me," repeated the saying in such a manner, that it appeared as if Avenant thought so much of himself and his beauty, and felt sure the princess would have followed him all over the world; which when it came to the ears of the King, as it was meant to do, irritated him so much that he commanded Avenant to be imprisoned in a high tower and left to die there of hunger. The guards accordingly carried off the young man, who had quite forgotten his idle speech, and had not the least idea what fault he had committed. They ill-treated him very much, and then left him with nothing to eat and only water to drink. This, however, kept him alive for a few days, during which he did not cease to complain aloud, and to call upon the King, saying: "Oh King, what harm have I done? You have no subject more faithful than I. Never have I had a thought which could offend you."

And it so befell that the King, coming by chance, or else with a sort of remorse, past the tower, was touched by the voice of the young Avenant, whom he had once so much regarded. In spite of all the courtiers could do to prevent him, he stopped to listen, and overheard these words. The tears rushed into his eyes; he opened the door of the tower, and called: "Avenant!" Avenant came, creeping feebly along, fell at the King's knees, and kissed his feet:

"Oh sire, what have I done that you should treat me so cruelly?"

"You have mocked me and my ambassador; for you said, if I had sent you to fetch the Fair One with Golden Locks, you would have been successful and brought her back."

"I did say it, and it was true," replied Avenant fearlessly; "for I should have told her so much about your majesty and your various high qualities, which no one knows so well as myself, that I am persuaded she would have returned with me."

"I believe it," said the King, with an angry look at those who had spoken ill of his favorite; he then gave Avenant a free pardon and took him back with him to the court.

After having supplied the famished youth with as much supper as he could eat, the King admitted him to a private audience, and said: "I am as much in love as ever with the Fair One with Golden Locks, so I will take thee at thy word, and send thee to try and win her for me."

"Very well, please your majesty" replied Avenant cheerfully; "I will depart to-morrow."

The King, overjoyed with his willingness and hopefulness would have furnished him with a still more magnificent equipage and suite than the first ambassador but Avenant refused to take anything except a good horse to ride, and letters of introduction to the Princess's father. The King embraced him and eagerly saw him depart.

It was on a Monday morning when, without any pomp or show, Avenant thus started on his mission. He rode slowly and meditatively, pondering over every possible means of persuading the Fair One with Golden Locks to marry the King; but, even after several days journey towards her country, no clear project had entered into his mind. One morning, when he had started at break of day, he came to a great meadow with a stream running through it, along which were planted willows and poplars. It was such a pleasant, rippling stream that he dismounted and sat down on its banks. There he perceived gasping on the grass a large golden Carp, which, in leaping too far after gnats, had thrown itself quite out of the water, and now lay dying on the greensward. Avenant took pity on it, and though he was very hungry, and the fish was very fat, and he would well enough have liked it for his breakfast, still he lifted it gently and put it back into the stream. No sooner had the Carp touched the fresh cool water than it revived and swam away; but shortly returning, it spoke to him from the water in this wise:

"Avenant, I thank you for your good deed. I was dying, and you have saved me; I will recompense you for this one day."

After this pretty little speech, the fish popped down to the bottom of the stream, according to the habit of Carp, leaving Avenant very much astonished, as was natural.

Another day he met with a Raven that was in great distress, being pursued by an Eagle, which would have swallowed him up in no time. "See," thought Avenant, "how the stronger oppress the weaker! What right has an Eagle to eat up a Raven?" So taking his bow and arrow, which he always carried, he shot the Eagle dead, and the Raven, delighted, perched in safety on an opposite tree.

"Avenant," screeched he, though not in the sweetest voice in the world, "you have generously succored me, a poor miserable Raven. I am not ungrateful, and I will recompense you one day."

"Thank you," said Avenant, and continued his road.

Entering in a thick wood, so dark with the shadows of early morning that he could scarcely find his way, he heard an Owl hooting, like an owl in great tribulation. She had been caught by the nets spread by bird-catchers to entrap finches, larks, and other small birds. "What a pity," thought Avenant, "that men must always torment poor birds and beasts who have done them no harm!" So he took out his knife, cut the net, and let the Owl go free. She went sailing up in the air, but immediately returned hovering over his head on her brown wings.

"Avenant," said she, "at daylight the bird-catchers would have been here, and I should have been caught and killed. I have a grateful heart; I will recompense you one day."

These were the three principal adventures that befell Avenant on his way to the kingdom of the Fair One with Golden Locks. Arrived there, he dressed himself with the greatest care, in a habit of silver brocade, and a hat adorned with plumes of scarlet and white. He threw over all a rich mantle, and carried a little basket, in which was a lovely little dog, an offering of respect to the Princess. With this he presented himself at the palace gates, where even though he came alone, his mien was so dignified and graceful, so altogether charming, that every one did him reverence, and was eager to run and tell the Fair One with Golden Locks, that Avenant, another ambassador from the King, her suitor, awaited an audience.

"Avenant!" repeated the Princess. "That is a pretty name; perhaps the youth is pretty too."

"So beautiful," said the ladies of honor, "that while he stood under the palace window we could do nothing but look at him."

"How silly of you!" sharply said the Princess. But she desired them to bring her robe of blue satin, to comb out her long hair, and adorn it with the freshest garland of flowers; to give her her high-heeled shoes, and her fan. "Also," added she, "take care that my audience-chamber is well swept and my throne well dusted. I wish in everything to appear as becomes the Fair One with Golden Locks."

This done she seated herself on her throne of ivory and ebony and gave orders for her musicians to play, but softly, so as not to disturb conversation. Thus, shining in all her beauty, she admitted Avenant to her presence.

He was so dazzled that at first he could not speak; then he began and delivered his harangue to perfection.

"Gentle Avenant," returned the Princess, after listening to all his reasons for her returning with him, "your arguments are very strong, and I am inclined to listen to them; but you must first find for me a ring, which I dropped into the river about a month ago. Until I recover it, I can listen to no proposition of marriage."

Avenant, surprised and disturbed, made her a profound reverence and retired, taking with him the basket and the little dog Cabriole, which she refused to accept. All night long he sat sighing to himself. "How can I ever find a ring which she dropped into the river a month ago? She has set me an impossibility."

"My dear master," said Cabriole, "nothing is an impossibility to one so young and charming as you are; let us go at daybreak to the river-side."

Avenant patted him, but replied nothing; until, worn out with grief, he slept. Before dawn Cabriole wakened him, saying: "Master, dress yourself and let us go to the river."

There Avenant walked up and down, with his arms folded and his head bent, but saw nothing. At last he heard a voice, calling from a distance, "Avenant, Avenant!"

The little dog ran to the water-side. — "Never believe me again, master, if it is not a golden Carp with a ring in its mouth!"

"Yes, Avenant," said the Carp, "this is the ring which the Princess has lost. You saved my life in the willow meadow, and I have recompensed you. Farewell!"

Avenant took the ring gratefully and returned to the palace with Cabriole, who scampered about in great glee.

Craving an audience, he presented the Princess with her ring, and begged her to accompany him to his master's kingdom. She took the ring, looked at it, and thought she was surely dreaming.

"Some fairy must have assisted you, fortunate Avenant," said she.

"Madam, I am only fortunate in my desire to obey your wishes."

"Obey me still," she said graciously. "There is a prince named Galifron, whose suit I have refused. He is a giant as tall as a tower, who eats a man as a monkey eats a nut: he puts cannons into his pockets instead of pistols; and when he speaks, his voice is so loud that every one near him becomes deaf. Go and fight him, and bring me his head."

Avenant was thunderstruck; but after a time he recovered himself. "Very well, madam, I shall certainly perish, but I will perish like a brave man. I will depart at once to fight the Giant Galifron."

The Princess, now in her turn surprised and alarmed, tried every persuasion to induce him not to go, but in vain. Avenant armed himself and started, carrying his little dog in its basket. Cabriole was the only creature that gave him consolation: "Courage, master! While you attack the giant, I will bite his legs: he will stoop down to strike me, and then you can knock him on the head." Avenant smiled at the little dog's spirit, but he knew it was useless.

Arrived at the castle of Galifron, he found the road all strewn with bones, and carcasses of men. Soon he saw the giant walking. His head was level with the highest trees, and he sang in a terrific voice:

"Bring me babies to devour;
More — more — more — more —

Men and women, tender and tough;
All the world holds not enough."

To which Avenant replied, imitating the tune:

"Avenant you here may see,
He is come to punish thee:
Be he tender, be he tough,
To kill thee, giant, he is enough."

Hearing these words, the giant took up his massive club, looked around for the singer, and perceiving him, would have slain him on the spot, had not a Raven, sitting on a tree close by, suddenly flown out upon him and picked out both his eyes. Then Avenant easily killed him and cut off his head, while the Raven, watching him, said:

"You shot the Eagle who was pursuing me: I promised to recompense you, and to-day I have done it. We are quits."

"No, it is I who am your debtor, Sir Raven," replied Avenant, as, hanging the frightful head to his saddle-bow, he mounted his horse and rode back to the city of the Fair One with Golden Locks.

There everybody followed him, shouting: "Here is brave Avenant, who has killed the giant," until the Princess, hearing the noise, and fearing it was Avenant himself who was killed, appeared, all trembling; and even when he appeared with Galifron's head, she trembled still, although she had nothing to fear.

"Madam," said Avenant, "your enemy is dead; so I trust you will accept the hand of the King my master."

"I cannot," replied she thoughtfully, "unless you first bring me a phial of the water in the Grotto of Darkness. It is six leagues in length, and guarded at the entrance by two fiery dragons. Within, it is a pit, full of scorpions, lizards, and serpents, and at the bottom of this place flows the Fountain of Beauty and Health. All who wash in it become, if ugly, beautiful, and if beautiful, beautiful forever; if old, young; and if young, young forever. Judge then, Avenant, if I can quit my kingdom without carrying with me some of this miraculous water."

"Madam," replied Avenant, "you are already so beautiful that you require it not; but I am an unfortunate ambassador whose death you desire; I will obey you, though I know I shall never return."

So he departed with his only friends—his horse and his faithful dog Cabriole; while all who met him looked at him compassionately, pitying so pretty a youth bound on such a hopeless errand. But, however kindly they addressed him, Avenant rode on and answered nothing, for he was too sad at heart.

He reached a mountain-side, where he sat down to rest, leaving his horse to graze, and Cabriole to run after the flies. He knew that the Grotto of Darkness was not far off, yet he looked about him like one who sees nothing. At last he perceived a rock, as black as ink, whence came a thick smoke; and in a moment appeared one of the two dragons, breathing out flames. It had a yellow and green body, claws, and a long tail. When Cabriole saw the monster, the poor little dog hid himself in terrible fright. But Avenant resolved to die bravely; so taking a phial which the Princess had given him, he prepared to descend into the cave.

"Cabriole," said he, "I shall soon be dead; then fill this phial with my blood, and carry it to the Fair One with Golden Locks, and afterward to the King, my master, to show him I have been faithful to the last."

While he was thus speaking a voice called: "Avenant, Avenant!"—and he saw an Owl sitting on a hollow tree. Said the Owl: "You cut the net in which I was caught, and I vow to recompense you. Now is the time. Give me the phial; I know every corner of the Grotto of Darkness—I will fetch you the water of beauty."

Delighted beyond words, Avenant delivered up his phial; the Owl flew with it into the grotto, and in less than half an hour reappeared, bringing it quite full and well corked. Avenant thanked her with all his heart, and joyfully took once more the road to the city.

The Fair One with Golden Locks had no more to say. She consented to accompany him back, with all her suite, to his master's court. On the way thither she saw so much of him, and found him so charming, that Avenant might have married her himself had he chosen; but he would not have been false to his master for all the beauties under the sun. At length they arrived at the King's city, and the Fair One with Golden Locks became his spouse and Queen. But she still loved Avenant in her heart, and often said to the King her lord: "But for Avenant I should not be here; he has done all sorts of impossible deeds for my sake; he has fetched me the water of beauty, and I shall never grow old—in short, I owe him everything."

And she praised him in this sort so much that at length the King became jealous; and though Ayenant gave him not the slightest cause of offense, he shut him up in the same high tower once more—but with irons on his hands and feet, and a cruel jailer besides, who fed him with bread and water only. His sole companion was his little dog Cabriole.

When the Fair One with Golden Locks heard of this, she reproached her husband for his ingratitude, and then throwing herself at his knees, implored that Avenant might be set free. But the King only said: "She loves him!"

and refused her prayer. The Queen entreated no more, but fell into a deep melancholy.

When the King saw it, he thought she did not care for him because he was not handsome enough; and that if he could wash his face with her water of beauty, it would make her love him the more. He knew that she kept it in a cabinet in her chamber, where she could find it always.

Now it happened that a waiting-maid, in cleaning out this cabinet, had, the very day before, knocked down the phial, which was broken in a thousand pieces, and all the contents were lost. Very much alarmed, she then remembered seeing, in a cabinet belonging to the King, a similar phial. This she fetched, and put in the place of the other one, in which was the water of beauty. But the King's phial contained the water of death. It was a poison, used to destroy great criminals—that is, noblemen, gentlemen, and such like. Instead of hanging them or cutting their heads off, like common people, they were compelled to wash their faces with this water; upon which they fell asleep, and woke no more. So it happened that the King, taking up this phial, believing it to be the water of beauty, washed his face with it, fell asleep, and—died.

Cabriole heard the news, and, gliding in and out among the crowd which clustered round the young and lovely widow, whispered softly to her—"Madam, do not forget poor Avenant." If she had been disposed to do so, the sight of his little dog would have been enough to remind her of him—his many sufferings, and his great fidelity. She rose up, without speaking to anybody, and went straight to the tower where Avenant was confined. There, with her own hands, she struck off his chains, and putting a crown of gold on his head, and a purple mantle on his shoulders, said to him, "Be King—and my husband.

Avenant could not refuse: for in his heart he had loved her all the time. He threw himself at her feet, and then took the crown and scepter, and ruled her kingdom like a king. All the people were delighted to have him as their sovereign. The marriage was celebrated in all imaginable pomp, and Avenant and the Fair One with Golden Locks lived and reigned happily together all their days.

BEAUTY AND THE BEAST

By Mme. d'Aulnoy

There was once a very rich merchant, who had six children, three boys and three girls. As he was himself a man of great sense, he spared no expense for their education. The three daughters were all handsome, but particularly the youngest; indeed, she was so very beautiful, that in her childhood everyone called her the Little Beauty; and being equally lovely when she was grown up, nobody called her by any other name, which made her sisters very jealous of her. This youngest daughter was not only more handsome than her sisters, but also was better tempered. The two eldest were vain of their wealth and position. They gave themselves a thousand airs, and refused to visit other merchants' daughters; nor would they condescend to be seen except with persons of quality.

They went every day to balls, plays, and public walks, and always made game of their youngest sister for spending her time in reading or other useful employments. As it was well known that these young ladies would have large fortunes, many great merchants wished to get them for wives; but the two eldest always answered, that, for their parts, they had no thoughts of marrying anyone below a duke or an earl at least. Beauty had quite as many offers as her sisters, but she always answered, with the greatest civility, that though she was much obliged to her lovers, she would rather live some years longer with her father, as she thought herself too young to marry.

It happened that, by some unlucky accident, the merchant suddenly lost all his fortune, and had nothing left but a small cottage in the country. Upon this he said to his daughters, while the tears ran down his cheeks, "My children, we must now go and dwell in the cottage, and try to get a living by labor, for we have no other means of support." The two eldest replied that they did not know how to work, and would not leave town; for they had lovers enough who would be glad to marry them, though they had no longer any fortune. But in this they were mistaken; for when the lovers heard what had happened, they said, "The girls were so proud and ill-tempered, that all we wanted was their fortune; we are not sorry at all to see their pride brought down; let them show off their airs to their cows and sheep." But everybody pitied poor Beauty, because she was so sweet-tempered and kind to all, and several gentlemen offered to marry her, though she had not a penny; but Beauty still refused, and said she could not think of leaving her poor father in this trouble. At first Beauty could not help sometimes crying in secret for the hardships she was now obliged to suffer; but in a very short time she said to herself, "All the crying in the world will do me no good, so I will try to be happy without a fortune."

When they had removed to their cottage, the merchant and his three sons employed themselves in ploughing and sowing the fields, and working in the garden. Beauty also did her part, for she rose by four o'clock every morning, lighted the fires, cleaned the house, and got ready the breakfast for the whole family. At first she found all this very hard; but she soon grew quite used to it, and thought it no hardship; indeed, the work greatly benefited her health. When she had done, she used to amuse herself with reading, playing her music, or singing while she spun. But her two sisters were at a loss what to do to pass the time away; they had their breakfast in bed, and did not rise till ten o'clock. Then they commonly walked out, but always found themselves very soon tired; when they would often sit down under a shady tree, and grieve for the loss of their carriage and fine clothes, and say to each other, "What a mean-spirited, poor stupid creature our young sister is, to be so content within this low way of life!" But their father thought differently; and loved and admired his youngest child more than ever.

After they had lived in this manner about a year the merchant received a letter, which informed him that one of his richest ships, which he thought was lost, had just come unto port. This news made the two eldest sisters almost mad with joy; for they thought they should now leave the cottage, and have all their finery again. When they found that their father must take a journey to the ship, the two eldest begged he would not fail to bring them back some new gowns, caps, rings, and all sorts of trinkets. But Beauty asked for nothing; for she thought in herself that all the Ship was worth would hardly buy everything her sisters wished for. "Beauty," said the merchant, "how comes it that you ask for nothing: what can I bring you, my child?"

"Since you are so kind as to think of me, dear father," she answered, "I should be glad if you would bring me a rose, for we have none in our garden." Now Beauty did not indeed wish for a rose, nor anything else, but she only said this that she might not affront her sisters; otherwise they would have said she wanted her father to praise her for desiring nothing. The merchant took his leave of them, and set out on his journey; but when he got to the ship, some persons went to law with him about the cargo, and after a deal of trouble he came back to his cottage as poor as he had left it. When he was within thirty miles of his home, and thinking of the joy of again meeting his children, he lost his way in the midst of a dense forest. It rained and snowed very hard, and, besides, the wind was so high as to throw him twice from his horse. Night came on, and he feared he should die of cold and hunger, or be torn to pieces by the wolves that he heard howling round him. All at once, he cast his eyes toward a long avenue, and saw at the end a light, but it seemed a great way off. He made the best of his way toward it, and found that it came from a splendid palace, the windows of which were all blazing with light. It had great bronze gates, standing wide open, and fine court-yards, through which the merchant passed; but not a living soul was to be seen. There were stables, too, which his poor, starved horse, less scrupulous than himself, entered at once, and took a good meal of oats and hay. His master then tied him up, and walked toward the entrance hall, but still without seeing a single creature. He went on to a large dining parlor, where he found a good fire, and table covered with some very nice dishes, but only one plate with a knife and fork. As the snow and rain had wetted him to the skin, he went up to the fire to dry himself. "I hope," said he, "the master of the house or his servants will excuse me, for it surely will not be long now before I see them." He waited some time, but still nobody came: at last the clock struck eleven, and the merchant, being quite faint for the want of food, helped himself to a chicken, and to a few glasses of wine, yet all the time trembling with fear. He sat till the clock struck twelve, and then, taking courage, began to think he might as well look about him: so he opened a door at the end of the hall, and went through it into a very grand room, in which there was a fine bed; and as he was feeling very weary, he shut the door, took off his clothes, and got into it.

It was ten o'clock in the morning before he awoke, when he was amazed to see a handsome new suit of clothes laid ready for him, instead of his own, which were all torn and spoiled. "To be sure," said he to himself, "this place belongs to some good fairy, who has taken pity on my ill luck." He looked out of the window, and instead of the snow-covered wood, where he had lost himself the previous night, he saw the most charming arbors covered with all kinds of flowers. Returning to the hall where he had supper, he found a breakfast table, ready prepared. "Indeed, my good fairy," said the merchant aloud, "I am vastly obliged to you for your kind care of me." He then made a hearty breakfast, took his hat, and was going to the stable to pay his horse a visit; but as he passed under one of the arbors, which was loaded with roses, he thought of what Beauty had asked him to bring back to her, and so he took a bunch of roses to carry home. At the same moment he heard a loud noise, and saw coming toward him a beast, so frightful to look at that he was ready to faint with fear. "Ungrateful man!" said the beast in a terrible voice, "I have saved your life by admitting you into my palace, and in return you steal my roses, which I value more than anything I possess. But you shall atone for your fault—die in a quarter of an hour.

The merchant fell on his knees, and clasping his hands, said, "Sir, I humbly beg your pardon: I did not think it would offend you to gather a rose for one of my daughters, who had entreated me to bring her one home. Do not kill me, my lord!"

"I am not a lord, but a beast," replied. the monster, "I hate false compliments: so do not fancy that you can coax me by any such ways. You tell me that you have daughters; now I will suffer you to escape, if one of them will come and die in your stead. If not, profuse that you will yourself return in three months, to be dealt with as I may choose."

The tender-hearted merchant had no thoughts of letting any one of his daughters die for his sake; but he knew that if he seemed to accept the beast's terms, he should at least have the pleasure of seeing them once again. So he gave his promise, and was told that he might then set off as soon as he liked. "But," said the beast, "I do not wish you to go back empty handed. Go to the room you slept in, and you will find a chest there; fill it with whatsoever you like best, and I will have it taken to your own house for you."

When the beast had said this, he went away. The good merchant, left to himself, began to consider that as he must die—for he had no thought of breaking a promise, made even to a beast—he might as well have the comfort of leaving his children provided for. He returned to the room he had slept in, and found there heaps of gold pieces lying about.

He filled the chest with them to the very brim, locked it, and, mounting his horse, left the palace as sorrowful as he had been glad when he first beheld it. The horse took a path across the forest of his own accord, and in a few hours they reached the merchant's house. His children came running round him, but, instead of kissing them with joy, he could not help weeping as he looked at them. He held in his hand the bunch of roses, which he gave to Beauty, saying, "Take these roses, Beauty; but little do you think how dear they have cost your poor father;" and then he gave them an account of all that he had seen or heard in the palace of the beast.

The two eldest sisters now began to shed tears, and to lay the blame upon Beauty, who, they said, would be the cause of her father's death. "See," said they, "what happens from the pride of the little wretch; why did not she ask for such things as we did? But, to be sure, Miss must not be like other people;

and though she will be the cause of her father's death, yet she does not shed a tear."

"It would be useless," replied Beauty, "for my father shall not die. As the beast will accept one of his daughters, I will give myself up, and be only too happy to prove my love for the best of fathers."

"No, sister," said the three brothers with one voice, "that cannot be; we will go in search of this monster, and either he or we will perish."

"Do not hope to kill him," said the merchant, "his power is far too great. But Beauty's young life shall not be sacrificed; I am old, and cannot expect to live much longer; so I shall but give up a few years of my life, and shall only grieve for the sake of my children."

"Never, father!" cried Beauty; "if you go back to the palace, you cannot hinder my going after you; though young, I am not over-fond of life; and I would much rather be eaten up by the monster, than die of grief for your loss."

The merchant in vain tried to reason with Beauty who still obstinately kept to her purpose; which, in truth, made her two sisters glad, for they were jealous of her, because everybody loved her.

The merchant was so grieved at the thoughts of losing his child, that he never once thought of the chest filled with gold, but at night, to his great surprise, he found it standing by his bedside. He said nothing about his riches to his eldest daughters, for he knew very well it would at once make them want to return to town; but he told Beauty his secret, and she then said, that while he was away, two gentlemen had been on a visit at her cottage, who had fallen in love with her two sisters. She entreated her father to marry them without delay, for she was so sweet-natured, she only wished them to be happy.

Three months went by, only too fast, and then the merchant and Beauty got ready to set out for the palace of the beast. Upon this, the two sisters rubbed their eyes with an onion, to make believe they were crying; both the merchant and his sons cried in earnest. Only Beauty shed no tears. They reached the palace in a very few hours, and the horse, without bidding, went into the stable as before. The merchant and Beauty walked toward the large hall, where they found a table covered with every dainty and two plates laid already. The merchant had very little appetite; but Beauty, that she might the better hide her grief, placed herself at the table, and helped her father; she then began to eat herself, and thought all the time that, to be sure, the beast had a mind to fatten her before he ate her up, since he had provided such good cheer for her. When they had done their supper, they heard a great noise, and the good old man began to bid his poor child farewell, for he knew it was the beast coming to them. When Beauty first saw that frightful form, she was very much terrified, but tried to hide her fear. The creature walked up to her, and eyed her all over—then asked her in a dreadful voice if she had come quite of her own accord.

"Yes," said Beauty.

"Then you are a good girl, and I am very much obliged to you."

This was such an astonishingly civil answer that Beauty's courage rose: but it sank again when the beast, addressing the merchant, desired him to leave the palace next morning, and never return to it again. "And so good-night, merchant. And good-night, Beauty."

"Good-night, beast," she answered, as the monster shuffled out of the room.

"Ah! my dear child," said the merchant, kissing his daughter, "I am half dead already, at the thought of leaving you with this dreadful beast; you shall go back and let me stay in your place."

"No," said Beauty, boldly, "I will never agree to that; you must go home to-morrow morning."

They then wished each other good-night, and went to bed, both of them thinking they should not be able to close their eyes; but as soon as ever they had lain down, they fell into a deep sleep, and did not awake till morning. Beauty dreamed that a lady came up to her, who said, "I am very much pleased, Beauty, with the goodness you have shown, in being willing to give your life to save that of your father. Do not be afraid of anything; you shall not go without a reward."

As soon as Beauty awoke she told her father this dream; but though it gave him some comfort, he was a long time before he could be persuaded to leave the palace. At last Beauty succeeded in getting him safely away.

When her father was out of sight, poor Beauty began to weep sorely; still, having naturally a courageous spirit, she soon resolved not to make her sad case still worse by sorrow, which she knew was vain, but to wait and be patient. She walked about to take a view of all the palace, and the elegance of every part of it much charmed her.

But what was her surprise, when she came to a door on which was written, BEAUTY'S ROOM! She opened it in haste, and her eyes were dazzled by the splendor and taste of the apartment. What made her wonder more than all the rest, was a large library filled with books, a harpsichord, and many pieces of music. "The beast surely does not mean to eat me up immediately," said she, "since he takes care I shall not be at a loss how to amuse myself." She opened the library and saw these verses written in letters of gold in the back of one of the books: —

"Beauteous lady, dry your tears,
Here's no cause for sighs or fears.
Command as freely as you may,
For you command and I obey."

"Alas!" said she, sighing; "I wish I could only command a sight of my poor father, and to know what he is doing at this moment." Just then, by chance, she cast her eyes upon a looking-glass that stood near her, and in it she saw a picture of her old home, and her father riding mournfully up to the door. Her sisters came out to meet him, and although they tried to look sorry, it was easy to see that in their hearts they were very glad. In a short time all this picture disappeared, but it caused Beauty to think that the beast, besides being very powerful, was also very kind. About the middle of the day she found a table laid ready for her, and a sweet concert of music played all the time she was dining, without her seeing anybody. But at supper, when she was going to seat herself at table, she heard the noise of the beast, and could not help trembling with fear.

"Beauty," said he, "will you give me leave to see you sup?"

"That is as you please," answered she, very much afraid.

"Not in the least," said the beast; "you alone command in this place. If you should not like my company, you need only say so, and I will leave you that moment. But tell me, Beauty, do you not think me very ugly?"

"Why, yes," said she, "for I cannot tell a falsehood; but then I think you are very good."

"Am I?" sadly replied the beast; "yet, besides being ugly, I am also very stupid; I know well enough that I am but a beast."

"Very stupid people," said Beauty, "are never aware of it themselves."

At which kindly speech the beast looked pleased, and replied, not without an awkward sort of politeness, "Pray do not let me detain you from supper, and be sure that you are well served. All you see is your own, and I should be deeply grieved if you wanted for anything."

"You are very kind—so kind that I almost forgot you are so ugly," said Beauty, earnestly.

"Ah! yes," answered the beast, with a great sigh; "I hope I am good-tempered, but still I am only a monster."

"There is many a monster who wears the form of a man; it is better of the two to have the heart of a man and the form of a monster."

"I would thank you, Beauty, for this speech, but I am too senseless to say anything that would please you," returned the beast in a melancholy voice; and altogether he seemed so gentle and so unhappy that Beauty, who had the tenderest heart in the world, felt her fear of him gradually vanish.

She ate her supper with a good appetite, and conversed in her own sensible and charming way, till at last, when the beast rose to depart, he terrified her more than ever by saying abruptly, in his gruff voice, "Beauty, will you marry me?"

Now Beauty, frightened as she was, would speak only the exact truth; besides her father had told her that the beast liked only to have the truth spoken to him. So she answered, in a very firm tone, "No, beast."

He did not get into a passion, or do anything but sigh deeply, and depart.

When Beauty found herself alone, she began to feel pity for the poor beast. "Oh!" said she, "what a sad thing it is that he should be so very frightful, since he is so good-tempered!"

Beauty lived three months in this palace very well pleased. The beast came to see her every night, and talked with her while she supped; and though what he said was not very clever, yet, as she saw in him every day some new goodness, instead of dreading the time of his coming, she soon began continually looking at her watch, to see if it were nine o'clock; for that was the hour when he never failed to visit her. One thing only vexed her, which was that every night before he went away, he always made it a rule to ask her if she would be his wife, and seemed very much grieved at her steadfastly replying "No." At last, one night, she said to him, "You wound me greatly, beast, by forcing me to refuse you so often; I wish I could take such a liking to you as to agree to marry you; but I must tell you plainly that I do not think it will ever happen. I shall always be your friend; so try to let that content you.

"I must," sighed the beast, "for I know well enough how frightful I am; but I love you better than myself. Yet I think I am very lucky in your being pleased to stay with me; now promise, Beauty, that you will never leave me.

Beauty would almost have agreed to this, so sorry was she for him, but she had that day seen in her magic glass, which she looked at constantly, that her father was dying of grief for her sake.

"Alas!" she said, "I long so much to see my father, that if you do not give me leave to visit him, I shall break my heart."

"I would rather break mine, Beauty," answered the beast; "I will send you to your father's cottage: you shall stay there, and your poor beast shall die of sorrow."

"No," said Beauty, crying, "I love you too well to be the cause of your death; I promise to return in a week. You have shown me that my sisters are married, and my brothers are gone for soldiers, so that my father is left all alone. Let me stay a week with him."

"You shall find yourself with him to-morrow morning," replied the beast; "but mind, do not forget your promise. When you wish to return, you have nothing to do but to put your ring on a table when you go to bed. Good-by, Beauty!" The beast sighed as he said these words, and Beauty went to bed very sorry to see him so much grieved. When she awoke in the morning, she found herself in her father's cottage. She rang a bell that was at her bedside, and a servant entered; but as soon as she saw Beauty the woman gave a loud shriek; upon which the merchant ran upstairs, and when he beheld his daughter he ran to her, and kissed her a hundred times. At last Beauty began to remember that she had brought no clothes with her to put on; but the servant told her she had just found in the next room a large chest full of dresses, trimmed all over with gold, and adorned within pearls and diamonds.

Beauty, in her own mind, thanked the beast for his kindness, and put on the plainest gown she could find among them all. She then desired the servant to lay the rest aside, for she intended to give them to her sisters; but, as soon as she had spoken these words, the chest was gone out of sight in a moment. Her father then suggested, perhaps the beast chose for her to keep them all for herself: and as soon as he had said this, they saw the chest standing again in the same place. While Beauty was dressing herself, a servant brought word to her that her sisters were come with their husbands to pay her a visit. They both lived unhappily with the gentlemen they had married. The husband of the eldest was very handsome, but was so proud of this that he thought of nothing else from morning till night, and did not care a pin for the beauty of his wife. The second had married a man of great learning; but he made no use of it, except to torment and affront all his friends, and his wife more than any of them. The two sisters were ready to burst with spite when they saw Beauty dressed like a princess, and looking so very charming. All the kindness that she showed them was of no use; for they were vexed more than ever when she told them how happy she lived at the palace of the beast. The spiteful creatures went by themselves into the garden, where they cried to think of her good fortune.

"Why should the little wretch be better off than we?" said they. "We are much handsomer than she is."

"Sister!" said the eldest, "a thought has just come into my head; let us try to keep her here longer than the week for which the beast gave her leave; and then he will be so angry that perhaps when she goes back to him he will eat her up in a moment."

"That is well thought of," answered the other, "but to do this, we must pretend to be very kind."

They then went to join her in the cottage, where they showed her so much false love that Beauty could not help crying for joy.

When the week was ended, the two sisters began to pretend such grief at the thought of her leaving them that she agreed to stay a week more; but all that time Beauty could not help fretting for the sorrow that she knew her absence would give her poor beast for she tenderly loved him, and much wished for his company again. Among all the grand and clever people she saw, she found nobody who was half so sensible, so affectionate, so thoughtful, or so kind. The tenth night of her being at the cottage, she dreamed she was in the garden of the palace, that the beast lay dying on a grass plot, and with his last breath put her in mind of her promise, and laid his death to her forsaking him. Beauty awoke in a great fright, and she burst into tears. "Am not I wicked," said she, "to behave so ill to a beast who has shown me so much kindness? Why will I not marry him? I am sure I should be more happy with him than my sisters are with their husbands. He shall not be wretched any longer on my account; for I should do nothing but blame myself all the rest of my life."

She then rose, put her ring on the table, got into bed again, and soon fell asleep. In the morning she with joy found herself in the palace of the beast. She dressed herself very carefully, that she might please him the better, and thought she had never known a day pass away so slowly. At last the clock struck nine, but the beast did not come. Beauty, dreading lest she might truly have caused his death, ran from room to room, calling out: "Beast, dear beast;" but there was no answer. At last she remembered her dream, rushed to the grass plot, and there saw him lying apparently dead beside the fountain. Forgetting all his ugliness, she threw herself upon his body, and finding his heart still beating, she fetched some water and sprinkled it over him, weeping and sobbing the while.

The beast opened his eyes. "You forgot your promise, Beauty, and so I determined to die; for I could not live without you. I have starved myself to death, but I shall die content since I have seen your face once more."

"No, dear beast," cried Beauty, passionately, "you shall not die; you shall live to be my husband. I thought it was only friendship I felt for you, but now I know it was love."

The moment Beauty had spoken these words, the palace was suddenly lighted up, and all kinds of rejoicings were heard around them, none of which she noticed, but hung over her dear beast with the utmost tenderness. At last, unable to restrain herself, she dropped her head over her hands, covered her eyes, and cried for joy; and, when she looked up again, the beast was gone. In his stead she saw at her feet a handsome, graceful young prince, who thanked her with the tenderest expressions for having freed him from enchantment.

"But where is my poor beast? I only want him and nobody else," sobbed Beauty.

"I am he," replied the prince. "A wicked fairy condemned me to this form, and forbade me to show that I had any wit or sense, till a beautiful lady should consent to marry me. You alone, dearest Beauty, judged me neither by my looks nor by my talents, but by my heart alone. Take it then, and all that I have besides, for all is yours."

Beauty, full of surprise, but very happy, suffered the prince to lead her to his palace, where she found her father and sisters, who had been brought there by the fairy-lady whom she had seen in a dream the first night she came.

"Beauty," said the fairy, "you have chosen well, and you have your reward, for a true heart is better than either good looks or clever brains. As for you, ladies," and she turned to the two elder sisters, "I know all your ill deeds, but I have no worse punishment for you than to see your sister happy. You shall stand as statues at the door of her palace, and when you repent of, and have amended your faults, you shall become women again. But, to tell you the truth, I very much fear you will remain statues forever."

JACK AND THE BEANSTALK

Anonymous

Once upon a time there was a poor widow who lived in a little cottage with her only son Jack.

Jack was a giddy, thoughtless boy, but very kindhearted and affectionate. There had been a hard winter, and after it the poor woman had suffered from fever and ague. Jack did no work as yet, and by degrees they grew dreadfully poor. The widow saw that there was no means of keeping Jack and herself from starvation but by selling her cow; so one morning she said to her son, "I am too weak to go myself, Jack, so you must take the cow to market for me, and sell her."

Jack liked going to market to sell the cow very much; but as he was on his way, he met a butcher who had some beautiful beans in his hand. Jack stopped to look at them, and the butcher told the boy that they were of great value, and persuaded the silly lad to sell the cow for these beans. When he brought them home to his mother instead of the money she expected for her nice cow, she was very vexed and shed many tears, scolding Jack for his folly. He was very sorry, and mother and son went to bed very sadly that night; their last hope seemed gone.

At daybreak Jack rose and went out into the garden.

"At least," he thought, "I will sow the wonderful beans. Mother says that they are just common scarlet-runners, and nothing else; but I may as well sow them."

So he took a piece of stick, and made some holes in the ground, and put in the beans.

That day they had very little dinner, and went sadly to bed, knowing that for the next day there would be none, and Jack, unable to sleep from grief and vexation, got up at day-dawn and went out into the garden.

What was his amazement to find that the beans had grown up in the night, and climbed up and up till they covered the high cliff that sheltered the cottage, and disappeared above it! The stalks had twined and—twisted themselves together till they formed quite a ladder.

"It would be easy to climb it," thought Jack.

And, having thought of the experiment, he at once resolved to carry it out, for Jack was a good climber. However, after his late mistake about the cow, he thought he had better consult his mother first.

So Jack called his mother, and they both gazed in silent wonder at the Beanstalk, which was not only of great height, but it was thick enough to bear Jack's weight.

"I wonder where it ends," said Jack to his mother; "I think I will climb up and see."

His mother wished him not to venture up this strange ladder, but Jack coaxed her to give her consent to the attempt, for he was certain there must be something wonderful in the Beanstalk; so at last she yielded to his wishes.

Jack instantly began to climb, and went up and up on the ladder-like bean till everything he had left behind him — the cottage, the village, and even the tall church tower — looked quite little, and still he could not see the top of the Beanstalk.

Jack felt a little tired, and thought for a moment that he would go back again; but he was a very persevering boy, and he knew that the way to succeed in anything is not to give up. So, after resting for a moment, he went on.

After climbing higher and higher, till he grew afraid to look down for fear he should be giddy, Jack at last reached the top of the Beanstalk, and found himself in a beautiful country, finely wooded, with beautiful meadows covered with sheep. A crystal stream ran through the pastures; not far from the place where he had got off the Beanstalk stood a fine, strong castle.

Jack wondered very much that he had never heard of or seen this castle before; but when he reflected on the subject, he saw that it was as much separated from the village by the perpendicular rock on which it stood as if it were in another land.

While Jack was standing looking at the castle, a very strange-looking woman came out of the wood and advanced toward him.

She wore a pointed cap of quilted red satin turned up with ermine, her hair streamed loose over her shoulders, and she walked with a staff. Jack took off his cap and made her a bow.

"If you please, ma'am," said he, "is this your house?"

"No," said the old lady. "Listen, and I will tell you the story of that castle."

"Once upon a time there was a noble knight, who lived in this castle, which is on the borders of Fairyland. He had a fair and beloved wife and several lovely children; and as his neighbors, the little people, were very friendly toward him, they bestowed on him many excellent and precious gifts.

"Rumor whispered of these treasures; and a monstrous giant who lived at a great distance, and who was a very wicked being, resolved to obtain possession of them.

"So he bribed a false servant to let him inside the castle, when the knight was in bed and asleep, and he killed him as he lay. Then he went to the part of the castle which was the nursery, and also killed all the poor little ones he found there.

"Happily for her, the lady was not to be found. She had gone with her infant son, who was only two or three months old, to visit her old nurse, who lived in the valley; and she had been detained all night there by a storm.

"The next morning, as soon as it was light, one of the servants at the castle, who had managed to escape, came to tell the poor lady of the sad fate of her husband and her pretty babes. She could scarcely believe him at first, and was eager at once to go back and share the fate of her dear ones; but the old nurse, with many tears, besought her to remember that she had still a child, and that it was her duty to preserve her life for the sake of the poor innocent.

"The lady yielded to this reasoning, and consented to remain at her nurse's house as the best place of concealment; for the servant told her that the Giant had vowed, if he could find her, he would kill both her and her baby. Years rolled on. The old nurse died, leaving her cottage and the few articles of furniture it contained to her poor lady, who dwelt in it, working as a peasant for her daily bread. Her spinning-wheel and the milk of a cow which she had purchased with the little money she had with her, sufficed for the scanty subsistence of herself and her little son. There was a nice little garden attached to the cottage, in which they cultivated peas, beans, and cabbages, and the lady was not ashamed to go out at harvest time and glean in the fields to supply her little son's wants.

"Jack, that poor lady is your mother. This castle was once your father's, and must again be yours."

Jack uttered a cry of surprise.

"My mother! oh, madam, what ought I to do? My poor father! My dear mother!"

"Your duty requires you to win it back for your mother. But the task is a very difficult one, and full of peril, Jack. Have you courage to undertake it?"
"I fear nothing when I am doing right," said Jack.

"Then," said the lady in the red cap, "you are one of those who slay giants. You must get into the castle, and if possible possess yourself of a hen that lays golden eggs, and a harp that talks. Remember, all the Giant possesses is really yours."

As she ceased speaking, the lady of the red hat suddenly disappeared, and of course Jack knew she was a fairy.

Jack determined at once to attempt the adventure; so he advanced, and blew the horn which hung at the castle portal. The door was opened in a minute or two by a frightful Giantess, with one great eye in the middle of her forehead.

As soon as Jack saw her he turned to run away, but she caught him, and dragged him into the castle.

"Ho, ho!" she laughed terribly. "You didn't expect to see me here, that is clear! No, I shan't let you go again. I am weary of my life. I am so overworked, and I don't see why I should not have a page as well as other ladies. And you shall be my boy. You shall clean the knives, and black the boots, and make the fires, and help me generally when the Giant is out. When he is at home I must hide you, for he has eaten up all my pages hitherto, and you would be a dainty morsel, my little lad."

While she spoke she dragged Jack right into the castle. The poor boy was very much frightened, as I am sure you and I would have been in his place. But he remembered that fear disgraces a man; so he struggled to be brave and make the best of things. "I am quite ready to help you, and do all I can to serve you, madam," he said, "only I beg you will be good enough to hide me from your husband, for I should not like to be eaten at all."

"That's a good boy," said the Giantess, nodding her head; "it is lucky for you that you did not scream out when you saw me, as the other boys who have been here did, for if you had done so my husband would have awakened and have eaten you, as he did them, for breakfast. Come here, child; go into my wardrobe: he never ventures to open that; you will be safe there."

And she opened a huge wardrobe which stood in the great hall, and shut him unto it. But the keyhole was so large that it admitted plenty of air, and he could see everything that took place through it. By and by he heard a heavy tramp on the stairs, like the lumbering along of a great cannon, and then a voice like thunder cried out:

"Fe, fa, fi-fo-fum,
I smell the breath of an Englishman.
Let him be alive or let him be dead,
I'll grind his bones to make my bread."

"Wife," cried the Giant, "there is a man in the castle. Let me have him for breakfast."

"You are grown old and stupid," cried the lady, in her loud tones. "It is only a nice fresh steak off an elephant, that I have cooked for you, which you smell. There, sit down and make a good breakfast."

And she placed a huge dish before him of savory steaming meat, which greatly pleased him, and made him forget his idea of an Englishman being in the castle. When he had breakfasted he went out for a walk, and then the Giantess opened the door, and made Jack come out to help her. He helped her all day. She fed him well, and when evening came put him back in the wardrobe.

The Giant came in to supper. Jack watched him through the keyhole, and was amazed to see him pick a wolf's bone, and put half a fowl at a time into his capacious mouth.

When the supper was ended he bade his wife bring him his hen that laid the golden eggs.

"It lays as well as it did when it belonged to that paltry knight," he said; "indeed, I think the eggs are heavier than ever."

The Giantess went away, and soon returned with a little brown hen, which she placed on the table before her husband.

"And now, my dear," she said, "I am going for a walk, if you don't want me any longer."

"Go, said the Giant; "I shall be glad to have a nap by and by."

Then he took up the brown hen and said to her:

"Lay!" And she instantly laid a golden egg.

"Lay!" said the Giant again. And she laid another.

"Lay!" he repeated the third time. And again a golden egg lay on the table.

Now, Jack was sure this hen was that of which the fairy had spoken.

By and by the Giant put the hen down on the floor, and soon after went fast asleep, snoring so loud that it sounded like thunder.

Directly Jack perceived that the Giant was fast asleep, he pushed open the door of the wardrobe and crept out; very softly he stole across the room, and, picking up the hen, made haste to quit the apartment. he knew the way to the kitchen, the door of which he found was left ajar; he opened it, shut and locked it after him, and flew back to the Beanstalk, which he descended as fast as his feet would move.

When his mother saw him enter the house she wept for joy, for she had feared that the fairies had carried him away, or that the Giant had found him. But Jack put the brown hen down before her, and told her how he had been in the Giant's castle, and all his adventures. She was very glad to see the hen, which would make them rich once more.

Jack made another journey up the Beanstalk to the Giant's castle one day while his mother had gone to market; but first he dyed his hair and disguised himself. The old woman did not know him again, and dragged him in as she had done before, to help her to do the work; but she heard her husband coming, and hid him in the wardrobe, not thinking that it was the same boy who had stolen the hen. She bade him stay quite still there, or the Giant would eat him. Then the Giant came in, saying:

"Fe, fa, fi-fo-furn,
I smell the breath of an Englishman.
Let him he alive or let him be dead,
I'll grind his bones to make my bread."

"Nonsense!" said the wife, "it is only a roasted bullock that I thought would be a titbit for your supper; sit down and I will bring it up at once.

The Giant sat down, and soon his wife brought up a roasted bullock on a large dish, and they began their supper. Jack was amazed to see them pick the bones of the bullock as if it had been a lark. As soon as they had finished their meal, the Giantess rose and said:

"Now, my dear, with your leave I am going up to my room to finish the story I am reading. If you want me, call for me."

"First," answered the Giant, "bring me my money bags, that I may count my golden pieces before I sleep." The Giantess obeyed. She went and soon returned with two large bags over her shoulders, which she put down by her husband.

"There," she said: "that is all that is left of the knight's money. When you have spent it you must go and take another baron's castle."

"That he shan't, if I can help it," thought Jack.

The Giant, when his wife was gone, took out heaps and heaps of golden pieces, and counted them, and put them in piles, till he was tired of the amusement. Then he swept them all back into their bags, and leaning back in his chair fell fast asleep, snoring so loud that no other sound was audible.

Jack stole softly out of the wardrobe, and taking up the bags of money (which were his very own, because the Giant had stolen them from his father), he ran off, and with great difficulty descending the Beanstalk, laid the bags of gold on his mother's table. She had just returned from town, and was crying at not finding Jack. "There, mother, I have brought you the gold that my father lost."

"Oh, Jack! you are a very good boy, but I wish you would not risk your precious life in the Giant's castle. Tell me how you came to go there again."

And Jack told her all about it.

Jack's mother was very glad to get the money, but she did not like him to run any risk for her.

But after a time Jack made up his mind to go again to the Giant's castle.

So he climbed the Beanstalk once more, and blew the horn at the Giant's gate. The Giantess soon opened the door; she was very stupid, and did not know him again,. but she stopped a minute before she took him in. She feared another robbery; but Jack's fresh face looked so innocent that she could not resist him, and so she bade him come in, and again hid him away in the wardrobe.

By and by the Giant came home, and as soon as he had crossed the threshold he roared out:

"Fe, fa, li-fo-fum,
I smell the breath of an Englishman.
Let him be alive or let him be dead,
I'll grind his bones to make my bread."

"You stupid old Giant," said his wife, "you only smell a nice sheep, which I have grilled for your dinner.'

And the Giant sat down, and his wife brought up a whole sheep for his dinner. When he had eaten it all up, he said:

"Now bring me my harp, and I will have a little music while you take your walk."

The Giantess obeyed, and returned with a beautiful harp. The framework was all sparkling with diamonds and rubies, and the strings were all of gold.

"This is one of the nicest things I took from the knight," Said the Giant. "I am very fond of music, and my harp is a faithful servant."

So he drew the harp toward him and said:

"Play!"

And the harp played a very soft, sad air.

"Play something merrier!" said the Giant.

And the harp played a merry tune.

"Now play me a lullaby," roared the Giant; and the harp played a sweet lullaby, to the sound of which its master fell asleep.

Then Jack stole softly out of the wardrobe, and went into the huge kitchen to see if the Giantess had gone out; he found no one there, so he went to the door and opened it softly, for he thought he could not do so with the harp in his hand.

Then he entered the Giant's room and seized the harp and ran away with it; but as he jumped over the threshold the harp called out: "MASTER! MASTER!"

And the Giant woke up.

With a tremendous roar he sprang from his seat, and in two strides had reached the door.

But Jack was very nimble. He fled like lightning with the harp, talking to it as he went (for he saw it was a fairy), and telling it he was the son of its old master, the knight.

Still the Giant came on so fast that he was quite close to poor Jack, and had stretched out his great hand to catch him. But, luckily, just at that moment he stepped upon a loose stone, stumbled, and fell flat on the ground, where he lay at his full length.

This accident gave Jack time to get on the Bean stalk and hasten down it; but just as he reached their own garden he beheld the Giant descending after him.

"Mother! mother!" cried Jack, "make haste and give me the ax."

His mother ran to him with a hatchet in her hand, and Jack with one tremendous blow cut through all the Beanstalks except one.

"Now, mother, stand out of the way!" said he. Jack's mother shrank back, and it was well she did so, for just as the Giant took hold of the last branch of the Beanstalk, Jack cut the stem quite through and darted from the spot.

Down came the Giant with a terrible crash, and as he fell on his head, he broke his neck, and lay dead at the feet of the woman he had so much injured.

Before Jack and his mother had recovered from their alarm and agitation, a beautiful lady stood before them.

"Jack," said she, "you have acted like a brave knight's son, and deserve to have your inheritance restored to you. Dig a grave and bury the Giaint, and then go and kill the Giantess."

"But," said Jack, "I could not kill any one unless I were fighting with him; and I could not draw my sword upon a woman. Moreover, the Giantess was very kind to me."

The Fairy smiled on Jack.

"I am very much pleased with your generous feeling," she said. "Nevertheless, return to the castle, and act as you will find needful."

Jack asked the Fairy if she would show him the way to the castle, as the Beanstalk was now down. She told him that she would drive him there in her chariot, which was drawn by two peacocks. Jack thanked her, and sat down in the chariot with her.

The Fairy drove him a long distance round, till they reached a village which lay at the bottom of the mill. Here they found a number of miserable-looking men assembled. The Fairy stopped her carriage and addressed them:

"My friends," said she, "the cruel Giant who oppressed you and ate up all your flocks and herds is dead, and this young gentleman was the means of your being delivered from him, and is the son of your kind old master, the knight."

The men gave a loud cheer at these words, and pressed forward to say that they would serve Jack as faithfully as they had served his father. The Fairy bade them follow her to the castle, and they marched thither in a body, and Jack blew the horn and demanded admittance.

The old Giantess saw them coming from the turret loophole. She was very much frightened, for she guessed that something had happened to her husband; and as she came downstairs very fast she caught her foot in her dress, and fell from the top to the bottom and broke her neck.

When the people outside found that the door was not opened to them, they took crowbars and forced the portal. Nobody was to be seen, but on leaving the mall they found the body of the Giantess at the foot of the stairs.

Thus Jack took possession of the castle. The Fairy went and brought his mother to him, with the hen and the harp. He had the Giantess buried, and endeavored as much as lay in his power to do right to those whom the Giant had robbed.

Before her departure for fairyland, the Fairy explained to Jack that she had sent the butcher to meet him with the beans, in order to try what sort of lad he was.

"If you had looked at the gigantic Beanstalk and only stupidly wondered about it," she said, "I should have left you where misfortune had placed you, only restoring her cow to your mother. But you showed an inquiring mind, and great courage and enterprise, therefore you deserve to rise; and when you mounted the Beanstalk you climbed the Ladder of Fortune."

She then took her leave of Jack and his mother.

HOP-O'-MY-THUMB

Retold by Joseph Jacobs

Once upon a time there was a Wood-cutter and his wife who had seven children, all boys. The eldest was only ten years old. They were very poor, and their seven children were a great burden, since not one of them was able to earn his living.

What troubled them still more was the fact that the youngest was not only very delicate, but silent, which they took for stupidity, but which was really a mark of his good sense. He was very small, and when he was born he was scarcely bigger than one's thumb, which caused him to be called little "Hop-o'-My-Thumb." This poor child was the scapegoat of the house, and was blamed for everything. He was, however, sharper and wiser than all his brothers, and though he spoke little, he listened a great deal.

At last there came a bad year, and so great a famine, that the poor people resolved to rid themselves of their children. One evening, when the children were all in bed, and the Wood-cutter with a sorrowful heart, was sitting by the fire with his wife, he said to her: "You know that we can no longer support our children. I cannot let them die of hunger before my eyes, and I am resolved to take them to the wood to-morrow, and lose them. It will be easy to do this, for, while they amuse themselves tying my sticks, we have only to slip away without their seeing us."

"Ah!" cried his Wife, "would you then destroy your children?" In vain did her husband set forth to her their great poverty: she would not consent. She was poor, she said. But she was their mother. At last, having considered what a grief it would be to her to have them die of hunger before her eyes, she agreed to her husband's plan, and went, weeping, to bed.

Hop-o'-My-Thumb had listened to all that they had said, for having heard them, from his bed, talking of family matters, he had risen softly and slipped under his father's stool, in order to hear without being seen. He then went back to bed, but lay awake the rest of the night, thinking what he should do. He rose early and went to a brook, where he filled his pocket with little white pebbles, and then returned to the house.

Soon after, they all set off, but Hop-o'-My-Thumb did not tell his brothers anything of what he knew. They went into a forest, so thick that they could not see each other at a distance of ten paces. The Wood-cutter began to fell a tree, while the children gathered sticks to make up into bundles. The father and mother, seeing them thus employed, slipped away unnoticed, and then fled rapidly, by a little winding path.

When the children found they were alone, they began to scream and cry with all their strength. Hop-o'-My-Thumb let them cry, knowing well how to get home; for, while walking, he had dropped along the path the little white pebbles which he had in his pockets.

He therefore said to them, "Fear not, brothers, my father and mother have left us here, but I will lead you to the house only follow me."

They obeyed at once, and he led them home along the same path by which they had come into the forest at first. They did not dare to go into the house, but placed themselves near the door, in order to hear what their father and mother were saying.

Now it had so happened that, just as the Woodcutter and his Wife reached home, the lord of the village had sent them ten crowns, which he had long owed them, and which they had never hoped to obtain. This gave them new life, for the poor creatures were almost dead from hunger.

The Wood-cutter immediately sent his Wife to the butcher's, where, as it was long since they had eaten anything, she bought three times as much meat as was needed for the supper of two people.

When they were seated at table, the Wife said, "Alas! where now are our poor children? They would make good cheer with what we have left. But it is you who wished to lose them. I always said we should repent it. What are they doing now in the forest? Alas! alas! perhaps the wolves have already eaten them! You were most cruel thus to lose your children."

The Wood-cutter at last grew impatient, for she repeated more than twenty times that they would repent what they had done, and that she had told him so. He threatened to beat her if she was not silent. The Wood-cutter did not do this because he was less sorry than his Wife, but because her reproaches angered him. His Wife now shed tears, and cried out, "Alas! where are my children, my poor children?"

She said this so loud that the children, who were at the door, heard her, and all cried out together, "Here we are! here we are!"

She ran quickly to open the door, and said, as she embraced them, "How overjoyed I am to see you again, my darling children! you must be very tired and very hungry; and you, Peter, how muddy you are! come, let me brush you." Peter was her eldest son, whom she loved more than all the others.

The children then sat down at the table, and ate with an appetite which delighted their father and mother, to whom they described, all speaking at once, how frightened they had been in the forest.

These good people were filled with joy to have their children with them again, and this joy lasted as long as the ten crowns held out. But when the money was spent, they fell back into their former misery, and resolved to lose them once more; and in order not to fail again, they determined to take them much further into the forest than the first time.

They could not, however, speak of this so secretly but that they were overheard by Hop-o'-My-Thumb, who laid his plans to escape as before. Although he got up early in order to go out and pick up some little stones, he could not succeed in his purpose, for he found the door of the house shut and double-bolted. He was wondering what he should do, when, his mother having given them each a bit of bread for breakfast, he thought that he might use his bread instead of pebbles by dropping crumbs along the paths as they walked. He therefore slipped the bread into his pocket.

Their father and mother led them this time into the thickest and darkest part of the forest, and, as soon as they were there, ran away and left them.

Hop-o'-My-Thumb was not much troubled, because he believed he could easily find his way by means of the bread which he had scattered as he passed along. What was his surprise when he could not find a single crumb: the birds had come and eaten it all.

Now was their lot indeed wretched; the more they wandered about, the deeper they buried themselves in the forest. Night came, and a great wind arose which frightened them terribly. They thought they heard on all sides the howling of hungry wolves coming to eat them up. They did not dare to speak, or even turn their heads. Rain began to fall, which wet them to the skin. They slipped at every step, and, if they fell, got up so covered with mud that they could hardly move their hands.

Finally, Hop-o'-My-Thumb climbed to the top of a tree, to see if he could not discover something. Having looked on all sides, he at last saw a little gleam of light, like that from a candle, but it was very far off, beyond the forest. He got down from the tree: but when he was on the ground he no longer saw anything, which troubled him greatly. However, having walked for some time with his brothers in the direction where he had seen the light, he again saw it as they came out of the wood. At last they reached the house where the candle was, though not without many alarms, for they lost sight of it whenever they descended unto a hollow place.

They knocked at the door, which was opened to them by a woman. She asked them what they wanted. Hop-o'-My-Thumb replied that they were poor children who had lost themselves in the forest, and who asked, for charity's sake, a place to sleep.

The woman, seeing how bitter they were, began to weep, and said to them, "Alas! my poor children, whence do you come? Do you not know that this is the house of an Ogre, who eats little children?"

"Alas, madam," said Hop-o'-My-Thumb, who like his brothers was shaking with fear, "what shall we do? The wolves of the forest will certainly devour us to-night, if you will not give us shelter. This being the case, we had rather be eaten by the Ogre, and he, perhaps, will take pity on us, if you will beg him to do so."

The Ogre's wife, who thought she might be able to conceal them from her husband till the next morning, let them come in, and placed them near a good fire, where a whole sheep was roasting for the Ogre's supper.

When they had begun to get warm, they heard three or four heavy knocks at the door. It was the Ogre. His wife hastily hid the children under the bed, and then opened the door.

The Ogre asked first if supper was ready, and the wine drawn; and then sat down at the table. The mutton was nearly raw, but he liked it all the better on that account.

He then began to sniff about, saying that he smelled fresh meat.

"It must be this calf which I have just been dressing that you smell," said the wife.

"I smell fresh meat, I tell you again," said the Ogre, looking fiercely at his wife; "and there is something more of which I do not know."

Saying these words, he rose from the table and went straight to the bed, where he found the poor children.

"Ah!" said he, "this, then, is the way you wish to deceive me, wicked woman. I know not what prevents me from eating you, too. Here is game, which comes to me very conveniently to treat three Ogres of my acquaintance, who are coming to visit me about this time."

He then drew the little boys from under the bed, one after another. The poor children threw themselves on their knees begging for pardon. But they had to do with the most cruel of all the Ogres, who, far from having pity, devoured them already with his eyes, and said to his wife that they would be delicious morsels fried, when she had made a good sauce for them.

He took out a great knife, and, approaching the poor children, began to sharpen it on a long stone, which he held in his left hand. He then seized one of them, when his wife said to him, "Why do you begin at this time of night? Shall you not have time to-morrow?"

"Be silent," replied the Ogre; "they will be more tender if I kill them now."

"But you have already so much meat on hand," replied his wife. "Here are a calf, two sheep, and half a pig."

"You are right," said the Ogre; "give them a good supper, that they may not grow thin, and put them to bed."

The good woman was overcome with joy, and brought them their supper at once; but they were too frightened to eat.

As for the Ogre, he set himself to drinking, delighted to have something with which to regale his friends. He drank a dozen cups more than usual, which went to his head, and obliged him to go early to bed.

Now this Ogre had seven daughters, who were still only children. These little Ogresses all had beautiful complexions, for they ate fresh meat like their father. They had little round gray eyes, crooked noses, and great mouths filled with long teeth, very sharp and far apart. They were not yet very wicked, but they promised well, for they already bit little children whenever they got the chance. They had been put to bed early, and were all seven in one bed, each having a golden crown on her head.

There was in the same room another bed of the same size. Here it was that the Ogre's wife put the seven little boys, after which she went to bed in her own chamber.

Hop-o'-My-Thumb, who had remarked that the Ogre's daughters had golden crowns on their heads, was afraid that the Ogre might regret not having killed him and his brothers that evening. So he rose about the middle of the night, and, taking his nightcap and those of his brothers, he went very softly and placed them on the heads of the Ogre's seven daughters, after having removed their golden crowns. He then put the crowns on his brothers' heads and on his own, so that the Ogre might mistake them for his daughters, and his daughters for the boys whom he wished to kill.

The plan succeeded as he had expected. The Ogre, having awakened about midnight, was sorry that he had put off till next day what he might have done that evening. He jumped quickly out of bed, and, taking his great knife, "Let us see," said he, "how our little friends are getting on."

He went on tiptoe to the room of his daughters, and approached the bed where the little boys were all asleep, except Hop-o'-My-Thumb, who was terribly frightened when he felt the Ogre's hand touching his head, as he had already touched his brothers'. But when the Ogre felt the golden crowns, he said, "Indeed, I was near making a nice piece of work of it. I see that I drank too much in the evening."

He then went to the bed of his daughters, where he felt the boys' little nightcaps. "Ah! here they are," said he, "the fine fellows! I must go boldly to work." Saying these words, and without hesitating, he cut the throats of his seven daughters. Very well pleased with his expedition, he went back to bed. As soon as Hop-o'-My-Thumb heard the Ogre snoring, he awakened his brothers, and told them to dress themselves quickly and follow him. They went softly down unto the garden, and leaped over the walls. They hurried away, and ran almost all night, without knowing whither they went.

The Ogre, when he woke up, said to his wife, "Go upstairs and dress those little fellows who were here last night."

The Ogress was very much astonished at the kindness of her husband, not suspecting for a moment the way in which he meant that she should dress them. Believing that he simply wished her to put on their clothes, she went upstairs, where she was amazed to see her seven daughters with their throats cut. She was so overcome that she immediately fainted. The Ogre, thinking his wife was too slow, went upstairs to assist her. He was no less astonished than his wife when the frightful sight met his eyes.

"Ah! what have I done here?" he cried; "but those little wretches shall pay for this, and at once."

He then threw a bucket of water into his wife's face, and, having revived her, said, "Give me quickly my seven-league boots, that I may go after those boys and catch them."

He then started out into the country at once, and, having rushed about in all directions, came at last to the road where the poor children were walking, and then not more than a hundred steps from their father's house. They saw the Ogre striding from mountain to mountain, and crossing rivers as if they were little brooks.

Hop-o'-My-Thumb, who saw a hollow rock near the place where they were, hid himself and his six brothers there, and watched carefully what became of their enemy. The Ogre, who was very tired with his long and fruitless journey, wished to rest himself, and sat down, by chance, on the very rock where the little boys were hidden.

As he was overcome with fatigue, he soon fell asleep, and began to snore so frightfully that the poor children were as much frightened as when he held his knife ready to cut their throats. Hop-o'-My-Thumb was less afraid, and told his brothers to run into the house while the Ogre slept, and not to worry about him. They followed his counsel, and quickly reached the house.

Hop-o'-My-Thumb then approached the Ogre, softly drew off his boots, and put them on himself. The boots were very long and very large; but, as they were fairy boots, they had the gift of becoming larger or smaller, according to the size of the wearer's leg. In fact, they fitted Hop-o'-My-Thumb as if they had been made for him.

He then went straight to the Ogre's house, where he found his wife weeping over her daughters.

"Your husband," said Hop-o'-My-Thumb, "is in great danger, for he has been taken by a band of robbers, who will kill him if he does not give them all his gold and silver. Just when they held their knives to his throat he perceived me, and besought me to come and tell you of the state in which he was, and to direct you to give me all that he has, without retaining anything, since otherwise they would slay him without mercy. As time passed, he wished that I should take his seven-league boots, as you see, in order to make haste, and also that you might not think me an impostor."

The good woman, very much frightened, gave him all she had; for this Ogre was a good husband, although he did eat little children.

Hop-o'-My-Thumb, being then loaded with all the Ogre's treasures, returned to his father's house, where he was welcomed with great joy and where they all lived happily ever after.

THE GOOSE-GIRL

Anonymous

There was once upon a time an old Queen whose husband had been dead for many years, and she had a beautiful daughter. When the princess grew up she was betrothed to a prince who lived at a great distance. When the time came for her to be married, and she had to ,journey forth into the distant kingdom, the aged Queen packed up for her many costly vessels of silver and gold, and trinkets also of gold and silver; and cups and jewels, in short, everything which appertained to a royal dowry, for she loved her child with all her heart. She likewise sent her maid in waiting, who was to ride with her, and hand her over to the bridegroom, and each had a horse for the journey, but the horse of the King's daughter was called Falada, and could speak. So when the hour of parting had come, the aged mother went into her bedroom, took a small knife and cut her finger with it until it bled, then she held a white handkerchief to it into which she left three drops of blood fall, gave it to her daughter and said: "Dear child, preserve this carefully, it will be of service to you on your way."

So they took a sorrowful leave of each other: the princess put the piece of cloth in her bosom, mounted her horse, and then went away to her bridegroom. After she had ridden for a while she felt a burning thirst and said to her waiting-maid: "Dismount, and take my cup which thou hast brought with thee for me, and get me some water from the stream, for I should like to drink." "If you are thirsty," said the waiting-maid, "get off your horse yourself, and lie down and drink out of the water; I don't choose to be your servant." So in her great thirst the princess alighted, bent down over the water in the stream and drank, and was not allowed to drink out of the golden cup. Then she said, "Ah, Heaven!" and the three drops of blood answered:

"If thy mother knew this, her heart would break."

But the King's daughter was humble, said nothing, and mounted her horse again. She rode some miles further, but the day was warm, the sun scorched her, and she was thirsty once more, and when they came to a stream of water, she again cried to her waiting-maid: "Dismount, and give me some water in my golden cup," for she had long ago forgotten the girl's ill words.

But the waiting-maid said still more haughtily: "If you wish to drink, drink as you can, I don't choose to be your maid." Then in her great thirst the King's daughter alighted, bent over the flowing stream, wept and said: "Ah, heaven!" and the drops of blood again replied: "If thy mother knew this, her heart would break." And as she was thus drinking and leaning right over the stream, the handkerchief with the three drops of blood fell out of her bosom, and floated away with the water without her observing it, so great was her trouble.

The waiting-maid, however, had seen it, and she rejoiced to think that she had now power over the bride, for since the princess had lost the drops of blood, she had become weak and powerless. So now when she wanted to mount her horse again, the one that was called Falada, the waiting-maid said: "Falada is more suitable for me, and my nag will do for thee," and the princess had to be content with that. Then the waiting-maid, with many hard words, bade the princess exchange her royal apparel for her own shabby clothes; and at length she was compelled to swear by the clear sky above her, that she would not say one word of this to any one at the royal court, and if she had not taken this oath she would have been killed on the spot. But Falada saw all this, and observed it well.

The waiting-maid now mounted Falada, and the true bride the bad horse, and thus they traveled onward, until at length they entered the royal palace. There were great rejoicings over her arrival, and the prince sprang forward to meet her, lifted the waiting-maid from her horse, and thought she was his consort. She was conducted upstairs, but the real princess was left standing below. Then the old King looked out of the window and saw her standing in the courtyard, and how dainty and delicate and beautiful she was, and instantly went to the royal apartment, and asked the bride about the girl she had with her who was standing down below in the courtyard, and who she was. "I picked her up on my way for a companion; give the girl something to work at, that she may not stand idle." But the old King had no work for her, and knew of none, so he said: "I have a little boy who tends the geese, she may help him." The boy was called Conrad, and the true bride had to help him to tend the geese.

Soon afterward the false bride said to the young King: "Dearest husband, I beg you to do me a favor." He answered: "I will do so most willingly." "Then send for the knacker, and have the head of the horse on which I rode here cut off, for it vexed me on the way." In reality she was afraid that the horse might tell how she had behaved to the King's daughter. Then she succeeded in making the King promise that it should be done, and the faithful Falada was to die; this came to the ears of the real princess, and she secretly promised to pay the knacker a piece of gold if he would perform a small service for her.

There was a great dark-looking gateway in the town, through which morning and evening she had to pass with the geese: would he be so good as to nail up Falada's head on it, so that she might see him again, more than once. The knacker's man promised to do that, and cut off the head, and nailed it fast beneath the dark gateway.

Early in the morning, when she and Conrad drove out their flock beneath this gateway, she said in passing:

"Alas, Falada, hanging there

Then the head answered:

"Alas, young Queen, how ill you fare!
If this your tender mother knew,
Her heart would surely break in two."

Then they went still further out of the town, and drove their geese into the country. And when they had come to the meadow, she sat down and unbound her hair which was like pure gold, and Conrad saw it and delighted in its brightness, and wanted to pluck out a few hairs. Then she said:

"Blow, blow, thou gentle wind, I say,
Blow Conrad's little hat away,
And make him chase it here and there,
Until I have braided all my hair,
And bound it up again.

And there came such a violent wind that it blew Conrad's hat far away across country, and he was forced to run after it. When he came back she had finished combing her hair and was putting it up again, and he could not get any of it. Then Conrad was angry, and would not speak to her, and thus they watered the geese until the evening, and then they went home.

Next day when they were driving the geese out through the dark gateway, the maiden said:

"Alas, Falada, hanging there

Falada answered:

"Alas, young Queen, how ill you fare!
If this your tender mother knew,
Her heart would surely break in two."

And she sat down again in the field and began to comb out her hair, and Conrad ran and tried to clutch it, so she said in haste:

"Blow, blow, thou gentle wind, I say,
Blow Conrad's little hat away,
And make him chase it here and there,
Until I have braided all my hair,
And bound it up again.

Then the wind blew, and blew his little hat off his head and far away, and Conrad was forced to run after it, and when he came back, her hair had been put up a long time, and he could get none of it, and so they looked after their geese till evening came.

But in the evening after they had got home, Conrad went to the old King, and said: "I won't tend the geese with that girl any longer!" "Why not?" inquired the aged King. "Oh, because she vexes me the whole day long." Then the aged King commanded him to relate what it was that she did to him. And Conrad said: "In the morning when we pass beneath the dark gateway with the flock, there is a sorry horse's head on the wall and she says to it:

"Alas, Falada, hanging there!"

And the head replies:

"Alas, young Queen, how ill you fare!
If this your tender mother knew,
Her heart would surely break in two."

And Conrad went on to relate what happened on the goose pasture, and how when there he had to chase his hat.

The aged King commanded him to drive his flock out again next day, and as soon as morning came, he placed himself behind the dark gateway, and heard how the maiden spoke to the head of Falada, and then he too went into the country, and hid himself in the thicket in the meadow. There he soon saw with his own eyes the goose-girl and the goose-boy bringing their flock, and how after a while she sat down and unplaited her hair, which shone with radiance. And soon she said:

"Blow, blow, thou gentle wind, I say,
Blow Conrad's little hat away,
And make him chase it here and there,
Until I have braided all my hair,
And bound it up again."

Then came a blast of wind and carried off Conrad's hat, so that he had to run far away, while the maiden quietly went on combing and plaiting her hair, all of which the King observed. Then, quite unseen, he went away, and when the goose-girl came home in the evening, he called her aside, and asked why she did all these things. "I may not tell you that, and I dare not lament my sorrows to any human being, for I have sworn not to do so by the heaven which is above me; if I had not done that, I should have lost my life." He urged her and left her no peace, but he could draw nothing from her. Then said he: "If thou wilt not tell me anything, tell thy sorrows to the iron stove there," and he went away. Then she crept into the iron stove, and began to weep and lament, and emptied her whole heart, and said: "Here am I deserted by the whole world, and yet I am a King's daughter, and a false waiting-maid has by force brought me to such a pass that I have been compelled to put off my royal apparel, and she has taken my place with my bridegroom, and I have to perform menial service as a goose-girl. If my mother did but know that, her heart would break."

The aged King, however, was standing outside by the pipe of the stove, and was listening to what she said and heard it. Then he came back again, and bade her come out of the stove. And royal garments were placed on her, and it was marvellous how beautiful she was! The aged King summoned his son, and revealed to him that he had got the false bride who was only a waiting-maid, but that the true one was standing there, as the sometime goose-girl. The young King rejoiced with all his heart when he saw her beauty and youth, and a great feast was made ready to which all the people and all good friends were invited. At the head of the table sat the bridegroom with the King's daughter at one side of him and the waiting-maid on the other, but the waiting-maid was blinded, and did not recognize the princess in her dazzling array. When they had eaten and drunk, and were merry, the aged King asked the waiting-maid as a riddle, what a person deserved who had behaved in such and such a way to her master, and at the same time related the whole story, and asked what sentence such an one merited? Then the false bride said: "She deserves no better fate than to be stripped entirely naked, and put in a barrel which is studded inside with pointed nails, and two white horses should be harnessed to it, which will drag her along through one street after another, till she is dead." "It is thou," said the aged King, "and thou must pronounce thine own sentence, and thus shall it be done unto thee." And when the sentence had been carried out, the young King married his true bride, and both of them reigned over their kingdom in peace and happiness.

HE WHO KNEW NOT FEAR

Anonymous

A certain father had two sons, the elder of whom was sharp and sensible, and could do everything, but the younger was stupid and could neither learn nor understand anything, and when people saw him they said: "There's a fellow who will give his father some trouble!" When anything had to be done, it was always the elder who was forced to do it; but if his father bade him fetch anything when it was late, or in the night-time, and the way led through the churchyard, or any other dismal place, he answered: "Oh, no, father, I'll not go there, it makes me shudder!" for he was afraid. Or when stories were told by the fire at night which made the flesh creep, the listeners often said: "Oh, it makes us shudder!" the younger sat in a corner and listened with the rest of them, and could not imagine what they could mean. "They are always saying: 'It makes me shudder, it makes me shudder!' It does not make me shudder," thought he. "That, too, must be an art of which I understand nothing!"

Now it came to pass that his father said to him one day: "Hearken to me, thou fellow in the corner there, thou art growing tall and strong, and thou, too, must learn something by which thou canst earn thy living. Look how thy brother works, but thou dost not even earn thy salt." "Well, father," he replied, "I am quite willing to learn something—indeed, if it could but be managed, I should like to learn how to shudder. I don't understand that at all yet." The elder brother smiled when he heard that, and thought to himself:

"Good God, what a blockhead that brother of mine is! He will never be good for anything as long as he lives! He who wants to be a sickle must bend himself betimes."

The father sighed, and answered him: "Thou shalt soon learn what it is to suffer, but thou wilt not earn thy living by that."

Soon after this the sexton came to the house on a visit, and the father bewailed his trouble, and told him how his younger son was so backward in every respect that he knew nothing and learned nothing. "Just think," said he, "when I asked him how he was going to earn his bread, he actually wanted to learn to shudder." "If that be all," replied the sexton, "he can learn that with me. Send him to me, and I will soon polish him." The father was glad to do it, for he thought: "It will train the boy a little." The sexton, therefore, took him into his house, and he had to ring the bell. After a day or two the sexton awoke him at midnight, and bade him arise and go up into the church tower and ring the bell. "Thou shalt soon learn what shuddering is," thought he, and secretly went there before him; and when the boy was at the top of the tower and turned around, and was just going to take hold of the bell rope, he saw a white figure standing on the stairs opposite to the sounding hole. "Who is there?" cried he, but the figure made no reply, and did not move or stir. "Give an answer," cried the boy, "or take thyself off; thou hast no business here at night."

The sexton, however, remained standing motionless, that the boy might think he was a ghost. The boy cried a second time: "What dost thou want here? — speak if thou art an honest fellow, or I will throw thee down the steps!" The sexton thought, "He can't intend to be as bad as his words," uttered no sound and stood as if he were made of stone. Then the boy called to him for the third time, and as that was also to no purpose, he ran against him and pushed the ghost down the stairs, so that it fell down ten steps and remained lying there in a corner. Thereupon he rang the bell, went home, and without saying a word went to bed and fell asleep. The sexton's wife waited a long time for her husband, but he did not come back. At length she became uneasy, and wakened the boy, and asked, "Dost thou not know where my husband is? He went up the tower before thou didst." "No, I don't know," replied the boy, "but someone was standing by the sounding hole on the other side of the steps, and as he would neither give an answer nor go away, I took him for a scoundrel, and threw him down stairs; just go there and you will see if it was he, I should be sorry if it were." The woman ran away and found her husband, who was lying moaning in the corner, and had broken his leg.

She carried him down, and then with loud screams she hastened to the boy's father. "Your boy," cried she, "has been the cause of a great misfortune! He has thrown my husband down the steps and made him break his leg. Take the good-for-nothing fellow away from our house." The father was terrified, and ran thither and scolded the boy. "What wicked tricks are these?" said he; "the devil must have put this into thy head." "Father," he replied, "do listen to me. I am quite innocent. He was standing there by night like one who is intending to do some evil. I did not know who it was, and I entreated him three times either to speak or to go away." "Ah," said the father, "I have nothing but unhappiness with thee. Go out of my sight. I will see thee no more."

"Yes, father, right willingly, wait only until it is day. Then will I go forth and learn how to shudder, and then I shall, at any rate, understand one art which will support me." "Learn what thou wilt," spake the father, "it is all the same to me. Here are fifty thalers for thee. Take these and go into the wide world, and tell no one from whence thou comest, and who is thy father, for I have reason to be ashamed of thee." "Yes, father, it small be as you will. If you desire nothing more than that, I can easily keep it in mind."

When day dawned, therefore, the boy put his fifty thalers into his pocket, and went forth on the great highway, and continually said to himself, "If I could but shudder! If I could but shudder!"

Then a man approached who heard this conversation which the youth was holding with himself, and when they had walked a little further to where they could see the gallows, the man said to him, "Look, there is the tree where seven men have married the ropemaker's daughter, and are now learning how to fly. Sit down below it, and wait till night comes, and thou wilt soon learn how to shudder." "If that is all that is wanted," answered the youth, "it is easily done; but if I learn how to shudder as quickly as that, thou shalt have my fifty thalers. Just come back to me early in the morning." Then the youth went to the gallows, sat down below it, and waited till evening came. And as he was cold, he lighted himself a fire, but at midnight the wind blew so sharp that in spite of his fire he could not get warm. And as the wind knocked the hanged men against each other, and they moved backward and forward, he thought to himself: "Thou shiverest below by the fire, but how those up above must freeze and suffer!" And as he felt pity for them, he raised the ladder, and climbed up, unbound one of them after the other, and brought down all seven. Then he stirred the fire, blew it, and set them all round it to warm themselves. But they sat there and did not stir, and the fire caught their clothes. So he said:

"Take care, or I will hang you up again." The dead men, however, did not hear, but were quite silent, and let their rags go on burning. On this he grew angry, and said: "If you will not take care, I cannot help you, I will not be burned with you, and he hung them up again each in his turn.

Then he sat down by his fire and fell asleep, and next morning the man came to him and wanted to have the fifty thalers, and said: "Well, dost thou know how to shudder?" "No," answered he, "how was I to get to know? Those fellows up there did not open their mouths, and were so stupid that they let the few old rags which they had on their bodies get burned." Then the man saw that he would not carry away the fifty thalers that day, and went away saying:

"One of this kind has never come in my way before."

The youth likewise went his way, and once more began to mutter to himself: "Ah, if I could but shudder! Ah, if I could but shudder!" A wagoner who was striding behind him heard that and asked: "Who art thou?" "I don't know," answered the youth. Then the wagoner asked:

"From whence comest thou?" "I know not." "Who is thy father?" "That I may not tell thee." "What is it that thou art always muttering between thy teeth?" "Ah," replied the youth, "I do so wish I could shudder, but no one can teach me how to do it." "Give up thy foolish chatter," said the wagoner. "Come go with me, I will see about a place for thee." The youth went with the wagoner, and in the evening they arrived at an inn where they wished to pass the night. Then at the entrance of the room the youth again said quite loudly, "If I could but shudder! If I could but shudder!" The host who heard that, laughed and said: "If that is your desire, there ought to be a good opportunity for you here." "Ah, be silent," said the hostess; "so many inquisitive persons have already lost their lives, it would be a pity and a shame if such beautiful eyes as these should never see the daylight again."

But the youth said: "However difficult it may be, I will learn it, and for this purpose indeed have I journeyed forth." He let the host have no rest, until the latter told him, that not far from thence stood a haunted castle where any one could very easily learn what shuddering was, if he would but watch in it for three nights. The King had promised that he who would venture this should have his daughter to wife, and she was the most beautiful maiden the sun shone on. Great treasures likewise lay in the castle, which were guarded by evil spirits, and these treasures would then be freed, and would make a poor man rich enough. Already many men had gone into the castle, but as yet none had come out again. Then the youth went next morning to the King, and said that if he were allowed he would watch three nights in the enchanted castle. The King looked at him, and as the youth pleased him, he said: "Thou mayst ask for three things to take into the castle with thee, but they must be things without life." Then he answered, "Then I ask for a fire, a turning-lathe, and a cutting-board with the knife." The King had these things carried into the castle for him during the day. When night was drawing near, the youth went up and made himself a bright fire in one of the rooms, placed the cutting-board and knife beside it, and seated himself by the turning-lathe. "Ah, if I could but shudder!" said he, "but I shall not learn it here either." Toward midnight he was about to poke his fire, and as he was blowing it, something cried suddenly from one cornier, "Au, miau! how cold we are!" "You simpletons!" cried he, "what are you crying about? If you are cold, come and take a seat by the fire and warm yourselves." And when he had said that, two great black cats came with one tremendous leap and sat down on each side of him, and looked savagely at him with their fiery eyes. After a short time, when they had warmed themselves, they said: "Comrade, shall we have a game at cards?" "Why not?" he replied, "but just show me your paws. Then they stretched out their claws. "Oh," said he, "what long nails you have! Wait, I must first cut them a little for you." Thereupon he seized them by the throats, put them on the cutting-board and screwed their feet fast. "I have looked at your fingers," said he, "and my fancy for card-playing has gone, and he struck them dead and threw them out into the water. But when he had made away with these two, and was about to sit down again by his fire, out from every hole and corner came black cats and black dogs with red-hot chains, and more and more of them came until he could no longer stir, and they yelled horribly, and got on his fire, pulled it to pieces, and wanted to put it out. He watched them for a while quietly, but at last when they were going too far, he seized his cutting knife, and cried: "Away with ye, vermin," and began to cut them down. Part of them ran away, the others he killed, and threw out into the fish pond. When he came back he blew up the embers of his fire again and warmed himself. And as he thus sat, his eyes would keep open no longer, and he felt a desire to sleep. Then he looked round and saw a great bed in the corner. "That is the very thing for me," said he, and got into it. When he was just going to shut his eyes, however, the bed began to move of its own accord, and went over the whole of the castle. "That's right," said he, "but go faster." Then the bed rolled on as if six horses were harnessed to it, up and down, over thresholds and steps, but suddenly, hop, hop, it turned over upside down, and lay on him like a mountain. But he threw quilts and pillows up in the air, got out and said: "Now any one who likes may drive," and lay down by his fire, and slept until it was day. In the morning the King came, and when he saw him lying there on the ground, he thought the spirits had killed him and he was dead. Then said he: "After all it is a pity—he is a handsome man." The youth heard it, got up, and said: "It has not come to that yet." Then the King was astonished, but very glad, and asked how he had fared. "Very well indeed," answered he; "one night is over, the two others will get over likewise." Then he went to the innkeeper, who opened his eyes very wide, and said: "I never expected to see thee alive again! Hast thou learned how to shudder yet?" "No," said he, "it is all in vain. If some one would but tell me!"

The second night he again went up into the old castle, sat down by the fire, and once more began his old song: "If I could but shudder!" When midnight came, an uproar and noise of tumbling about was heard; at first it was low, but it grew louder and louder. Then it was quiet for a while, and at length with a loud scream, half a man came down the chimney and fell before him. "Hollo!" cried he, "another half belongs to this. This is too little!" Then the uproar began again, there was a roaring and howling, and the other half fell down likewise. "Wait," said he, "I will just blow up the fire a little for thee." When he had done that and looked round again, the two pieces were joined together, and a frightful man was sitting in his place. "That is no part of our bargain," said the youth, "the bench is mine." The man wanted to push him away; the youth, however, would not allow that, but thrust him off with all his strength, and seated himself again, in his own place. Then still more men fell down, one after the other; they brought nine dead men's legs and two skulls, and set them up and played at ninepins with them. The youth also wanted to play and said: "Hark you, can I join you?" "Yes, if thou hast any money." "Money enough," replied he, "but your balls are not quite round." Then he took the skulls and put them in the lathe and turned them till they were round. "There, now, they will roll better!" said he. "Hurrah! now it goes merrily!" He played with them and lost some of his money, but when it struck twelve, everything vanished from his sight. He lay down and quietly fell asleep. Next morning the King came to inquire after him. "How has it fared with thee this time?" asked he. "I have been playing at ninepins," he answered, "and have lost a couple of farthings." "Hast thou not shuddered then?" "Eh, what?" said he, "I have made merry. If I did but know what it was to shudder!"

The third night he sat down again on his bench and said quite sadly: "If I could but shudder." When it grew late, six tall men came in and brought a coffin. Then said he: "Ha, ha, that is certainly my little cousin, who only died a few days ago," and he beckoned with his finger, and cried: "Come, little cousin, come." They placed the coffin on the ground, but he went to it and took the lid off, and a dead man lay therein. He felt his face, but it was cold as ice. "Stop," said he, "I will warm thee a, little," and went to the fire and warmed his hand and laid it on the dead man's face, but he remained cold. Then he took him out, and sat down by the fire and laid him on his breast and rubbed his arms that the blood might circulate again. As this also did no good, he thought to himself: "When two people lie in bed together, they warm each other," and carried him to bed, covered him over and lay down by him. After a short time the dead man became warm too, and began to move. Then said the youth: "See, little cousin, have I not warmed thee?" The dead man, however, got up and cried, "Now will I strangle thee."

"What!" said he, "is that the way thou thankest me? Thou shalt at once go into thy coffin again," and he took him up, threw him into it, and shut the lid.

Then came the six men and carried him away again. "I cannot manage to shudder," said he. "I shall never learn it here as long as I live."

Then a man entered who was taller than all others, and looked terrible. He was old, however, and had a long white beard. "Thou wretch," cried he, "thou shalt soon learn what it is to shudder, for thou shalt die." "Not so fast," replied the youth, "If I am to die, I shall have to have a say in it." "I will soon seize thee," said the fiend. "Softly, softly, do not talk so big. I am as strong as thou art, and perhaps even stronger." "We shall see," said the old man. "If thou art stronger, I will let thee go—come, we will try." Then he led him by dark passages to a smith's forge, took an ax, and with one blow struck an anvil into the ground. "I can do that better still," said the youth, and went to the other anvil. The old man placed himself near and wanted to look on, and his white heard hung down. Then the youth seized the ax, split the anvil with one blow, and struck the old man's beard in with it. "Now I have thee," said the youth. "Now it is thou who wilt have to die." Then he seized an iron bar and beat the old man till he moaned and entreated him to stop, and he would give him great riches. The youth drew out the ax and let him go. The old man led him back into the castle, and in a cellar showed him three chests full of gold. "Of these," said he, "one part is for the poor, the other is for the king, the third is thine." In the meantime it struck twelve, and the spirit disappeared; the youth, therefore, was left in darkness. "I shall still be able to find my way out," said he, and felt about, found the way into the room, and slept there by his fire. Next morning the King came and said, "Now thou must have learned what shuddering is?" "No," he answered; "what can it be? My dead cousin was here, and a bearded man came and showed me a great deal of money down below, but no one told me what it was to shudder." "Then," said the King, "thou hast delivered the castle, and shalt marry my daughter." "That is all very well," said he, "but still I do not know what it is to shudder!"

Then the gold was brought up and the wedding celebrated; but howsoever much the young King loved his wife, and however happy he was, he still said always: "If I could but shudder—if I could but shudder." And at last she was angry at this. Her waiting-maid said, "I will find a cure for him; he shall soon learn what it is to shudder." She went out to the stream which flowed through the garden, and had a whole bucketful of gudgeons brought to her. At night when the young King was sleeping, his wife was to draw the clothes off him and empty the bucketful of cold water with the gudgeons in it over him, so that the little fishes would sprawl about him. When this was done, he woke up and cried: "Oh, what makes me shudder so?—what makes me shudder so, dear wife? Ah! now I know what it is to shudder!"

ÆSOP'S FABLES

This has come to be the commonly accepted name for the well-known collection of stories about animals, though we cannot be sure that any of them, were written by the Greek slave of that name, who, Herodotus tells us, lived about the year 550 B.C. The fable about animals is probably the oldest form of story known. Its object is to teach a lesson to men and women, without seeming to do so, and because of this concealed lesson it has always been a great favorite with all nations. In Russia, for example, where a man did not dare say what he thought about a Government officer, he could tell a fable about the Dog in the Manger.

THE TOWN MOUSE AND Th COUNTRY MOUSE

Now you must know that a Town Mouse once upon a time went on a visit to his cousin in the country. He was rough and ready, this cousin, but he loved his town friend and made him heartily welcome. Beans and bacon, cheese and bread, were all he had to offer, but he offered them freely. The Town Mouse rather turned up his long nose at this country fare, and said: "I cannot understand, Cousin, how you can put up with such poor food as this, but of course you cannot expect anything better in the country; come you with me and I will show you how to live. When you have been in town a week you will wonder how you could ever have stood a country life." No sooner said than done: the two mice set off for the town and arrived at the Town Mouse's residence late at night. "You will want some refreshment after our long journey," said the polite Town Mouse, and took his friend into the grand dining-room. There they found the remains of a fine feast, and soon the two mice were eating up jellies and cakes and all that was nice. Suddenly they heard growling and barking. "What is that?" said the Country Mouse. "It is only the dogs of the house," answered the other. "Only!" said the Country Mouse. "I do not like that music at my dinner." Just at that moment the door flew open, in came two huge mastiffs, and the two mice had to scamper down and run off. "Good-by, Cousin," said the Country Mouse. "What! going so soon?" said the other. "Yes," he replied;

"BETTER BEANS AND BACON IN PEACE
THAN CAKES AND ALE IN FEAR."

THE MAN, THE BOY, AND DONKEY

A man and his son were once going with their Donkey to market. As they were walking along by its side a countryman passed them and said: "You fools, what is a Donkey for but to ride upon?"

So the Man put the Boy on the Donkey and they went on their way. But soon they passed a group of men, one of whom said: "See that lazy youngster, he lets his father walk while he rides."

So the Man ordered his Boy to get off, and got on himself. But they hadn't gone far when they passed two women, one of whom said to the other: "Shame on that lazy lout to let his poor little son trudge along."

Well, the Man didn't know what to do, but at last he took his Boy up before him on the Donkey. By this time they had come to the town, and the passers-by began to jeer and point to them. The Man stopped and asked what they were scoffing at. The men said: "Aren't you ashamed of yourself for overloading that poor Donkey of yours — you and your hulking son?"

The Man and Boy got off and tried to think what to do. They thought and they thought, till at last they cut down a pole, tied the Donkey's feet to it, and raised the pole and the Donkey to their shoulders. They went along amid the laughter of all who met them till they came to Market Bridge, when the Donkey, getting one of his feet loose, kicked out and caused the Boy to drop his end of the pole. In the struggle the Donkey fell over the bridge, and his fore-feet being tied together he was drowned.

"That will teach you," said an old man who had followed them:

"PLEASE ALL, AND YOU WILL PLEASE NONE."

THE SHEPHERD'S BOY

There was once a young Shepherd Boy who tended his sheep at the foot of a mountain near a dark forest. It was rather lonely for him all day, so he thought upon a plan by which he could get a little company and some excitement. He rushed down toward the village calling out "Wolf, Wolf," and the villagers came out to meet him, and some of them stopped with him for a considerable time.

This pleased the boy so much that a few days afterward he tried the same trick, and again the villagers came to his help.

But shortly after this a Wolf actually did come out from the forest, and began to worry the sheep, and the boy of course cried out "Wolf, Wolf," still louder than before. But this time the villagers who had been fooled twice before, thought the boy was again deceiving them, and nobody stirred to come to bis help.

So the Wolf made a good meal off the boy's flock, and when the boy complained, the wise man of the village said:

"A LIAR WILL NOT BE BELIEVED, EVEN
WHEN HE SPEAKS THE TRUTH."

ANDROCLES

A slave named Androcles once escaped from his master and fled to the forest. As he was wandering about there he came upon a Lion lying down moaning and groaning.

At first he turned to flee, but finding that the Lion did not pursue him, he turned back and went up to him.

As he came near, the Lion put out his paw, which was all swollen and bleeding, and Androcles found that a huge thorn had got into it, and was causing all the pain. He pulled out the thorn and bound up the paw of the Lion, who was soon able to rise and lick the hand of Androcles like a dog.

Then the Lion took Androcles to his cave, and every day used to bring him meat from which to live.

But shortly afterward both Androcles and the Lion were captured, and the slave was sentenced to be thrown to the Lion, after the latter had been kept without food for several days. The Emperor and all his Court came to see the spectacle and Androcles was led out into the middle of the arena. Soon the Lion was let loose from his den, and rushed bounding and roaring toward his victim. But as soon as he came near to Androcles he recognized his friend, and fawned upon him, and licked his hands like a friendly dog. The Emperor, surprised at this, summoned Androcles to him, who told him the whole story. Whereupon the slave was pardoned and freed, and the Lion let loose to his native forest.

"GRATITUDE IS THE SIGN OF NOBLE SOULS."

THE FOX AND THE STORK

At one time the Fox and the Stork were on visiting terms and seemed very good friends. So the Fox invited the Stork to dinner, and for a joke put nothing before her but some soup in a very shallow dish. This the Fox could easily lap up, but the Stork could only wet the end of her long bill in it, and left the meal as hungry as when she began.

"I am sorry," said the Fox, "the soup is not to your liking."

"Pray do not apologize," said the Stork. "I hope you will return this visit, and come and dine with me soon."

So a day was appointed when the Fox should visit the Stork; but when they were seated at table all that was for their dinner was contained in a very long-necked jar with a narrow mouth, in which the Fox could not insert his snout, so all he could manage to do was to lick the outside of the jar.

"I will not apologize for the dinner," said the Stork:

"ONE BAD TURN DESERVES ANOTHER."

THE CROW AND THE PITCHER

A crow, half-dead with thirst, came upon a Pitcher which had once been full of water; but when the Crow put its beak into the mouth of the Pitcher he found that only very little water was left in it, and that he could not reach far enough down to get at it.

He tried, and he tried, but at last had to give up in despair.

Then a thought came to him, and he took a pebble and dropped it into the Pitcher. Then he took another pebble and dropped it into the Pitcher. Then he took another pebble and dropped that into the Pitcher. Then he took another pebble and dropped that into the Pitcher. Then he took another pebble and dropped that into the Pitcher. Then he took another pebble and dropped that into the Pitcher.

At last, at last, he saw the water mount up near him; and after casting in a few more pebbles he was able to quench his thirst and save his life.

"LITTLE BY LITTLE DOES THE TRICK."

THE FROGS DESIRING A KING

The Frogs were living as happy as could be in a marshy swamp that just suited them; they went splashing about caring for nobody and nobody troubling with them. But some of them thought that this was not right, that they should have a King and a proper constitution, so they determined to send up a petition to Jove to give them what they wanted. "Mighty Jove," they cried, "send unto us a King that will rule over us and keep us in order." Jove laughed at their croaking, and threw down into the swamp a huge Log, which came down—kerplash—into the swamp. The Frogs were frightened out of their lives by the commotion made in their midst, and all rushed to the bank to look at the horrible monster; but after a time, seeing that it did not move, one or two of the boldest of them ventured out toward the Log, and even dared to touch it; still it did not move. Then the greatest hero of the Frogs jumped upon the Log and commenced dancing up and down upon it, thereupon all the Frogs came and did the same; and for sometime the Frogs went about their business every day without taking the slightest notice of the new King Log lying in their midst.

But this did not suit them, so they sent another petition to Jove, and said to him: "We want a real King; one that will really rule over us." Now this made Jove angry, so he sent among them a big Stork that soon set to work gobbling them all up. Then the Frogs repented when too late.

"BETTER NO RULE THAN CRUEL RULE."

THE FROG AND THE OX

"Oh, father," said a little Frog to the big one sitting by the side of a pool, "I have seen such a terrible monster! It was as big as a mountain, with horns on its head, and a long tail, and it had hoofs divided in two."

"Tush, child, tush," said the old Frog, "that was only Farmer White's Ox. It isn't so big either; he may be a little bit taller than I, but I could easily make myself quite as broad; just you see." So he blew himself out, and blew himself out, and blew himself out. "Was he as big as that?" asked he.

"Oh, much bigger than that," said the young Frog.

Again the old one blew himself out, and asked the young one if the Ox was as big as that.

"Bigger, father, bigger," was the reply.

So the Frog took a deep breath, and blew and blew and blew, and swelled and swelled and swelled. And then he said: "I'm sure the Ox is not as big as _____" But at this moment he burst.

"SELF-CONCEIT MAY LEAD TO SELF-DESTRUCTION."

THE COCK AND THE PEARL

A cock was once strutting up and down the farmyard among the hens when suddenly he espied something shining and the straw. "Ho! ho!" quoth he, "that's for me," and soon rooted it out from beneath the straw. What did it turn out to be but a Pearl that by some chance had been lost in the yard? "You may be a treasure," quoth Master Cock, "to men that prize you, but for me I would rather have a single barley corn than a peck of pearls."

"PRECIOUS THINGS ARE FOR THOSE THAT CAN PRIZE THEM."

THE FOX WITHOUT A TAIL

It happened that a Fox caught its tail in a trap, and in struggling to release himself lost all of it but the stump. At first he was ashamed to show himself among his fellow foxes. But at last he determined to put a bolder face upon his misfortune, and summoned all the foxes to a general meeting to consider a proposal which he had to place before them.

When they had assembled together the Fox proposed that they should all do away with their tails. He pointed out how inconvenient a tail was when they were pursued by their enemies, the dogs; how much it was in the way when they desired to sit down and hold a friendly conversation with one another. He failed to see any advantage in carrying about such a useless encumbrance.

"That is all very well," said one of the older foxes; "but I do not think you would have recommended us to dispense with our chief ornament if you had not happened to lose it yourself."

"DISTRUST INTERESTED ADVICE."

THE FOX AND THE CAT

A fox was boasting to a Cat of its clever devices for escaping its enemies. "I have a whole bag of tricks," he said, "which contains a hundred ways of escaping my enemies."

"I have only one," said the Cat; "but I can generally manage with that." Just at that moment they heard the cry of a pack of hounds coming toward them, and the Cat immediately scampered up a tree and hid herself in the boughs. "This is my plan," said the Cat. "What are you going to do?" The Fox thought first of one way, then of another, and while he was debating the hounds came nearer and nearer, and at last the Fox in his confusion was caught up by the hounds and soon killed by the huntsmen. Miss Puss, who had been looking on, said:

"BETTER ONE SAFE WAY THAN A HUNDRED
ON WHICH YOU CANNOT RECKON."

THE DOG IN THE MANGER

A dog looking out for its afternoon nap jumped into the Manger of an Ox and lay there cosily upon the straw. But soon the Ox, returning from its afternoon work, came up to the Manger and wanted to eat some of the straw. The Dog in a rage, being awakened from its slumber, stood up and barked at the Ox, and whenever it came near attempted to bite it. At last the Ox had to give up the hope of getting at the straw, and went away muttering:

"AH, PEOPLE OFTEN GRUDGE OTHERS WHAT THEY CANNOT ENJOY THEMSELVES."

THE FOX AND THE GOAT

By an unlucky chance a Fox fell into a deep well from which he could not get out. A Goat passed by shortly afterward, and asked the Fox what he was doing down there. "Oh, have you not heard?" said the Fox; "there is going to be a great drought, so I jumped down here in order to be sure to have water by me. Why don't you come down, too?" The Goat thought well of this advice, and jumped down into the well. But the Fox immediately jumped on her back, and by putting his foot on her long horns managed to jump up to the edge of the well. "Good-by, friend," said the Fox; — "remember next time,

"NEVER TRUST THE ADVICE OF A MAN IN DIFFICULTIES."

BELLING THE CAT

Long ago, the mice held a general council to consider what measures they could take to outwit their common enemy, the Cat. Some said this, and some said that; but at last a young mouse got up and said he had a proposal to make, which he thought would meet the case. "You will all agree," said he, "that our chief danger consists in the sly and treacherous manner in which the enemy approaches us. Now, if we could receive some signal of her approach, we could easily escape from her. I venture, therefore, to propose that a small bell be procured, and attached by a ribbon round the neck of the Cat. By this means we should always know when she was about, and could easily retire while she was in the neighborhood."

This proposed met with general applause, until an old mouse got up and said: "That is all very well, but who is to bell the Cat?" The mice looked at one another and nobody spoke. Then the old mouse said:

"IT IS EASY TO PROPOSE IMPOSSIBLE REMEDIES."

THE JAY AND THE PEACOCK

A jay venturing into a yard where Peacocks used to walk, found there a number of feathers which had fallen from the Peacocks when they were moulting. He tied them all to his tail and strutted down toward the Peacocks. When he came near them they soon discovered the cheat, and striding up to him pecked at him and plucked away his borrowed plumes. So the Jay could do no better than go back to the other Jays, who had watched his behavior from a distance; but they were equally annoyed with him, and told him

"IT IS NOT ONLY FINE FEATHERS THAT MAKE FINE BIRDS."

THE ASS AND THE LAP-DOG

A farmer one day came to the stables to see to his beasts of burden: among them was his favorite Ass, that was always well fed and often carried his master. With the Farmer came his Lap-dog, who danced about and licked his hand and frisked about as happy as could be. The Farmer felt in his pocket, gave the Lap-dog some dainty food, and sat down while he gave his orders to his servants. The Lap-dog jumped into his master's lap, and lay there blinking while the Farmer stroked his ears. The Ass, seeing this, broke loose from his halter and commenced prancing about in imitation of the Lap-dog. The Farmer could not hold his sides with laughter, so the Ass went up to him, and putting his feet upon the Farmer's shoulder attempted to climb into his lap. The Farmer's servants rushed up with sticks and pitchforks and soon taught the Ass that

"CLUMSY JESTING IS NO JOKE."

THE ANT AND THE GRASSHOPPER

In a field one summer's day a Grasshopper was hopping about, chirping and singing to its heart's content. An Ant passed by, bearing along with great toil an ear of corn he was taking to the nest.

"Why not come and chat with me," said the Grasshopper, "instead of toiling and moiling in that way?"

"I am helping to lay up food for the winter," said the Ant, "and recommend you to do the same."

"Why bother about winter?" said the Grasshopper; "we have got plenty of food at present."

But the Ant went on its way and continued its toil.

Then the winter came the Grasshopper had no food, and found itself dying of hunger, while it saw the ants distributing every day corn and grain from the stores they had collected in the summer. Then the Grasshopper knew

IT IS BEST TO PREPARE FOR THE DAYS OF NECESSITY.

THE WOODMAN AND THE SERPENT

One wintry day a Woodman was tramping home from his work when he saw something black lying on the snow. When he came closer, he saw it was a Serpent to all appearance dead. But he took it up and put it in his bosom to warm while he hurried home. As soon as he got indoors he put the Serpent down on the hearth before the fire. The children watched it and saw it slowly come to life again. Then one of them stooped down to stroke it, but the Serpent raised its head and put out its fangs and was about to sting the child to death. So the Woodman seized his axe, and with one stroke cut the Serpent in two. "Ah," said he,

"NO GRATITUDE FROM THE WICKED."

THE MILKMAID AND HER PAIL

Patty, the Milkmaid, was going to market carrying her milk in a Pail on her head. As she went along she began calculating what she would do with the money she would get for the milk. "I'll buy some fowls from Farmer Brown," said she, "and they will lay eggs each morning, which I will sell to the parson's wife. With the money that I get from the sale of these eggs I'll buy myself a new dimity frock and a chip hat; and when I go to market, won't all the young men come up and speak to me! Polly Shaw will be that jealous; but I don't care. I shall just look at her and toss my head like this." As she spoke, she tossed her head back, the Pail fell off it and all the milk was spilt. So she had to go home and tell her mother what had occurred. "Ah, my child," said her mother,

DO NOT COUNT YOUR CHICKENS BEFORE THEY ARE HATCHED.

THE LION AND THE MOUSE

Once when a Lion was asleep a little Mouse began running up and down upon him; this soon wakened the Lion, who placed his huge paw upon him, and opened his big jaws to swallow him. "Pardon, O King," cried the little Mouse; "forgive me this time, I shall never forget it: who knows but what I may be able to do you a turn some of these days?" The Lion was so tickled at the idea of the Mouse being able to help him, that he lifted up his paw and let him go. Some time after the Lion was caught in a trap, and the hunters, who desired to carry him alive to the King, tied him to a tree while they went in search of a wagon to carry him on. Just then the little Mouse happened to pass by, and seeing the sad plight in which the Lion was, went up to him and soon gnawed away the ropes that bound the King of the Beasts. "Was I not right?" said the little Mouse.

"LITTLE FRIENDS MAY PROVE GREAT FRIENDS."

HERCULES AND THE WAGONER

A wagoner was once driving a heavy load along a very muddy way. At last he came to a part of the road where the wheels sank halfway into the mire, and the more the horses pulled, the deeper sank the wheels. So the Wagoner threw down his whip, and knelt down and prayed to Hercules the Strong. "O Hercules, help me in this my hour of distress," quote he. But Hercules appeared to him, and said:

"Tut, man, don't sprawl there. Get up and put your shoulder to the wheel."

"THE GODS HELP THEM THAT HELP THEMSELVES."

THE LION'S SHARE

The Lion went once a-hunting along with the Fox, the Jackal, and the Wolf. They hunted and they hunted till at last they surprised a Stag, and soon took its life. Then came the question how the spoil should be divided. "Quarter me this Stag," roared the Lion; so the other animals skinned it and cut it into four parts. Then the Lion took his stand in front of the carcass and pronounced judgment: "The first quarter is for me in my capacity as King of Beasts; the second is mine as arbiter; another share comes to me for my part in the chase; and as far the fourth quarter, well, as for that, I should like to see which of you will dare to lay a paw upon it."

"Humph!" grumbled the Fox as he walked away with his tail between his legs; but he spoke in a low growl—

"YOU MAY SHARE THE LABORS OF THE GREAT,
BUT YOU WILL NOT SHARE THE SPOIL."

THE FOX AND THE CROW

A fox once saw a Crow fly off with a piece of cheese in its beak and settle on a branch of a tree. "That's for me, as I am a Fox," said Master Reynard, and he walked up to the foot of the tree. "Good-day, Mistress Crow," he cried. "How well you are looking to-day: how glossy your feathers; how bright your eye. I feel sure your voice must surpass that of other birds, just as your figure does; let me hear but one song from you that I may greet you as the Queen of Birds." The Crow lifted up her head and began to caw her best, but the moment she opened her mouth the piece of cheese fell to the ground, only to be snapped up by Master Fox. "That will do," said he. "That was all I wanted. In exchange for your cheese I will give you a piece of advice for the future—

"DO NOT TRUST FLATTERERS.

THE DOG AND THE SHADOW

It happened that a Dog had got a piece of meat and was carrying it home in his mouth to eat it in peace. Now on his way home he had to cross a plank lying across a running brook. As he crossed, he looked down and saw his own shadow reflected in the water beneath. Thinking it was another dog with another piece of meat, he made up his mind to have that also. So he made a snap at the shadow in the water, but as he opened his mouth the piece of meat fell out, dropped into the water and was never seen more.

"BEWARE LEST YOU LOSE THE SUBSTANCE
BY GRASPING AT THE SHADOW."

THE WOLF AND THE LAMB

Once upon a time a Wolf was lapping at a spring on a hillside, when, looking up, what should he see but a Lamb just beginning to drink a little lower down. "There's my supper," thought he, "if only I can find some excuse to seize it." Then he called out to the Lamb, "How dare you muddle the water from which I am drinking?"

"Nay, master, nay," said Lambikin; "if the water be muddy up there, I cannot be the cause of it, for it runs down from you to me."

"Well, then," said the Wolf, "why did you call me bad names this time last year?"

"That cannot be," said the Lamb; "I am only six months old."

"I don't care," snarled the Wolf; "if it was not you it was your father;" and with that he rushed upon the poor little Lamb and—

WARRA WARRA WARRA WARRA WARRA—

ate her all up. But before she died she gasped out—

"ANY EXCUSE WILL SERVE A TYRANT."

THE BAT, THE BIRDS, AND THE BEASTS

A great conflict was about to come off between the Birds and the Beasts. When the two armies were collected together the Bat hesitated which to join. The Birds that passed his perch said: "Come with us;" but he said: "I am a Beast." Later on, some Beasts who were passing underneath him looked up and said: "Come with us;" but he said: "I am a Bird." Luckily at the last moment peace was made, and no battle took place, so the Bat came to the Birds and wished to join in the rejoicings, but they all turned against him and he had to fly away. He then went to the Beasts, but soon had to beat a retreat, or else they would have torn him to pieces. "Ah," said the Bat, "I see now

HE THAT IS NEITHER ONE THING NOR
THE OTHER HAS NO FRIENDS."

THE BELLY AND THE MEMBERS

One fine day it occurred to the Members of the Body that they were doing all the work and the Belly was having all the food. So they held a meeting, and after a long discussion, decided to strike work till the Belly consented to take its proper share of the work. So for a day or two the Hands refused to take the food, the Mouth refused to receive it, and the Teeth had no work to do. But after a day or two the Members began to find that they themselves were not in a very active condition: the Hands could hardly move, and the Mouth was all parched and dry, while the Legs were unable to support the rest. So thus they found that even the Belly in its dull quiet way was doing necessary work for the Body, and that all must work together or the Body will go to pieces.

THE FOX AND THE GRAPES

One hot summer's day a Fox was strolling through an orchard till he came to a bunch of Grapes just ripening on a vine which had been trained over a lofty branch. "Just the thing to quench my thirst," quoth he. Drawing back a few paces, he took a run and a jump, and just missed the bunch. Turning round again with a One, Two, Three, he jumped up, but with no greater success. Again and again he tried after the tempting morsel, but at last had to give it up, and walked away with his nose in the air, saying: "I am sure they are sour."

"IT IS EASY TO DESPISE WHAT YOU CANNOT GET."

THE SWALLOW AND THE OTHER BIRDS

It happened that a Countryman was sowing some hemp seed in a field where a Swallow and some other birds were hopping about picking up their food. "Beware of that man," quoth the Swallow. "Why, what is he doing?" said the others. "That is hemp seed he is sowing; be careful to pick up every one of the seeds, or else you will repent it." The birds paid no heed to the Swallow's words, and by and by the hemp grew up and was made into cord, and of the cords nets were made, and many a bird that had despised the Swallow's advice was caught in nets made out of that very hemp. "What did I tell you?" said the Swallow.

"DESTROY THE SEED OF EVIL, OR IT
WILL GROW UP TO YOUR RUIN."